J.-A.-S. Collin de Plancy

Irish Saints in Great Britain

J.-A.-S. Collin de Plancy
Irish Saints in Great Britain
ISBN/EAN: 9783337335663

Printed in Europe, USA, Canada, Australia, Japan

Cover: Foto ©Lupo / pixelio.de

More available books at **www.hansebooks.com**

LEGENDS

OF THE

BLESSED VIRGIN.

COLLECTED FROM AUTHENTIC SOURCES,

BY

J. COLLIN DE PLANCY.

𝕿ranslated from the 𝕱rench.

LONDON:
CHARLES DOLMAN, 61, NEW BOND STREET,
AND 22, PATERNOSTER ROW.
1852.

PRINTED BY
COX (BROTHERS) AND WYMAN, GREAT QUEEN STREET,
LINCOLN'S-INN FIELDS.

APPROBATION.

DENIS AUGUSTUS AFFRE, by the Divine Mercy and favour of the Holy Apostolic See, Archbishop of Paris.

A volume, entitled "Legends of the Blessed Virgin," by M. Collin de Plancy (forming one of the series of *Library of Legends*), having been submitted to us for our approbation,

We have had it examined, and from the report made to us thereupon, we consider it to be a work affording much safe and interesting reading.

Given at Paris, under the signature of our Vicar-General, the seal of our arms, and the counter signature of our Secretary, the 18th of September, 1845.

F. DUPANLOUP,
Vicar-General.
By order of His Grace the Archbishop of Paris.

P. CRUICE,
Secretary to the Commission.

PREFACE.

The Translator of the following work feels that some apology is due to his Catholic readers for the title under which the sacred narratives which compose it are introduced. The word "Legend," although in its etymological and proper sense quite unobjectionable, has acquired a meaning in the eyes of the world which makes it necessary for a Catholic, addressing himself to Catholics, to draw attention to its derivation and ecclesiastical use. "Legends," or readings, then, are pieces of sacred literature (*legenda*, "to be read," as distinct from things *credenda*, or *agenda*, "to be believed or done"), not matters of faith, and therefore not of precept, but edifying narratives which the faithful may read with profit, and which may, by God's blessing, be the means of arresting the attention of others to the marvels of the spiritual world. But Protestants, who assume as a first principle that all miracles in the present day are impossible, treat, as a consequence, all miraculous histories as fables. Hence the term "legend," which in itself implies neither truth nor falsehood, has come, in Protestant countries, to be identified with fiction.

In the title-page of the present work, the term is applied in its only legitimate sense, to signify histories of a sacred character, ranging as to their degrees of credibility between historical certainty and that measure of probability, whether greater or less, which results from their having been accepted by a religious people as pious and edifying traditions. A cursory survey of the titles in the Index will be sufficient to show how wrong it would be to class all the narratives together, as if possessing equal authority; for no one would pretend to consider the history of the "Council of Ephesus" (which this series includes) as a "legend," in any other sense of the term than one which was entirely consistent with historical truth.

Another history in the present volume, is that of the Holy House, which is credibly believed to have been wonderfully translated by angels in the thirteenth century, first from Nazareth to Dalmatia, and thence to Loreto in Italy. The truth of this miraculous account has been recognised by successive pontiffs, of whom some have written in its favour, some have authorized its introduction into canonical books of the Church, and others have bestowed upon the sanctuary with which it is connected, numerous privileges.*

---

* The evidence upon which this history rests has been collected and ably exhibited by a contributor to the *Rambler*, for May, 1851; and it is earnestly hoped that no Catholic reader at least will allow himself to speak or

Other narratives are comprehended in the present series, the evidence of which is mainly local, and which the Translator does not profess to have examined. Catholic countries are full of spots which may be said to be haunted by religious associations. The traditions, which are rife in them, will be received with various feelings, according to the preconceived notions of those to whom they are presented. By such as are determined to admit no extraordinary interposition of Divine Providence, by whatsoever tokens authenticated, they will share the fate of all miraculous histories of modern times, and be rejected, simply because they involve the supernatural. By such as feed on the thoughts of the invisible world, they will often be embraced, it may be with an eagerness which too readily despises the laborious process of critical inquiry. The truer estimate of their claims to acceptance, is likely to be formed by such as approach them with no antecedent prejudice on the ground of a supposed impossibility, while feeling at the same time, that it is a duty to religion itself to discriminate between such narratives, according to the degrees of historical testimony by which they are supported; the practice of hastily admitting all miraculous stories without examination, being one which,

think slightingly of it on the ground of any supposed improbability, without a careful study of the facts which are brought forward in that masterly paper.

however different in its moral nature and tendency from that to which it is opposed, may, in its results, be possibly no less prejudicial to the cause of God and His Church.

Of our own age and country, the dangers lie in the contrary direction to that of credulity. All our habits, associations, and modes of thought have a tendency to rivet us to this present world, and to make us measure events by the standard of our own experience. The present volume will answer a purpose far beyond that of mere amusement, if it awaken some among us to the truth, that, in the words of our great poet—

> "There are more things in heaven and earth
> Than are dreamed of in our philosophy "—

if it accustom us to the idea of providential interpositions, not regulated according to those general laws, by which we are accustomed to bind down the ways of the Infinite, but directed by a wisdom which is altogether above us, to the advancement of ends far beyond our search, and of which we know only that they must be good and gracious as He is, who ordains them.

LONDON, *May*, 1852.

NOTE.—The Translator has arranged the Legends in the order of the Litany of the B. V.; adapted to many of them English titles, expressive of the devotion to which they are attached; and omitted several notes unnecessary for the elucidation of the text.—*G. W.*

CONTENTS.

The Christian Name	*Page* 1
The Sparrow	4
The Council of Ephesus	7
Our Lady of Deliverance	13
The Poor Priest	20
The Jubilee of our Lady of Hanswyck	25
Our Lady's Knight	32
Our Lady of Paris	41
The Huguenots	47
Our Lady's Tourney	53
The Lion of Brussels	58
The Prisoner's Mother	61
Our Lady of Verviers	64
The Legend of Sister Beatrice	67
The Saint	77
The Keys of Poictiers	83
Our Lady's Image	87
The Precipice	91
The Chorister of our Lady of Puy	95
Our Lady the Deliverer	104
The Pilgrim of our Lady of Hal	110
Mary of Flanders	120
The Scholar's Vision	128
The Three Knights of St. John	139

CONTENTS.

The Oak of Hildesheim .... *Page*	152
The Wooden Candlestick	155
The Holy House	159
The Indian's Cloak	174
The Jew's Child...	182
The Siege of Guelders	186
Our Lady of the Hermits.....................................	189
The Choir Boy of our Lady of Chartres......................	196
Our Lady Help of Mariners	204
The Hour of Death	210
The Rock of Betharram	215
The Poor Sick Woman	218
The Demoniac	223
Legend of the Lord of Crequy................................	227
The Battle of Lepanto	242
Our Lady ad Nives	247
Our Lady of the Angels	252
The Scapular	256
Our Lady of the Pillar......................................	261
A Legend of the Rosary	268
The Iconoclasts	274
The Cure	284
The Abbey of Afflighem	288
A Legend of Duns Scot	292
Legend of the Lord of Champfleury	295
Epilogue	306
Index to the Images and Sanctuaries mentioned in this work	309

LEGENDS

OF THE

BLESSED VIRGIN.

𝕮𝖍𝖊 𝕮𝖍𝖗𝖎𝖘𝖙𝖎𝖆𝖓 𝕹𝖆𝖒𝖊.

"Jesus et Maria." "Jesus and Mary."

IN ancient times there lived in a village in Hainault, between Valenciennes and Maubeuge ("where," says the old chronicle, "God was loyally served, and his holy Mother worthily honoured"), a simple country girl, whose youth and grace, candour and gentleness, attracted the general esteem of the villagers. She grew up little versed in worldly matters, but confidently walking before God in innocence and truth, not dreaming of evil.

Unendowed with the gift of memory, and still less with that of knowledge, the village maid knew but one prayer, which was JESUS AND MARY! And even when her lips ceased to move, the echo of these sweet names fluttered in her heart.*

---

* "This short prayer, *Jesus and Mary!* is easy to remember; it sweetly fills the mind, and is most powerful in the hour of need."—*Thomas à Kempis.*

Let us now follow the popular legend. The devil, whom our fathers—ignorant as we esteem them to have been—perceived to be at work at various times and in different circumstances in which we, with our pride of intellect, will not allow him to have any part, failing to recognise the demon who goeth about continually seeking whom he may devour—the devil then could not behold, without rage, the constant and simple piety of this poor maid, so confiding, so ingenuous, so simple, and so beautiful. He therefore sought her ruin. He enticed many amorous youths to court her. With her short and simple, but powerful prayer, she repulsed them without suspecting their object.

"These peasants are dull, stupid fellows," said the devil, who, like many others, judged of the talents of those employed by the success of his designs.

He roused the passions of the gallants at the court of Count William VI. The noblest of them, having heard of the charms of the young village maiden, came to the neighbourhood gaily dressed, and offered her the homage of their praise. The powerful little prayer triumphed over the courtiers as it had done over the rustics. The humble heart breathed it with a firm hope. She had been told, and firmly believed, that JESUS was her GOD, and *Mary* her patroness.

"Well, this is astounding!" said the devil: "nothing remains now but for me to go and see what *I* can do." He knew that innocence is defended by the Divine protection, and that God guards simple hearts. He was enraged.

He then assumed human form, says the naïve tradition, and presented himself before the maiden. He had the most seducing appearance and engaging manners; and so lively was his conversation, that the maiden was delighted with him; and so overcome by the confusion he caused in her, that she forgot her holy prayer.

The demon secretly rejoiced; he redoubled his efforts, until believing he had secured his prey, carelessly asked the simple girl,

"What is your name, fair maid?"

Why did the devil ask this question? And what could have instigated the demand?

"Mary!" she replied.

At the sound of this name, the channel of grace and source of strength, the demon started, and disappeared.

Surprised and alarmed at his sudden disappearance, the poor girl felt the danger she had run. But she had been saved, and never afterwards was her short and sweet prayer "JESUS and MARY" out of her mind.

The Sparrow.

"Sancta Maria."   "Holy Mary."

HOLY Mary! How many charming legends are attached to the sweet name of Mary! Here is one which is generally regarded as a pious tale or parable.

In the early ages of Christianity, a pious solitary, great in the sight of God, but little known to men (though St. Bernard twice preached his panegyric, and composed the office for his festival), lived on the borders of the Aube, in a forest of Champagne. The ancient Gauls had here worshipped one of their gloomy divinities, for whom the Romans had substituted Saturn. The spot was thence called *Saturniacum*, when the solitary, whose name was Victor de Plancy, came there, and built a chapel and small hermitage.

Numerous miraculous events followed this work. Among the most surprising were conversions, by which souls sold to perdition were redeemed to heaven; and hearts once frozen by egotism, and corrupted by vicious practices, were inflamed with charity, and brought forth such flowers of virtue as even the world is constrained to admire, phenomena which perplex the mind, but are easily explained by faith.

The saint felt that the hours which he passed

alone in his cell were the sweetest of his life. The only living creature near him was a tame sparrow, which he fed and cherished, regarding him as the emblem of solitude.* Tenderly devoted to the Blessed Virgin, the holy hermit invoked her incessantly, and the only words he uttered aloud were, *Ave Maria!*

Long accustomed to hear these words, and only these words, the sparrow learned to form them; and great (as may be imagined) was the joy of the recluse the first time the bird flew on his shoulder and cried in his ears *Ave Maria!*

At first imagining some holy spirit had come on a divine mission, the saint fell on his knees in reverence; but the bird continuing to chirp *Ave Maria! Ave Maria!* soon made him aware of the real source of those sweet sounds. The bird, from an innocent distraction, became a friend—almost a brother—a praying creature of God. He redoubled his care of him, and henceforth his solitude was agreeably enlivened.

The modest bird, to whom the people gave the name of "The little Monk," seemed on his part to share in his master's joy. At dawn of day his first cry was, *Ave Maria!* When Victor threw him his crumbs, the little bird sang a grace of Ave Marias; and on the hermit kneeling to his devotions, the bird would perch on his shoulder and softly whisper, *Ave Maria!*

Victor cultivated a small garden. Could he for one instant have lost sight of the constant object of his thoughts, the faithful sparrow on a tree would have instantly recalled it by his *Ave Maria!*

The Christians of the country, who came to consult the holy hermit in their troubles and doubts,

* "Like a sparrow all alone on the house top."—*Ps.* ci.

much esteemed the little bird; and on saluting them with his little prayer, they could not consider it to be otherwise than a miraculous favour accorded to the solitary by our Blessed Lady.

The sparrow, when free, took short flights into the country; and when the hermit, in his meditative walks, had rambled further than his wont from his cell, he was sure to be reminded by the bird chirping an *Ave Maria!*

One day in spring, as Victor lay ill upon his mat, he opened the wicket of his cell, and his little friend flew out, as was his custom. A few minutes afterwards, Victor was alarmed at seeing a sparrow-hawk pursuing his favourite. The bird of prey opened his beak, and spread his talons to seize and devour the poor sparrow, when the little bird, almost feeling the sharp claws of his enemy, screamed out, *Ave Maria!*

At this wonder, the hawk, startled and terrified, arrested his course; and the gentle sparrow had time to reach the cell; and falling on the breast of Victor, faintly chirped an *Ave Maria!* and died.

The Council of Ephesus.

"Sancta Dei Genitrix."   "Holy Mother of God."

HE following is more properly a page from ecclesiastical history than a legend. But we have thought that a rapid sketch of the council held at Ephesus might occupy a most appropriate place in a volume devoted to the relation of the wonders wrought through the intercession of the ever blessed "Mother of God." The council, in confirming this sublime title to the Blessed Virgin, has taught us that we can never conceive too high a notion of the power and majesty of her to whom we fly in our necessities.

In the fifth century, whilst illustrious doctors were contending against Arianism, and all the other little sects which attacked the impregnable rock on which is placed the chair of Peter, there appeared among the defenders of the Church, a man of great merit, powerful in speech, rich in learning, and honoured for the austerity of his life; he was called Nestorius, and became patriarch of Constantinople. His vanity was excited by the great applause he received. He said in one of his sermons to the young Theodosius,—"Purge the earth of heresies, and I promise you the joys of heaven." It was a bold saying. He combated

Arianism, but he replaced the zeal of charity with violence; he excited the people against the Arians, whom he drove from their assemblies by force, and whose churches he levelled to the ground. Yet he himself entertained all this time an erroneous doctrine.

He admitted that there were two natures in Christ, which acted in concert. "Jesus Christ," said he, "as man, was born of the Blessed Virgin, suffered and died; but Christ, as God, directed the man Jesus, with whom he was joined by a moral union only."

He first obtained the assistance of weak men to preach this doctrine, which he afterwards asserted himself, in the year 428. The people saw at once that he would deprive them of their grand invocation of Mary, as the "Holy Mother of God," and they rose in a mass against this innovation.

But the inflexible stubbornness of Nestorius would not give way. St. Cyril of Alexandria wrote in vain to the faithless patriarch; equally fruitless were the supplications of the faithful and the warnings and exhortations of the guardian of the faith, the holy Pope St. Celestine. Nestorius heeded no remonstrance, but persecuted his opponents with great warmth. He was cut off from the communion of the Church, but still persisted in his errors.

The contest became so violent, that it was thought necessary to convoke a general council, to condemn the heresy broached by Nestorius. This was done with the concurrence of the Emperor Theodosius the Younger, and it was convoked, doubtless, by special design of Almighty Providence, to meet at Ephesus; for the blessed Mother of our Saviour had lived in that town, with the beloved disciple, after the ascension of her divine Son. The tradition of this fact was kept with great fidelity by the Ephesians, who were noted for the warmth of their devotion to our blessed Lady. Delighted were they then to learn, that from their city was to proceed the justification of her most sacred character.

On the 7th of June, in the year 431, two hundred and sixty bishops were assembled at Ephesus. Nestorius also arrived with a numerous escort, but was more than ever puffed up with pride and self-conceit. John of Antioch, and other prelates, being on their way to join the council, it was with some regret (the seventh being the feast of Pentecost) put off to the 22nd. But these prelates being personal friends of Nestorius, and not wishing to assist at his condemnation, had not arrived when the first session was opened on that day. The assembled bishops and doctors of the Church walked in procession to the church at Ephesus, dedicated to God under the special patronage of his holy Mother. In this edifice the council was held.

All the townspeople refrained from labour, and in their eagerness to learn the decision of the fathers, surrounded the church, invoking our blessed Lady to direct their proceedings and to vindicate her dignity.

Could such an assemblage of worthy pastors of the Church, met in a city so devoted to Mary, fail to be unanimous in their decision? Nestorius foresaw that they could not, he therefore refused to appear. St. Cyril presided over the council as representative of the Sovereign Pontiff, and delivered a discourse at one of the sessions, of which the following are some sentences:—

"Hail, Mary! treasure of the world!

"Hail, Mary, Mother of God. It is through you that the prophets raise their voices, and that the pastors of the Church celebrate the praises of the Almighty, singing with the angels that sublime canticle,—'Glory be to God on high, and on earth, peace to men of good will.'

"Hail, Mary, Mother of God! through you the Magi offered their presents, guided by a resplendent star.

"Hail, Mary, Mother of God! through you the glorious college of the apostles was elected by our Redeemer.

"Hail, Mary, Mother of God! through you St. John leaped in his mother's womb; the torch fluttered in the presence of the source of light.

"Hail, Mary, Mother of God! through you that ineffable grace has descended upon mankind, of which the apostle speaks, when he says, it hath appeared to all men.

"Hail, Mary, Mother of God! from you proceeded the true light, of which the evangelist said, 'I am the light of the world.'

"Hail, Mary, Mother of God! from you came forth Him, who conquered death and hell.

"Hail, Mary, Mother of God! you gave birth to the Creator and Redeemer of men, our guide to the kingdom of heaven.

"Hail, Mary, Mother of God! by you is every faithful soul saved."*

The whole discourse thus contained in each

---

* "How can it be called in question that the Blessed Virgin is entitled to be called *Mother of God*, for as Jesus Christ our Saviour is truly God, so is the Blessed Virgin Mother of God."—*Letter of St. Cyril.*

sentence an invocation to Mary, under the title of which it had been attempted to deprive her.

The question was decided on the first day; so unanimous were the fathers, that it was not necessary to put it to each one; for they all cried out in chorus, "Sancta Dei Genitrix! Mater divinæ gratiæ! Mater Creatoris! Mater Salvatoris!"—"Holy Mother of God! Mother of divine grace! Mother of our Creator! Mother of our Redeemer!"

A few friends of Nestorius, indeed, sought to defend him, but in vain; he was condemned. He went into exile, and remained obstinate, proud, and unbending, until his death, which took place in Libya, after having a long time wandered from city to city. It is said that his tongue was found, immediately after his death, to have been eaten by worms.

The people of Ephesus, who heard the acclamations before the decision was announced to them, readily conjectured the result, and great was their joy thereat. When, at the close of the sermon, the bishops and fathers left the church, they all assembled and reconducted them to their abodes, accompanied by bands of music, bearing torches and laurel-branches, and strewing the ground with flowers, through the streets illuminated in honour of the occasion. The women and children prostrated themselves, kissing the robes of the prelates, singing their praises, and extolling our blessed Lady, in whose honour throughout the night the city resounded with cries of "Live, Mary, Mother of God!"

Since this time, to the angelic salutation, "*Hail, Mary! full of grace, the Lord is with thee;*" and the words of St. Elizabeth, at the

Visitation, *"Blessed art thou amongst women, and blessed is the fruit of thy womb, Jesus,"* has ever been added the conclusion adopted by the Council of Ephesus:—

"*Holy Mary,* MOTHER OF GOD, *pray for us sinners, now and at the hour of our death.*" *Amen.*

Our Lady of Deliverance.*

"Sancta Virgo Virginum."   "Holy Virgin of Virgins."

THE history of the iniquities of the Parliament of Paris would fill a large volume. We will give an instance which might occupy a page in such a work.

On the 6th of February, 1737, a year after the government of the Two Sicilies had fallen into the hands of the Bourbons, and the same year in which the duchy of Tuscany passed into the house of Lorraine, the Parliament of Paris was bold in its pride. On that day it was in the humour to show, by some arbitrary act, its great power and good pleasure. It solemnly suppressed a confraternity.

What was this confraternity? That of our Lady of Deliverance, which had had a quiet existence of upwards of two centuries in the church of St. Etienne-des-Grés,† at Paris.

"Well," said a citizen, who supped that night with a member of parliament, to his host, "it was a strange act of yours to suppress the good confraternity of our Lady!"

"It has been done, however," was the answer.

* Notre Dame de Bonne-délivrance.

† This church no longer exists; it formerly stood at the corner of the Rues St. Jacques and St. Etienne-des-Grés, so called from the steps in front of the principal entrance.

"But on what grounds?" asked the other; "it was established in 1533 by good citizens and Christians, and it has been confirmed by the bulls of four Sovereign Pontiffs. Louis XIII., Anne of Austria, Louis XIV., the Great Condé, and many other princes have thought it an honour to have their names inscribed in its register. St. Francis of Sales and St. Vincent of Paul were members of it. And it was before the image of our Lady of Deliverance that the young Francis, as you know, was freed from the most cruel temptations.

"He was pursuing his studies at Paris, being in his sixteenth year, when the evil spirit filled his mind with the dreadful thought that he was of the number of the reprobate,—that he would never reach heaven. So fearfully did the tempter try him, that he neither ate, drank, nor took repose, and his body became visibly emaciated. His tutor, who saw him become worse and worse each day, feeling a disgust for every occupation, sought in vain to obtain from him the cause of his dejection. The demon who suggested this illusion was one of those called dumb, on account of the silence which it imposes on those it afflicts. Francis, although deprived of those sweet feelings which the love of God imparts to the Christian soul, remained faithful to grace, and did his best to repulse the assaults of the evil one; but when he called to mind the calm and happiness which he had enjoyed before this trial, he could but weep and be sad. He remained in this agony for the space of a month. After this time his fidelity was doubtless rewarded. A divine inspiration led him to the church of St. Etienne-des-Grés. He entered, and threw himself at the feet of the statue of our Lady of Deliverance, and besought her intervention in his behalf:—'Obtain for me, from the bounty of God, that if I am to be eternally separated from Him, I may at least be allowed to love Him here with all my heart.' Such was his prayer. He knew the power of the *Memorare*,* and recited it with fervour. When he finished it, he found a sweet sensation stealing over him, and his fears entirely dissipated. Overcome with joy, he hastened to publish the benefit he had received; and he ever retained a great devotion towards our Lady of Deliverance and the confraternity attached to it, which you have just abolished. Should not such a testimony as this have pleaded in its favour?"

"The decree has passed," said the legislator.

"But consider the disquieted, the sick, and women in labour, who have great devotion to our Lady of Deliverance. Travellers, prisoners, and the troubled in heart, address their vows to her."

"Our law does not prevent their aspirations. We have only suppressed the confraternity."

"I give you credit for your consideration in not *putting down* our blessed Lady," replied the citizen with a malicious smile. "But the confraternity was an admirable institution. Besides the care it took of the sick, the alms it distributed to the poor, it particularly sought to justify its title by procuring the release of prisoners. Every year it obtained the liberty of a great many imprisoned for debt. The royal authority itself had recognised the utility of so benevolent an institution. It confirmed its stability by many royal edicts in its favour. What is there in it which can excite your displeasure? Its sole employments were

* See note to the succeeding legend.

works of piety, charitable reunions, simple processions,* and beautiful and edifying ceremonies. Tell me what are your reasons?"

"I will give you but one, and that shall be a royal one: 'It hath seemed meet to us.'"

"To which, of course, I must bow in submission," replied the good citizen.

And thus, the confraternity was suppressed by Act of Parliament.

But the venerated image of our Lady of Deliver-

---

* The processions of the confraternity of our Lady of Deliverance were very plain when compared with those of our Lady of Hanswyck (which we shall shortly describe); yet they were not without some interest.

First came our Lady's banner, richly worked, and borne by a clerk in surplice, crowned with a wreath of flowers.

The silver cross came next, carried between two acolyths, bearing lighted tapers, who were also crowned with flowers. Then the mace of the confraternity, adorned with two angels, bearing tapers, the whole of silver gilt, was carried between two torch-bearers. The herald of the confraternity marched after this; he was clad in a blue velvet tunic, covered with golden fleurs-de-lis, and wore on his head a wreath of flowers. Then came another cross containing a portion of the precious wood of the holy cross.

A beautiful statue of our Lady, surrounded by angels and rays of light, all of silver.

A figure of St. Peter, of silver.

That of St. John the Baptist, with the lamb, of silver.

A figure of St. Roche, with the angel and dog, likewise of silver.

A representation of St. Sebastian, attached to a tree, having an angel over him crowning him, the whole in silver.

Thirty young men, and then the whole confraternity, followed by the clergy.

All who walked in this procession wore wreaths of flowers round their heads.

Read the descriptions given by Jacques Doublet, the old historian of St. Etienne-des-Grés, and then tell me whether they do not beat our civic shows? (If this be the case in France, how much more is it so in this country?)

ance, the Queen of the confraternity, remained in the hands of the people; and all in distress fled to her sanctuary.

It is an ancient statue of black stone, rudely carved, and held in great veneration since the eleventh century. There are many traditions attached to it, but as they rest on uncertain testimony, we will not mention them.

What the Parliament of 1737 did not, the Revolution of 1793 effected. They suppressed the worship of God and our blessed Lady and shut up their temples.

The church of St. Etienne-des-Grés, stript of its riches, was sold and pulled down! They, who carried off the crosses, and silver images, and other works in brass and metal, cared not for the stone statue of our Lady of Deliverance, which was of no material value. A pious woman, the Countess de Carignan St. Maurice, a devout servant of our Lady, who had great confidence in her protection, commissioned a person, unknown in the place, to buy it, who having paid for it, brought it to the countess, who placed it in a little oratory in her house, and then she thought herself secure. But her name was already written in the list of the proscribed. She was arrested and thrown into prison. There she was comforted by the companionship of the Superioress, Mother Valois, and many of the Sister Hospitallers of St. Thomas of Villanova, who with her threw themselves upon the compassion of our Lady of Deliverance. Thus did these good women pray and hope in the asylum which the tender mercy of the revolutionists had procured them. Nor did they hope in vain. The day of their liberation came; it was the 4th of October, 1794.

The Sister Hospitallers, fearing they should have no house to go to, felt troubled at separating from their companion. The convents had all been suppressed and their property confiscated; their houses were converted into prisons, barracks, or military depôts. But by a singular protection of Providence, the house of the Hospitallers had escaped notice. The sisters re-entered it, clad in a secular costume; but three months afterwards they were denounced to the club of their district, as disguised nuns, and it was immediately decided that the buildings occupied by the community should be sold, and accordingly they were covered with notices of public sale.

Madam de Carignan, on hearing this, made a vow to bestow her wealth and her dear image on the Sister Hospitallers, whom she again placed under the special protection of our Lady of Deliverance. All the sisters joined her in a novena, and great was their astonishment to see in ten days after, that all the placards had disappeared; no one thought of the sale, and the sisters remained in quiet possession of their convent. Time passed, and by a privilege almost unique, the daughters of St. Thomas of Villanova passed through the revolution in this convent, without being molested, as were all the other religious in the city.*

The holy image was erected in the house of the Hospitallers† in 1806, and Pius VII. attached several indulgences to it. The pretty little chapel

* The Convent of the English Augustinian nuns, in the Rue des Fossés St. Victor, affords another instance of the singular protection of Divine Providence during the French revolution.—*Trans.*

† Situated in the Rue de Sévres, nearly opposite L'Abbaye aux Bois.—*Trans.*

in which it is now honoured was not finished till 1830. Thus surrounded by faithful virgins, the image of our Lady of Deliverance, who drew St. Francis of Sales from the depths of despair, who opened the prison doors of so many in distress, and who saved the pious inheritance of the good Hospitallers, still protects Paris, which hath need to be delivered from many snares.

The Poor Priest.

"Mater-Christi." "Mother of Christ."

THIS is no embellished legend, but a simple anecdote of unquestionable veracity; and it claims a page in this collection, although doubtless known to many of our readers. Its subject is a prayer—the *Memorare*—dear to every Catholic heart, from the pen of that great servant of Mary, St. Bernard.*

In the days of Louis XIII., a courtier, freeing himself from the busy life of the world, its follies and its pleasures, had the happiness, moved by God's grace, to embrace the solid, pure, and calm life of the service of God. He was of a noble family, and he quitted the splendours of wealth to live in the straits of poverty. At the commencement of his new career, a great temptation surprised him, in the shape of one of those enticements which the world so alluringly throws out to

---

* The following is the English translation of the "*Memorare*," so called from the first word of the Latin version: "Remember, O most sweet Virgin Mary, that no one has ever been known in any age to have had recourse to your protection, implored your assistance, or sought your intercession in vain. Animated with this confidence, I run to thee, O Virgin Mother of Virgins, I come to thee, I kneel before thee, an afflicted sinner. Do not despise my prayer, O mother of the Word incarnate, but favourably and graciously hear me. Amen."

entrap those it is on the point of losing; instead of vainly braving the danger, the new soldier of Christ took refuge in a church in Paris, which, alas! like so many others, does not now exist. He humbly, but confidently, threw himself at the feet of our Lady of Deliverance, whose history we have just recounted, and the temptation and its object vanished.

He shortly afterwards was ordained; and sung his first mass in the church of St. Julien-the-Poor, at the Hôtel-Dieu,* surrounded by the poor, whom he henceforth adopted as his family. A fortune of £18,000 fell to his share, which he eagerly seized upon, not for his own use, but for the solacing of the miseries and wants of his new friends. But so numerous was his adopted family, that his fortune soon disappeared; and he began to seek the wealthy, and beg alms from them. Devoted to the care of the poor and unfortunate members of society, this priest had abandoned everything, and, possessed of nought but his warm heart, performed prodigies of charity, and effected numerous conversions. His care was not confined to the free poor; he went into the prisons, and carried consolation to their wretched inmates, and often accompanied them to the scene of their terrible death. It is difficult to believe that a man, in the hour of distress and prostration, at the threshold of a violent death, can still forget God. It is, however, of too frequent occurrence. The holy priest, of whom we write, had a particular compassion for these poor creatures. Bernard by name, he was more generally known throughout Paris by the title of "The poor priest."

* "God's house," the principal hospital in Paris, served by Sisters of Charity of St. Augustine.—*Trans.*

Full of confidence and love of the Blessed Virgin, to her he had recourse in all the conversions he desired to make. His favourite prayer was that of his namesake—the *Memorare*. He always carried about with him this prayer, printed on small pieces of paper, of which he distributed several hundred thousand copies. How much good must these have effected, for assuredly this sweet prayer has been the means of procuring a thousand times more graces than it contains words.* It was the strength of the good priest, whose quiet disinterestedness was not more remarkable than was his sanctity. Many pleasing instances of this might be cited. Cardinal Richelieu, who entertained great admiration for him, insisted on bestowing some patronage upon him. But finding he could not prevail on the humble priest to accept it, he one day said to him, " Tell me, then, any other way in which I can be of service to you ; and ask me for some favour."

"Willingly will I profit by your Eminence's goodness," replied the priest : " may I beg of your Grace to order new planks to be placed in the cart in which the prisoners are conducted to the place of execution, so that their attention may not be distracted from the love of God, and preparing to meet Him, by the fear of falling through the cart. . . . . "

One morning he was told that there lay, in the prison of Châtelet a wretched man, condemned to be broken alive on the wheel, who persisted in denying his guilt, and in refusing to see or hear a minister of religion. Bernard hastened to his cell, saluted, embraced, and consoled him. He used

* The same expression was used by St. Francis of Sales, in speaking of the spiritual exercises of St. Ignatius.

his most persuasive language to try and soften this heart of granite. All his charity was in vain; his zeal thrown away. The sullen prisoner raised not his eyes, nor gave the least sign of attention; he replied not, but while the priest exhausted his store of patience, remained motionless, seated on a stone bench. Now was the time to try the efficacy of his favourite prayer. Bernard said, "Come, brother, you will not refuse to say a little prayer to our Blessed Mother to obtain her assistance in your hour of need."

The prisoner remained like a rock in his state of impassible taciturnity.

"Well, I will recite it alone," said the priest, kneeling by the side of the prisoner: "do you merely unite your intention with mine, and if you suffer too much to speak, you will participate in my prayer by answering, Amen."

He took one of his little prayers out of his breviary. He recited it aloud; and when he had finished, waited an instant to see whether the prisoner's heart had relented; but he only saw an impatient movement, and heard a brutal exclamation. Wrung with grief, the priest listened only to his zeal. He raised his trembling hand, and placing the holy prayer on the criminal's lips, tried to force it into his mouth, saying, "Since you will not recite it, you shall swallow it."

The prisoner was chained and could not resist, and quietly suffered what he had not the power of preventing. He opened his mouth, till now fixed in despair, and promised to recite the prayer which had doubtless already purified the lips which it had touched. While, trembling with joy, the good priest again repeated the prayer, he saw, with visible emotion, that each word proceeded from the prisoner's lips with increasing warmth of devotion; at length he sighed, sobbed, and wept; and as the prayer was ended, his hardened heart had relented. He was overcome with deep contrition; he was no longer the obstinate infidel, but the repentant sinner. Through the tears which choked his utterance, he confessed the many and grievous sins of his life; he accepted, with humble submission, the sacrifice of his life, which he acknowledged to be too small for such a series of wickedness as his career had been composed of. So deeply indeed had the feeling of contrition sunk into his soul, that he fainted. The sinner, saved by the power of Mary, died at the poor priest's feet, who had just bestowed on him with the plenitude of his office the entire pardon of his transgressions.

Father Bernard, full of good works, departed this life on the 23rd of March, 1641, and was interred in the cemetery attached to the Hospital of Charity.*

* An almshouse for aged priests in Paris.—*Trans.*

The Jubilee of our Lady of Hanswyck.

"Mater divinæ gratiæ."   "Mother of Divine Grace."

ALINES, or Mechlin, is perhaps the only city in the world which has preserved in all their original perfection the religious *fêtes* or shows of the middle ages. In 1825, at the Jubilee of St. Rombould, to whom it is indebted for the knowledge of the Gospel, and in 1838, at the Jubilee of our Lady of Hanswyck (the name of a venerated image held in great esteem), this old Christian city exhibited the magnificent and popular spectacle of those gigantic processions, rich in allegory, and studded with those attractive costumes which delight the crowd, whose appearance reminds one of the times of Philip the Good, when the same *fêtes* took place exactly in the same manner, the spectators alone differing.

We will here faithfully describe in all its details the grand procession of 1838, in the persuasion that they will be appreciated by our readers, few of whom perhaps have ever assisted at any *fête* of so remarkable a nature.

First marched a band of music on foot, in the costume of the present day, after which rode a squadron of cavalry. This formed as it were a modern preface to an ancient work. The following was the order of the procession.

A group of sixteen angels on horseback, with

large extended wings and azure bodies, sounding golden trumpets, around the herald who carried the standard of the Jubilee. They announced the coming of the representation of the Litany of the Blessed Virgin of Loretto.

This sweet and favourite devotion of the people was represented by emblematical figures. First came thirty-six maidens, mounted on horses, elegantly dressed in white, in the modest and becoming fashion of Christian art, wearing crowns on their heads, from which fell rich lace veils. Each one carried in her left hand the attribute she represented—the *Tower of David*, the *House of Gold*, the *Tower of Ivory*, the *Mystical Rose*, the *Mirror of Justice, &c.*; and from their right hands waved banners of white silk. On every banner was worked, in letters of gold, some title given to our blessed Lady; as, *Amiable Mother, Admirable Mother, Powerful Virgin, Clement Virgin, Cause of our Joy, Health of the Sick, Refuge of Sinners, Consolatrix of the Afflicted,* and *Help of Christians, &c.* Thus the show was for the people a continual prayer.

The concluding portion of the Litany, in which the dignity of queen is so justly attributed to Mary, called forth still more majestic representation. Eight triumphal chariots bore the groups emblematic of these glorious titles of our heavenly queen.

Before the cars rode choirs of angels, with snow-white wings and starry foreheads, playing on harps and psaltering, mounted on palfreys magnificently caparisoned. The *Queen of Angels* was in the first car, drawn by six cream-coloured horses. She was raised on a golden throne, around which knelt many heavenly spirits. Seraphim, cherubim, archangels, and angels surrounded their Queen, the powers, principalities, and dominations carried crowns and sceptres. All these characters were borne by young girls, taken from the noblest families of Malines.

The *Queen of Patriarchs* was in the second car, attended by the venerable personages of the old law,—Adam, Noah, Abraham, Jacob, &c.

Next came the *Queen of Prophets*, round whose throne might be seen the inspired men, whose voices recorded the future, as plainly as the past, from Abraham to St. John the Baptist.

The fourth car bore the *Queen of Apostles*, who sat on a high throne, covered by a canopy, over which was raised the arms of the See of Peter, the eternal emblem of the Church. Among the twelve Apostles, the chosen ones of Christ, who were directly commissioned by him to propagate His Holy Gospel, might be seen their successors who had been chiefly instrumental in spreading the Christian religion in the north of Gaul; St. Rombauld, St. Servais, St. Amand, St. Lambert, St. Lievin, St. Gomer, and St. Willibrod.

The *Queen of Martyrs* sat in the fifth chariot, which represented the whole of the earth; for where has not the blood of Christians been shed for the faith? Princesses and recluses, bishops and soldiers, children and old men, young girls and mothers—all were there bearing their palms of triumph.

The sixth car was formed like a pulpit, and carried the *Queen of Confessors* and her militant court; the young girl who held the reins bore also a naked sword, to show that they who laboured in the propagation of the faith must always be ready to shed their blood, if necessary, in its defence.

Next came the *Queen of Virgins*. The fair charioteer of this car trod the pleasures of the world under her feet; behind her was a wheel and a palm, and on her right a lamb, emblem of innocence.

The eighth chariot was made to represent the heavens, in which reigned the *Queen of All Saints*, surrounded by her heavenly court, round whom shone a brilliant glory. The Grand Harmonic Society of Malines followed the Litany; but it sadly marred the effect of the whole, to see the members dressed in the modern costume. Better had it been to give them the characters of the court of David, or some others corresponding with the allegorical nature of the festival. But see, here is *Malines* herself, represented by a beautiful child crowned with towers, and surrounded by nine maidens, bearing emblems of the virtues of the city,—*Faith, Prudence, Charity, Union, Constancy, Fidelity, Valour, Modesty,* and *Justice.*

The cavalry officers, the king's aides-de-camp, and the grand officers of the court, followed on horseback. Behind them is a royal car, drawn by eight horses, in which are faithfully represented by children of twelve years of age, the King and Queen of the Belgians upon their throne. The attributes of the arts, commerce, justice, and war, group at their feet. The car is led by Fidelity, Religion, Justice, Goodness; Belgium, Wisdom, and Generosity are the attendants of their majesties. Four winged angels, at each corner of the car, bear aloft the national standard, surmounted by the lion.

A party of naval officers forms the transition to another spectacle. It is a ship, representing the *country's welfare*, an ingenious emblem;—navigation is to all countries the source of wealth.

The *country's welfare* is a three-masted ship, with her sails, cordage, flags, and cannon. An emblematic figure of Belgium commands her; she has her officers and sailors. She sails along the streets by mechanical contrivances, and is followed by fantastic personages, serving as forerunners to the horse, *Bayard*, an enormous animal, on whose back ride four mediæval knights : they are the sons of Aymon.

In the tradition of the country, Aymon was a count of Termonde. His four valiant sons defended Malines and Brabant, and Bayard, their trusty steed, often came to feed in the forest of Soigne, where he left the mark of his foot upon a rock ; he browsed formerly in the fertile plains watered by the Dyle.

After Bayard follow the Giants, for which the northern cities are so famous. Here come three children, fifteen feet high, whose father and mother look over the houses; the lady being a colossal princess, holding a fan as large as those with which domestics in the Indies cool their employers. The grandfather is even taller than his son, to show that each generation degenerated in size. He is seated in a monster tilbury of antique form, escorted by two monster camels mounted by cupids. This is, it is said, a relic of the crusaders, who were the first to import these animals into Europe.

After these great figures comes, as a kind of moral to the show, a good old man smoking his pipe, on a wretched nag, who draws Dame Fortune's wheel. The goddess herself is borne on high, around whom are grouped figures, who, as she makes a movement, rise or fall, showing what freaks the dame plays with mankind. These personages are well-dressed representations of harlequin and a beguine; a hunter and a milk-woman; a courtier and a coquette; a hermit and an old woman. Bursts of laughter greet the vicissitudes which these various persons undergo as they pass along. The cavalcade closed as it opened, with a large body of cavalry.

Such is a rapid glance at the curious procession which passed four times through the city of Malines, during the fifteen days of the jubilee, from the 15th of August to the 1st of September, in the year 1838. But what, you may ask, has this to do with our Lady of Hanswyck? The little we have been able to gather on this subject we will now relate.

In 1188, a ship, which bore the precious remains of a little ruined church, stopped of itself upon the waters of the Dyle, nor could all the efforts of the sailors cause it to advance. It stopped just before the little village of Hanswyck, where shortly afterwards a small chapel was dedicated to the Blessed Virgin, and received in its sanctuary a statue of our dear Lady, the most precious object the ship carried.

These circumstances becoming spread abroad, and it being evident that our Lady had herself chosen this spot for her sanctuary, numerous pilgrims visited it, and many and wonderful were the cures and blessings received by those who sought them.

The miraculous image, which still exists, holds in one arm her Divine Son, and in the other a sceptre. Innumerable have been the cures, both corporal and spiritual, obtained before this image.

In 1578, the church of Hanswyck was burnt down and the monastery destroyed by heretics.

From its vicinity, the religious took refuge in Malines, bearing as their only treasure this statue, which they concealed for some time. They eventually built a new monastery at Malines, near the gate of Louvain, in which they placed their precious charge.

In 1585, our Lady of Hanswyck, signalized her establishment in Malines, by delivering the city from a besieging enemy. One of its keys was henceforth confided to her keeping by the magistrates. Her shrine became so frequented, and so rich were the offerings deposited there, that they erected the church, with its beautiful cupola, which is the admiration of visitors to Malines.

At the last jubilee of our Lady of Hanswyck, one hundred thousand strangers visited the city. All the streets were decorated and illuminated, and beautiful transparencies exposed to view. The *railway trains* arrived every half-hour, and when we saw these beautiful processions and *fêtes*, how sadly did the thought of the cold and meaningless spectacles of home strike us.

Our Lady's Knight.

"Mater purissima."   "Mother most pure."

T the siege of Pampeluna, by the troops of Francis the First, in 1521, a gay and gallant officer, who had exhibited no great signs of sanctity, defended the town for Charles the Fifth. He was called Ignatius of Loyola.

In spite of all his efforts, the French army entered the city. Ignatius, faithful to his charge, retired to the citadel with a soldier, who was the only one who had sufficient courage to follow him; and though he found it garrisoned by a most insignificant number of men, he sustained several assaults, when a breach was made, and the victorious army entered. In the struggle, the young officer broke his right leg, and was wounded on the left one. He had behaved with such gallantry that the French spared the garrison for his sake. He was borne with honours to their general, who gave orders for him to be conveyed on a litter to the castle of Loyola, which was situated at a little distance from the city.

We will not dilate on the fortitude displayed by Ignatius during his illness, which was very severe, as the leg, which had been badly set, had to be rebroken, and a bone which protruded below the knee to be removed, besides other trying operations. This would involve the necessity of entering into details of the saint's life, which are sufficiently well known; our legend relates to one fact alone.

As he grew convalescent, the young officer became weary. He had spent his youth at courts, first as a page, then as a courtier, and lastly as an officer of merit. Born of a noble family, he had been nurtured to pleasures, and his vanity had ever been flattered. Hitherto (he was now twenty-nine years of age) he had paid little attention to his duties as a Christian; he had led the life which is commonly pursued by worldlings. He now asked for some books to amuse him and trifle away the time. What he desired were the romances and tales of chivalry, then so much in fashion. They knew he liked this reading; but whether no books of the kind were at hand, or a disposition of Divine Providence interfered, the attendants brought him the History of Christ, and some volumes of saints' lives.

Passionately addicted to romantic authors, he felt at first little taste for the books presented to him, but gradually he began to pay more attention to them. He admired acts of heroism he had not supposed practicable in other careers than his own; nor did he fail to perceive that the immortal crowns gained by the innumerable troops of martyrs, anchorites, confessors, and virgins, who had overcome in so many and such fierce combats, were far above the vain applause of this world. He felt a strong desire rapidly arise in him to follow the traces of those whose lives he now read with avidity. He asked himself if he were more timid than the virgins, less bold than the martyrs, whose wondrous deeds of mortification and painful torments so interested him? Whether God, whose rewards were so sure, was not more worthy of love than the inconstant creatures of earth? Whether heaven did not deserve more efforts to gain it than the riches and honours of such doubtful tenure here below? God gives his grace to the heart who desires and seeks it; Ignatius did not long wait for it. He saw his duty, and he resolved to perform it. He devoted himself entirely to God, forsook the worldly life he had hitherto led, and determined to follow in the path of the saints.

If the disorders, of what is called youthful folly, are made light of by worldly consciences, how differently does the soul, which enters seriously into herself, and examines her state by the help of God's light, regard them. Faults which men scarcely perceive, because they offend not their sense of propriety, are presented to the soul in their true light. Judged by the code of the saints, they are crimes, for they have outraged the majesty of God. They required expiation. Happy was he in having been born a member of that holy Church in which penance restores and raises the soul to God's affection. Repentance urged austerities; he willingly embraced them, feeling so inflamed with the love of God, as ready to undertake anything or make any sacrifice in his service. But he felt the want of some protector in his new career. Could he find one more potent or more kind than the ever Blessed Virgin Mary? Penetrated still with military spirit, he placed himself under her banner, and became her faithful knight. As soon as he was able to quit his couch, he mounted his charger, and set out, saying he was going to visit his uncle, the duke of Najare, who had frequently sent to inquire after him during his illness. After paying his respects to his relative, he sent away his servants, and set out alone for Montserrat.

Upon this steep mountain, whence such charming views of Catalonia are presented to the traveller's sight, there had long been venerated a celebrated image of the Blessed Virgin. Wondrous legends were attached to this famous pilgrimage. We fear to record them here, lest they should shock the sickly faith of this age. According to the historians of the image of our Lady of Montserrat, it was brought into Spain in the first age of the Christian era, if not by the apostle St. James, at least by some of his disciples. It was in great honour during the Roman domination at Barcelona. When the Moors invaded the country, it was concealed in a cavern at Montserrat, where it was discovered in the ninth century.

At this period we rest upon more certain ground. The annalists of Catalonia, upon the faith of an inscription found in 1239, and preserved in the monastery of Montserrat, relate that in the year 880, under the reign of Godfrey the Hairy, count of Barcelona, three young goatherds, who guarded their flocks on the mountain, saw, during the night, a great light issuing from a part of the rock, and rising up to the heavens. At the same time a superhuman melody struck their ears. They informed their parents of what they had seen and heard. The Bishop of Manrese, accompanied by the magistrates, and a large body of the Christian inhabitants, went the next night to the mountain. The wondrous light again appeared. The prelate, seized with admiration, fell on his knees, and remained some minutes in prayer; on rising, he went to the spot whence the light proceeded, where he found an ancient image of the Blessed Virgin. He desired to bring it to Manrese. But on arriving at the spot where the monastery had since been erected, the carriers found it impossible to move the image further, from which the good bishop understood that to be the place our Blessed Lady had chosen for her sanctuary.

Mabillon, who considers it certain that the image was venerated before the Saracenic invasion; and the venerable Canisius, who places this pilgrimage among the most celebrated, give implicit credence to these particulars.

Many miracles followed the recovery of the holy image.

A hermit, who led a retired life in a cave at Montserrat, hitherto a pious and austere man, received one day a companion, who was quite unknown to him, and who took up his abode in a neighbouring cell. The stranger soon gained his esteem by his apparent sanctity. But, say the popular legends, this man was no other than the devil in disguise. He knew the weak side of the hermit, who was somewhat vain of his rigorous penance. How miserable is the condition of the soul that discards humility! The poor hermit fell into the snares of his wily companion, and committed a great crime. The death of the count of Barcelona's daughter was imputed to him. It was at this time that the image was discovered. The tradition further states, that through the intercession of our Lady, the little child was restored to life, and the hermit to a sense of his fallen condition. There must have been some grounds for the accusation, for he fled the country, went to Rome, confessed his sins, and retired to the desert, where he spent seven years in severe penance.

Several other prodigies are told on credible evidence, and many were the sick restored to health after the physician's skill had failed; many the dying children restored to a parent's embrace; many the evils, both corporeal and spiritual, healed at this holy shrine.

It was before this sweet image that the young Spanish officer was going to accomplish the project he had formed. Knight of the Blessed Virgin! He dreamt but of this title, though he yet knew but little of its real import. Mixing his warlike fancies with Christian thoughts, he regarded this life as a warfare and a struggle, nor did he mistake therein. He desired to present, as a trophy, his material arms to our Lady of Montserrat, and receive from her those spiritual ones which enable her children to gain the good fight of salvation.

As he journeyed on alone, thinking over his resolutions, he was joined by a Moorish knight, who seemed to be following the same route. The travellers saluted one another; and as they rode side by side, exchanged words of courtesy. They soon came in sight of Montserrat, which Ignatius had declared to be the end of his journey. The renown of the place, its venerated image, and our dear Lady herself, offered natural subjects of conversation. The knight thought he perceived a contemptuous smile quiver on the lips of the Moor as he recounted one of the latest miracles which had been wrought by our Lady's intercession. Hard words ensued; and, as generally happens, Ignatius, growing warm, soon fell into a passion. The Christian disappeared; the soldier obtained the mastery. He would have the Moor, who was not of his faith, believe and reverence the same as he did. He was provoked at his obstinacy, and drew his sword, believing that to be an affair of honour, which was only one of prayer and persuasion. The Moor, seeing he had a valiant adversary to contend with, like his nation, not deeming it prudent to engage with superior force or skill, and trusting less to his sabre than to the swiftness of his Arab steed, stuck his spurs into his sides, and fled with the rapidity of an arrow. Ignatius, who was also well mounted, followed in pursuit; but on arriving at two cross roads, one of which led to the monastery, while the Moor had followed the other, he, like a true pilgrim, who had vowed to go directly to our Lady's shrine, paused for an instant. Could he give further pursuit without breaking his vow? He did not hesitate, but turned his horse's head direct to Montserrat. And now, his passion having cooled, he acknowledged the first intervention of his Blessed Queen in his behalf; for, thought he, "the saints of whom I read did not make converts by the means I was about to employ."

In the monastery he found a monk of eminent sanctity, who had formerly been grand vicar of Mirepoix, in France, whose name was John Chanones. Ignatius considered him a model of every Christian and monastic virtue. To him he had recourse, and with deep emotion and bitter tears made a confession of the sins of his whole life.

Being thus purified in the sight of God, he remembered having read in books of chivalry, that the candidate for knighthood passed the night watching and praying in his armour, which was called *the vigil of arms*, and wished, in like manner, to sanctify the object on which he was bent. In his military accoutrement, which he was soon to depose for ever, he watched and prayed the whole night in front of our Lady's altar, standing and kneeling, offering himself to Jesus and Mary, as their knight, according to the chivalric notions he had imbibed in the world, and which he now wished to sanctify in the service of God.* In the morning he suspended his sword to a pillar near the altar, as a sign of his renouncing the military profession; he gave his horse to the monastery, his clothes to a poor pilgrim; and clothing himself in a coarse linen suit, he received the holy communion, and set out seeking how best he could fulfil his engagements to our Lord and his Blessed Mother.

He now, doubtless, saw before him the glorious vision of the great work he was to begin. The Church, attacked and mined by the licentious advocates of a pretended reformation, stood in need of an intrepid champion. He conceived the project of his celebrated society, which was not fully established till 1534, when it was inaugurated in the crypt of our Lady of Montmartre (an oratory raised, according to tradition, on the very spot where the apostle of Gaul received the palm of martyrdom), near Paris, on the feast of the Assumption. It was afterwards confirmed by a papal bull, dated the 27th September, 1540.

We cannot here relate the further career of St. Ignatius (who became a great man and an eminent saint), of his companions, and of his society, and its persecutions by men who knew it not. It arrested the progress of the reformation, elevated education, spread abroad knowledge, encouraged and enlarged the study of the sciences, took the Gospel to the new world, and gave to mankind a

* Life of St. Ignatius, by Father Bouhours, book i.

host of great men in every branch of knowledge, and illustrated the pulpit by its eloquence. Always innocent, but attacked by weapons it disdains to employ in return, judged without a hearing, the Society of JESUS continues its steady path along *the royal highway of the cross*, traced out by its Divine Master. Its members, following the recommendation of the Gospel, do good to, and pray for, those who calumniate them.

Our Lady of Paris.

"Mater castissima."   "Mother most chaste."

HE veneration of the Blessed Virgin Mary, in Paris, can be traced to the first apostles of this great city. When Childebert, its king, in 537, rebuilt its church, it was dedicated to our Lady.

Fortunatus the poet wrote a pompous eulogy of this edifice, which he saw completed. The Normans left it untouched; but not so the hand of time, which gradually caused its decay until the commencement of the twelfth century, when it fell in ruins.

A poor scholar, named Maurice, born of an obscure family, at Sully, in Orléannais, had risen in the Church by his virtue and his learning. Being elected bishop of Paris, he resolved to rebuild Childebert's Church, and endow his adopted city with a cathedral, far surpassing any which had hitherto been built. He himself traced the plan, and the building was commenced in 1162. It is said that the first stone was laid by Pope Alexander III., who had taken refuge in France.

The first crusade carried into Asia not only hundreds of thousands of our warriors, but a multitude of priests and prelates, who earnestly undertook religious pilgrimages to the holy places in Palestine. On their return to Europe, they brought back a taste for the elegant Saracenic architecture.* The arts made also their conquests in the holy war. The religious edifices henceforth erected threw off that heavy massiveness, hitherto their principal characteristic, and put on the graceful lightness of the Pointed style. Then, during the twelfth, thirteenth, and fourteenth centuries, the spirit of religious zeal covered Europe with those productions of the mason's skill, which still excite our admiration and wonder. All the gold of their and our times, with ordinary resources, could not have erected a twentieth part of those gigantic cathedrals, and of those elegant churches, which, with all our boasted wealth, we are unable to keep in proper repair. Christian piety, sincere zeal, and national spirit, everywhere directed these grand works. Nationality, in those days, was more local than at present. Each Christian then saw his country in his church, which he dearly loved, and whose banner alone he would follow. The spirit of centralization has now placed all the religious edifices in France in the hands of the government, so that the parishioners no longer really possess their church. We know not whether this be the most prudent course to adopt.

In the times we write of, the sacred cause of religion was either forwarded by joining the crusades for the deliverance of the Holy Sepulchre, or in some other active labour for the benefit of

* The idea of the eastern origin of Pointed architecture has been quite abandoned by modern writers, who see in it a necessary development from the Norman or preceding style.—*Trans.*

the Church. They, whose courage failed at the thought of engaging in foreign warfare, built churches with their wealth or by their personal labour. During a great part of the century, under the direction of skilful masons, the works for the construction of our Lady's church of Paris were proceeded with. The number of workmen was immense; they were chiefly Parisians, though many others from distant parts, through devotion or a spirit of penance, devoted themselves to the great work.

Of those who were too feeble to work, some gave money, while others provided food for the workmen, which the women prepared. Indulgences were to be gained by all who in any way contributed to the erection of the sacred edifice; and who was not able, and did not yield some assistance? The possessor of a forest supplied the timber; farmers and others having carts and horses brought it to the spot; the less skilful drew the stone from the quarry and carried mortar to the masons. No helping hand, however humble, was refused. The poor widow mended the workmen's clothes, and asked for nothing in return. Every butcher sent a certain quantity of meat, and the gardeners supplied vegetables and fruit. Did any of the workmen's families stand in need of their absence from the works, they were readily allowed to depart.

When funds failed, processions of the statue of our Lady, or some saint's shrine, were proposed, and instantly some wealthy noble sent a sum of money to have the privilege of the procession passing through his grounds. And many were the offerings of jewels and precious stones made by noble lords and fair ladies.

The erection was surrounded by cabins, in which the workmen slept. They were awakened each morning by the sound of a bell. An altar had been erected, and the day's work was sanctified by attendance at the holy sacrifice of the mass. All were obliged to assist at it, and the holy chant announced to the neighbourhood that the day's work was about to commence. In the evening, tapers were lit, and, assembled round the statue of our Lady, canticles were sung, and prayers recited by the workmen, before they retired to rest.

It was by these means, and the concurrent assistance of the masses, that all the great churches were erected at this period. The cathedrals of our Lady, of Paris and of Rheims, were specially favoured by their heavenly patroness, in a manner which the people did not fail to appreciate. During the whole time of the erection of these churches, not one accident happened, and no labourer was killed, or even dangerously wounded. It is even said, that on several occasions our Lady herself appeared to the masons and brought them through their difficulties. The statuaries and carvers attributed the idea of some of their happiest efforts to the visions they had seen. And many an inspiration was obtained at prayer before her image, which is believed to be the same as the one which is now in the chapel on the right of the gates which separate the choir from the nave.

After nearly a century's labour, the vast cathedral, the pride and delight of the Parisians, was finished. The immaculate Virgin was their queen, to whom they had recourse in all their necessities. Nor did they ever apply to her in vain.

In 1304, King Philip the Fair, being hotly pursued by the Flemish, on the great day of Mons-en-puelle, gave himself and his army up for lost. He invoked our Lady of Paris in an ardent prayer; the contest was renewed, and he won the day. His first visit on his re-entering to his capital, was to the cathedral, to return thanks for his success. He also ordered a monument to be erected and placed before our Lady's image, representing him on horseback with his vizer down, as he was on the day of battle, at the moment he besought the assistance of the Blessed Virgin. This monument was destroyed at the Revolution.

When King John was made prisoner by the English, in 1356, at the battle of Poictiers, the Parisians vowed to our Lady, to offer her every year a wax candle, the same height as the tower, to obtain the deliverance of their king. The king returned, and the citizens faithfully fulfilled their vow for the space of two hundred and fifty years. But in 1605 they obtained permission to commute their vow by the present of a massive silver lamp, in the shape of a ship.

We must say one word concerning the vow of Louis XIII. Through the intercession of Mary, this king obtained a noble heir to his crown, and in thanksgiving the happy father of Louis XIV. placed his kingdom and people under the especial protection of the Queen of Heaven. The nation cordially seconded the pious vow of their king, and again recognised our Lady of Paris as their gracious patroness. The sole exterior sign of their homage consisted in an annual procession, dear to all Paris. It disturbed no other business, as it was observed on a holiday—the glorious day of Mary's Assumption. The empire afterwards re-established this custom, which was also observed in neighbouring cities. But Paris, of all cities, should ever celebrate this festival with the greatest pomp, for can she forget all that the Blessed Virgin has done for her? Has she not preserved and brought her through terrible trials, protected her Church from heresy and schism, constantly blessed her clergy, ever renowned for their learning and virtue; and did she not, when the schools of Paris were under her patronage, send missionaries to every part of the globe?

In 1793, some of the children of Paris, with horrid impiety, chased our Lady from her temple, and prostituted its sacred precincts to the Goddess of Reason! Yet did our dear Lady preserve her sacred shrine from destruction. The cathedral was actually offered for sale, *as affording a quantity of available material*, and the Marquis of St. Simon (then called Citizen Simon) bid 240,000 francs, with the intention of *pulling it down*. Happily it was necessary, before the destructive axe was allowed to strike its sacred walls, raised by the wealth, labour, and piety of its ancient citizens, to pay the whole sum at once, which the bidder was fortunately unable to do.

A complete restoration of this venerable sanctuary of our Blessed Mother has been projected, and in part effected. May our Lady obtain for those who are to be engaged in this holy work the same spirit of faith and devotion which animated the founders and builders of this magnificent cathedral!

The Huguenots.

"Mater inviolata." "Mother inviolate."

HE histories recording the crimes of those, who, during the religious troubles which afflicted the Church in the sixteenth century, desecrated and demolished the sacred edifices, holy images, and venerated shrines, also furnish proofs of their punishment. Sometimes hath Divine Justice seemed slow in inflicting the blow, but often it has fallen on the miscreants at the moment of their iniquity. How unsearchable are the ways of Divine Providence! Many creditable facts are recorded concerning the venerated images of our Blessed Lady. In the country where the sparrow chirped her sweet name (whose legend you have read in this book), there was an image of the Blessed Virgin, the size of life, known by the name, dear to so many Christians, of our Lady of Help. A man impiously boasted, in 1794, that "he would bring her down from her niche." Such was his gross expression. The church was opened, and he entered with his implements of destruction. Depositing his basket at the corner of the altar, he mounted on it to examine the figure. He found it was firmly attached to the wall by a strong iron bar, and that it would require a heavy instrument to displace it. He turned to descend, when he

slipped and fell from the altar. Wonderful to relate, the image, which was so firmly fixed, instantly detached itself, and falling on the man, killed him, without suffering the least injury itself.

In the same year, two men rushed into St. Paul's Church, at Orleans. Their object was to destroy a long-venerated image, representing the Blessed Virgin holding her Divine Son in her arms. One broke his leg on falling from an altar; the other fixed his ladder, mounted it, and placed his hands upon the image. No sooner had he touched it, than he was seen to tremble, and, to the astonishment of the lookers on, quietly descended, and feeling his way cautiously, to the amazement of the whole city, he left the church stone blind.

Instances of the like nature abound in every locality, and an authentic collection of them would form striking examples of divine justice.

In the following legend, the profanation was simply prevented, without being followed by an immediate punishment. We must transport ourselves to the department of the Landes, near Bordeaux, the country of St. Vincent of Paul. Three celebrated pilgrimages exist there within the circuit of a league: the cottage wherein Vincent was born in the village of Poy; the great oak in which, when a child, he retired to pray; and the renowned chapel of our Lady of Buglose, where, according to the local traditions, he sang his first mass.*

This chapel, and the homage shown to our Blessed Lady on this spot, are of very early origin. Every document which could illustrate this sub-

* Pélerinage de St. Vincent de Paul et de Notre Dame de Buglose, par M. Danos Chapelain, 1844.

ject, disappeared on the traces of the Huguenots, in 1570, when, by the order of Jane d'Albret, they laid waste this country, burning and destroying all that was dear to Catholic hearts.

At the first report of their approach, some of the faithful wishing at least to preserve the beloved image of our Lady, a beautiful marble statue, took it secretly from the chapel and concealed it within the briers of a marsh, not fearing that the armed bands would venture there in search of it. The image was thus saved from heretical violence. But thirty years elapsed before the country returned to perfect security; the Huguenots domineered over the inhabitants, and the men who had concealed the image died at the beginning of the seventeenth century, and their secret was buried with them. The old men who had repaired the sanctuary of their dear Lady remembered with regret her sweet image, which had smiled down upon them in their childhood, but sought in vain for any trace of it, and gave up the search in despair.

Time went on, the hydra of heresy was nearly extirpated by the efforts of Louis XIII.; meanwhile the marsh dried up. A young shepherd of the parish of Poy, in the year 1620, being accustomed to drive his herds to pasture on the land surrounding the marsh, remarked one day that one of his oxen had wandered into the marsh, and, half-buried in the briers, stopped at a certain spot, and began bellowing most violently. This being repeated two or three times, the shepherd thought there must be something extraordinary in it, and felt at first much afraid. Being, however, curious to discover the cause of this strange occurrence, he mounted a tree and discovered the bull licking a human form which lay buried in the briers. His fear increasing at this sight, he descended more quickly than he got up, and ran at his best speed to alarm the neighbourhood with the startling intelligence. The chief of the inhabitants, headed by the Rector of Poy, hastened to the spot, and making a way through the shrubs, found, to their great surprise, a marble image of the Blessed Virgin, beautiful and perfect, half-buried in the swamp.

There still remained one old couple, who, with tears of joy, recognised their much-regretted image of our Lady formerly placed in her chapel. Great demonstrations of joy were shown; fervent prayers and devout canticles burst from every mouth. The recovered image, which had lain hidden for half a century, was reverently taken up. It was placed on a temporary pedestal covered with verdure, and under a canopy of flowers. It remained there a twelvemonth, and many were the favours which Mary lavished on her devoted children during that period. So renowned did the image become, that the Bishop of Dax went to visit it in solemn procession. Among other wonders, a stream sprung up at its foot, and it still continues to flow at the present day.

This prelate, believing he discovered the hand of God in the graces which had flowed from prayers addressed to our Blessed Lady before this image, ordered it to be carried with great ceremony to the parish church of Poy. Everything being prepared for this translation, and the people collected together from neighbouring parts, the procession began to move. But when the statue had reached the remains of the ancient chapel, the beasts who drew it stood still, and could not be induced by any means to proceed further. This was considered an evident sign of our Lady's pleasure to reinstate her holy image in its ancient sanctuary. Accordingly it was erected in the chapel, which was immediately rebuilt with such zeal, that it was ready to be opened on Whit-Monday, in the year 1622. The circumstances of the recovery of the image were painted on the walls, and in allusion to the animal who discovered it, it was henceforth called our Lady of Buglose.*

The pilgrimage became much frequented, and in 1706, Bernard d'Abadie, Bishop of Dax, increased its celebrity by giving the chapel to the Lazarists, or Fathers of the Mission, founded by St. Vincent of Paul.

Surprising cures, wonderful conversions, and numberless graces were obtained at this venerated sanctuary of the Blessed Mother of God. At length the revolution came, in 1789. Its progress was rapid. Like the impetuous rush of whirlwinds and torrents, so is the unrestrained burst of human passions. But amidst the general plunder and destruction of the churches around, the chapel of our Lady of Buglose remained untouched, owing, not indeed to the forbearance of the mob, but the supernatural interference of providence.

A crowd of impious men invaded our Lady's sanctuary, armed with axes, hammers, and other destructive weapons. Ladders were planted against the walls to assist the work of destruction. While the most horrid blasphemies were uttered, some

* Buglose, in the local patois, signifies the bellowing of oxen. I cannot discover what name the pilgrimage bore before the time of its destruction by the Protestants.

mounted the ladders, and others began to dismantle the altar and other objects within their reach. But on a sudden every hand was arrested, every tongue was silenced, and every heart trembled, while a deep and awful sound seemed to issue from beneath the chapel. It increased with such vehemence, that, unable to comprehend its cause, and terrified with the fear of being swallowed up alive, the sacrilegious wretches fled in confusion, leaving everything behind them.

This circumstance was soon known to all the country, and excited such a dread, that no one ever afterwards dared even to think of pillaging our Lady's Chapel. Thus were pilgrims still able to visit their beloved shrine, undismayed by fear of the impious. The authorities of the place passed one not of the most absurd decrees of that epoch. They *tolerated* the opening of the chapel of Buglose, and *placed under their protection* the offerings of pilgrims to our Lady's shrine ...... Four or five years afterwards, religion was again proclaimed in the land, and this sanctuary was once more the universal refuge of the distressed and afflicted.

With regard to the impious crew who attacked the chapel, we have not been able to obtain any satisfactory information; but to judge from a host of examples, their end must have been most wretched.*

* For other instances of the fate of sacrilege, see the "Tale of the Beggars," in the *Legends of the Commandments of God*, page 17.

Our Lady's Tourney.

"Mater intemerata." "Mother undefiled."

LTHOUGH the last crusade of any importance took place in the reign of St. Louis, King of France, yet both political and religious necessity demanded that a stop should be put to the encroachments of the infidel hordes, who were about to take Constantinople, and would have invaded Europe and crushed the steady progress of civilization, had not their progress been arrested by the battle of Lepanto, that great feat of arms, directed by the holy Roman Church, which covered the Christian arms with glory. And as, throughout our countries, the defence of the faith was urged by preachers upon the Christian knights, many were the noble youths who, during the 15th century, on grand solemnities, made public vows to oppose the children of Mahomet. The order of the Golden Fleece, founded on the 10th of January, 1430, by Philip the Good, was at the outset composed of a few noblemen, nearly all engaged by oath to take the cross. Among these knights, the one most distinguished for his firm disposition and his acknowledged bravery was Sir Philip Pote, a gentleman of Burgundy, who possessed a large body of vassals. He had allowed several years to pass without taking arms for the accomplishment of his vow, when he

learned, in 1438, that Albert of Austria, having ascended the imperial throne, was about to march against the Turks. He hastened to join him with his company of men, and soon distinguished himself in valiant feats of arms.

Early in 1440, report was spread that the Emperor Albert had been killed, and his bravest knights slain around him in a fierce encounter with the enemy. The rumour being confirmed, great was the mourning in many noble families. Nevertheless, his friends entertained a hope that they should see once more the valiant Philip Pote; for, before his departure, he had had his arms blessed at the shrine of our Lady of Hope, at Dijon, and had fervently invoked her powerful assistance.

Our Lady of Hope had been venerated at Dijon from time immemorial. Her image bore the marks of antiquity; had existed, according to popular tradition, in the times of the first missionaries of the faith. It had been the channel of many graces and wonderful favours, as many illustrious persons had testified, and among others King Philip Augustus. Never had our Lady of Hope been known to desert any client, nor did she our Knight of the Golden Fleece.

A Christian prisoner, who had escaped from the Turkish camp, came to Burgundy, bearing the sad intelligence—which caused many a hope to perish—that most of the knight companions of Albert of Austria had indeed perished; that several, grievously wounded, had been taken by the enemy, and that among the latter was Philip Pote. He added, that all the captives, who had not the means of paying their ransom immediately, were put to death without mercy, some by the sword, others by drawing, several were hung, while many suffered the terrible death of impaling. He also stated that he had heard that Philip Pote, on account of his great bravery, had been condemned, as a particular mark of their consideration of his valour, to be torn in pieces by lions. His relatives and friends now lost all hope; they could but weep and pray for the repose of his soul, though they regarded him in some sense as a martyr, having fought and suffered death in the cause of the faith.

Six months elapsed, when further news arrived to the effect that Philip was not dead, but had escaped and returned by sea. The ship debarked at a port in Flanders, and the knight had gone to Bruges, where the Duke of Burgundy then kept his court, to get a votive picture to our Lady of Hope painted by a celebrated Flemish artist. Yet the soldier's tale was not devoid of truth. The Christian knight had not been given up to be destroyed by wild beasts; but being unable to ransom himself, had been condemned to encounter a fierce lion in the public theatre, a species of entertainment from which the Turks anticipated great sport. Being stripped of his arms and cuirass, for his enemies were bent on his destruction, Philip Pote was led forth into the arena. Yet he was not quite defenceless, for he had been allowed a short dagger, which his tormentors thought would be the means of his tormenting his savage antagonist, and thus exciting him to a state of fury. But the knight trusted in the little sword and the protection of our Lady of Hope, whom he now fervently invoked. So fortified was he by prayer, that the first bound of the lion did not have that terrific effect it generally produced upon its victims. He stood his ground firmly; and on the first opportunity, plunged the dagger into the lion's heart, who fell dead, while he himself remained perfectly unhurt. This hitherto unheard of achievement appeared so wonderful to the Turks, that by unanimous and spontaneous exclamations they demanded the freedom of the prisoner.

Grateful for his little less than miraculous preservation, the Christian knight returned to Europe, and caused his combat with the lion to be painted, in order that it might be suspended at the shrine of his Protectress.

The picture arrived at Dijon in May, 1441, and was presented, with great pomp, by the knight himself, in full costume, attended by his family, friends, and servants. There was a grand *fête* on the occasion, and great were the rejoicings of the citizens.

Another Knight of the Golden Fleece, Peter de Beaufremont, Count of Charny, Grand Chamberlain to the Duke of Burgundy, listening to the conversations held at the church porch by a noble company, concerning the supernatural protection which had been accorded to his friend, heard with impatience the cold and disdainful remarks which were made by some railers who sought to attribute human causes to superhuman effects. He suddenly rose in the midst of them, and, throwing his glove, declared that he would hold a tourney in honour of our Blessed Lady, and would break a lance with any one who offered to oppose him.

This bold defiance was met by boisterous cheering. The knights present ranged themselves on the side of Peter de Beaufremont; they were the Baron of Scey, William of Vienne, Andrew of Rabutin, two brothers of the house of Vaudrey, and many others who were dependants of the Great Chamberlain. But no one took up the glove, which remained in the church porch, in the very place it had fallen, for two years, until the time when the tournament took place two years after this time.

This singular pass of arms had been proclaimed in the two Burgundies, in Brabant, Flanders, the Low Countries, Portugal, Spain, England, Italy, and France, and it was not until the month of May, in the year 1443, that the tournament was opened with due splendour at Dijon.

The fifteen knights of our Lady issued out of the church, where they had assisted at a votive mass in her honour, and entered the lists, which were surrounded by a brilliant and eager assemblage. They were preceded by their esquires, all of whom bore a banner of the Blessed Virgin. Their retainers wore white blouses, with azure and gold trimmings, and bunches of roses were attached to their lances. But these bold champions had it all to themselves, say the old chronicles; no one dared to present himself to impugn the power of the Queen of Heaven. The vast assembly rent the air with their cries of joy, and went spontaneously to our Lady's Church, whither also followed the knights, whom the people called "Barons of the Blessed Virgin," who, while the *Magnificat* was sung in triumph, held their lances to the ground before her venerable image; and at its conclusion, liberally bestowed their *largess* upon the people.

The Lion of Brussels.

"Mater amabilis."   "Mother most loving."

AT the period of the first agitation caused by the pretended reformers of the sixteenth century, there was a lion in Brussels, concerning which the following curious anecdote is related. The fact, perhaps, is of equal merit with the lion of Florence, which has obtained the honour of being represented in painting.

The lion in question was taken during the last wars of Charles V. in Africa, tamed and apparently submissive; but, as is generally the case, in appearance only. Yet it was not confined in a cage, but suffered to go at large, and occasionally followed its master through the streets like a dog; and so accustomed did the people become to his calm and gentle behaviour, that his appearance excited no alarm. He was, however, greatly respected; it was held to be prudent not to seek a quarrel with him, as a lion is always a lion, with his fearful claws and terrible teeth. This truth had not, it appears, sunk deep into the mind of a little child. Alas! childhood is ever thoughtless. The boy, Daniel Pinus, was of noble family; and, accustomed daily to hear warlike exploits spoken of in his house as examples to inspire him with courage, the child thought that fear was a cowardly feeling never to be indulged in. At the time we write of, being between five and six years of age, he was walking by his mother's side in Carmelite-street, when he perceived the lion approaching in his usual quiet manner, taking no notice of anything around him. The child, who had disengaged his hand from his mother's, thinking that it would be a great thing to boast of, having braved the lion, on his approach struck the animal a smart blow on the head with his cane. The lion shook his mane; and, forgetting his education, sprung on the child, seized him round the middle, roaring with such fury as to alarm the neighbourhood. The civilized lion had disappeared; in his place appeared the furious host of the African deserts.

At this terrible sight, the poor mother fell on her knees. She knew not how to relieve her son from his perilous position; an imprudent act might cause his immediate destruction. She sought the aid of the Mother of Mercy; and seeing before her the Carmelite church, in which was established the pious and celebrated confraternity of the Scapular, in which the most noble gentlemen and ladies of Brussels were enrolled, she rushed into it; and throwing herself at the feet of our Lady of Carmel, cried out with vehemence,

"O Mary, Patroness of the Scapular! I give you my child. Do you take him from out of the lion's jaw, and he shall be consecrated to you for ever!"

This was the work of a few seconds. Scarcely had the prayer been pronounced, when the lion suddenly became appeased, dropped the child gently, and quietly continued his walk.

This event made a deep impression on the mind of the child, who warmly seconded his mother's vow. Daniel Pinus consecrated himself to our Lady of Carmel, and spent his life in the service of her to whom he owed his preservation. Sanderus adds, that the child's parents, in order to commemorate the event, presented to the church a magnificent altar frontal, on which the adventure was carved, with this inscription, "*De ore leonis, libera nos Domine!*"—"From the lion's jaw deliver us, O Lord!"

It is also recorded that the lion lost his liberty after this accident. But, alas! the Carmelite church fell in the destruction of churches in 1796. The confraternity of the Holy Scapular was transferred to the church of our Lady of Help, where also the image of the Holy Virgin of Carmel is still venerated.

The Prisoner's Mother.

"Mater admirabilis."   "Admirable Mother."

SHE who during three long sad days was separated from her Divine Son, and recovered him with joy in the temple, can never be insensible to a mother's grief.

In the beginning of the seventeenth century, a poor widow, of the Maritime Alps, whose support was derived from an only son, a fisherman, anxiously waited for his return one evening: but he came not.

There had been no tempest to excite her fear for his safety; so, though the morning dawned, and he had not returned, she still hoped that some delay, for which she could not account, had prevented his reaching home sooner. But in a few hours, news arrived that her dear son and his companions had been taken prisoners by the Turks, and carried to Algiers or Tunis.

The poor mother wept bitterly at the thought of her son's captivity, without any mixture of selfish feelings. She possessed no means of ransoming him herself, but her hopes were placed on the good Fathers of Mercy—those pious servants of Mary devoted to the liberation of captives.

But the religious, in her neighbourhood, were now occupied in collecting alms for the ransom of Christian slaves, and could not depart for the African coast until after the winter. In the mean time, how severe were the son's sufferings, how bitter the mother's tears!

One day, while indulging her grief, she said to herself, "The good Fathers of the Redemption of captives are the humble servants of the Holy Virgin. It is she who guides and protects the m. I will then have recourse to her immediate assistance. When was she known to despise a mother's tears?"

A few leagues from her hut, there was a much-frequented chapel of our Lady. It is still a celebrated pilgrimage, near Nice, and is called, *Our Lady's of the Little Lake* (Laghetto), and this is said to be the origin of its name. The spot on which the chapel now stands was formerly a small lake. Upon its waters something brilliant was seen floating one evening. Boats were put out, and it was discovered to be an image of our dear Lady. A venerable priest received it with honour, and the whole neighbourhood passed the night in singing the litany and hymns before the image. In the morning, they were astonished to see the lake dried up. Such has been the constant tradition. In the centre of the ground were discovered the ruins of an ancient chapel, which was immediately restored. Many miracles are recorded to have taken place in this chapel.

It was here, then, that the poor widow sought relief in her deep distress. She passed nine days on the spot praying, without ceasing, for the prisoner's return. After the novena, she went home, full of hope, as to the result. As she approached her cot, her fond eyes quickly discerned a figure, standing at the door. It was her son; he had escaped on the day she had commenced her novena, and had arrived at his mother's house on the day of its conclusion.

Our Lady of Verviers.

"Mater Creatoris."   "Mother of our Creator."

THE country round Liege is rarely visited by earthquakes, yet there have been occasions for fearing such accidents. Such was the feeling of the inhabitants of Verviers on the morning of the 18th September, 1692. The weather was lowering, the atmosphere underwent an unusual change, and the earth sent forth such fearful sounds, that the sages of the city declared that nature was suffering, and that the results would be most unfavourable. The almanac of Matthew Laensburg, which had then acquired some celebrity, was far from reassuring the people, for he announced for the season they were entering:—Phenomena, and derangements of nature.

When everything prospers, when our health, business, appetite, and sleep are good, we are bold and boastful; but when a change takes place, then we show the white feather and feel conscious of our weakness. Thus, said an old sage, fear is good, since it renders us humble. The tempest awakens the tepid soul, thunder instils good resolutions, the fear of some sudden disaster brings to our mind the remembrance of the slight tenure on which our lives depend, and the desire to pray, our only real strength here below, revives our troubled hearts. Thus were the churches of Verviers crowded on the day we record. The church of the Franciscan Father or Recollets, seemed to have attracted the largest congregation; for the city had great devotion to an image of the Blessed Virgin which belonged to that church, and which had been the source of many graces to the good townsfolk. This image, nearly of the natural size, was of stone, and placed over the porch in such a manner as to look down upon all who entered the sacred building; while the figure of the Infant Jesus stood on a globe at the distance of a foot from His mother, on her right, holding his hand up as it were to bless the faithful. Before entering the church, no one failed to raise his eyes to these sweet figures and to say his "Hail, Mary."

On the 18th of September, 1692, as the Father who said the mass was leaving the altar, the congregation rushed out of the church to see the cause of the clamour which was heard from without. A prodigy had taken place before an immense multitude of spectators, amounting to four thousand citizens, who testified to the truth of the event.

The two statues turned, faced, and approached each other. Their hands were joined by this movement. The sceptre which our Lady had before borne was thus held by her and her Divine Son jointly. They who half an hour before had seen the statues in their former position, were thunderstruck, as the reader may imagine. Was it a phenomenon of nature? But how could such a wondrous event take place by any natural means? No! it must be a miracle.

At the same time the sun shot his rays through the clouds, and fine weather appeared, which made the people imagine that this was a sign from the God of Nature of his Divine interposition.

In order to preserve a memorial of this wonderful event, the public notaries were charged to draw up a statement of the facts, the truth of which was attested on oath before the crucifix, by the most respectable townsmen who had seen the prodigy.

A few days afterwards, all Europe was terrified by hearing, that on the 18th of September, the very day of the miraculous movements of the images of our Lady and her Divine Son, at Verviers, a dreadful earthquake had desolated many countries; that several towns in Sicily had been destroyed by this disaster; and that a hundred and eight thousand souls had perished. The good people of Verviers now understood the reason of the wonders which they had seen, and that they had escaped by the special intervention of the Blessed Mother of God with her Divine Son, in favour of a pious and devout city.

Who will deny that this event was a miracle? It was followed by so many wonderful cures, supernatural gifts, and signal favours obtained at the feet of our Lady of Mercy of Verviers, that we may be permitted to believe that it was something more than a simple phenomenon.

The Legend of Sister Beatrice.

"Mater Salvatoris."   "Mother of our Savour."

HE first to recount the legend of Sister Beatrice, was Brother Cesar Heisterbach, a monk of Citeaux. He gives it as an event of his own times, and he wrote at the beginning of the thirteenth century, a period when sentiments of good feeling and of charity abounded.*

In a convent, whose name our chronicler does not consider it necessary to mention, there lived in the twelfth century a maiden called Beatrice. She had entered the holy dwelling in her childhood. Endowed with a pure and spotless mind, her youth had passed there delightfully, for she knew not nor thought of any other world beyond its precincts. The day came on which she was to make her vows. Happy day for her! For years had she longed to be clothed in the simple habit of the good community. Excited by the warmth of her devotion to our Blessed Lady, she consecrated herself to her service, and became by her virtues an honour and a blessing to her convent.

On attaining her eighteenth year, Sister Beatrice possessed an innocent heart, a conscience perfectly free from any shade of sin, and a calm, mild de-

* It is thought that Cesar Heisterbach died in 1240.

meanour. To these real and solid advantages were joined the gifts—too often, alas! fatal to youth,—of exquisite beauty of person and graceful manners. Yet, she considered not her beauty; nay, perhaps knew not she possessed so eminently charms which would have turned the head of many a worldly girl. She led the life of the saints, seeking to follow at a humble distance in the footsteps of the Queen of Virgins. Her great delight was prayer, in which she seemed to have a foretaste of the joys of heaven, and she was ever first to obey the summons to the holy hours of the divine office. She listened with the deepest attention to holy reading, that intellectual food which nourishes and strengthens our souls in our pilgrimage through life. Her sweetest occupation was to deck our Lady's altar, to work costly robes for her loved image, to renew daily the choicest flowers which were offered to her shrine, to weave them into crowns for her and her Divine Son, and to imitate during the winter season those flowers which Nature denies us, but which the fair sister excelled in producing in various materials. Beatrice was loved by the whole sisterhood, who did everything to show their admiration of her virtues, and all thought her an especial favourite of our dear Lady.

The life of Sister Beatrice passed thus smoothly along in the quiet discharge of those duties which it was her great happiness to fulfil, and which so well became her, when a young clerk was engaged for the service of the altar, who was more impressed with the spirit of the world than of that of the religious life. The good nuns dreamed not of the existence of any evil in the young man, but would have spurned any thought which would

have reflected on the character of any person who
ministered at the altar. Satan, however, had
unfortunately obtained possession of his heart.
Forgetting the sacred vows she had taken, he
dared to gaze on the beauty of Beatrice with
unholy passion. Instead of fighting with his
temptations, or rather flying from the object of
their suggestions, he entertained them, and sought
the company of the pure creature, whom he now
strove to draw with himself into the abyss of
crime.

Seizing the first opportunity of finding her
alone, he expressed, with well feigned hypocrisy,
the astonishment he felt at seeing her immured in
a cloister. How was it that at this first attack of
the enemy, the poor girl did not suspect his evil
designs? Did the suggestions of vanity so soon
gain possession of her mind? He drew a picture
of the world in colours so alluring, but at the
same time so false, that he caught the poor young
creature in his snare.

He employed all the resources of his mind to
shake her simple and confiding faith. No false-
hoods or exaggerations, or screened impiety, or
gross dissimulations, were spared to bring trouble
and doubt into the pure maid's mind. Oh! woe
be to her who allows the enemy to plant his foot
in the sacred enclosure of her virtue! Oh! woe
to the soul who ceases for one moment to watch,
and who flies not at the approach of the enemy,
and knows not that she alone is weakness itself!
Beatrice relaxed in the fervour of her devotions.
Her habitual serenity abandoned her, and a vague
kind of uneasiness took possession of her, and increased daily in gaining the mastery over her
conduct. She dreamed continually of a vain

liberty, until she had brought herself to believe that in abandoning God, she would receive the most delightful recompense in the false pleasures and delicious homage of the world. Foolish virgin!

After two other conferences, which were conducted with the greatest cunning by the wily clerk, Beatrice promised to run away from the convent—without so much as hinting her determination to those once dear guides of her youth—and to give herself up to the conduct of a young man she knew not, to see this world, of which he drew so flattering a picture, but whose real miseries she was, in her simplicity, far from imagining.

The only thing which caused her any concern was, that she did not *feel* happy, being ignorant that such is ever the case with those who abandon the course of rectitude. But, doubtless, she was not aware of the greatness of the crime she committed in treading her vows under feet.

Before leaving her convent, after midnight, when all the sisters had retired to their cells, the guilty nun was inspired with a desire of kneeling once more before the image of our dear Lady, whom, despite her late inconstancy, she had never ceased to love tenderly. She entered the chapel. For how many years had this sanctuary been her paradise! and now she was about to flee from it. She approached the altar, knelt, and scarce daring to raise her eyes to the figure of the Blessed Virgin, burst into tears. "O most holy Virgin," she at length murmured, with a troubled heart, "O most good Lady, my dear Mother and support to this day, I am now about to leave thee; still, as I ever was, I will remain faithful to thee, for I love thee dearly, my sweet Protectress. But thou seest how I am forced into the world. Alas! I feel that I am no longer worthy of serving thee. Take pity on me, I beseech thee!"

After this hasty prayer, she rose; and, as if fearful of being detained, she quickly placed her keys at the foot of the image, while, with downcast eyes, she said:

"Here are the keys thou didst confide to me, and which I can restore to no one else but thee, O Holy Virgin!"

As she spoke, a flower fell from the bouquets in our Lady's hand. She hurriedly picked it up, kissed it, and placing it in her bosom, determined never to part with it; she turned, and left our Lady's shrine. The clerk awaited her at a little distance with two fleet horses, which soon bore them far into the world.

After a few short months he abandoned her! Beatrice was alone in the wide world, covered with shame, remorse, and despair. She saw but one path before her; it was revolting to her sight, still she rushed into it.

Fifteen long wretched years had nigh passed over the head of the poor unhappy outcast, when she fell grievously sick. Then did the memory of Her whom she had never forgotten, but had still loved even in her career of guilt—of the holy one whose sweet flower she had ever preserved in her bosom—of Her who never rejects the guilty one, rush into her thoughts, till streams of tears filled her eyes, and sobs convulsed her breast. Fearing that the hour of death approached, and knowing the all-powerful Mary was her only refuge, she prayed most fervently; bitterly bewailing her fall, and its terrible consequences, and entreating her sweet Protectress to obtain for her one grace—the grace of once more being allowed to kneel in sorrow before her dear image, to kiss the floor of the little chapel of the convent in which the years of her innocence had been spent; that she might journey there as a beggar, and expiate her scandalous life by public penance was her ardent wish.

She now began to regain her strength. Faithful to her first intention, she distributed her little trinkets among the poor, and, clad in the meanest apparel, sought the road to her convent. *Her* convent! Oh, no! She dared not thus profane that sacred dwelling, even in thought. A hundred leagues were between her and the end of her journey. She passed over them without murmur or complaint, suffering everything for love of Mary, seeking neither pity nor consolation, and almost feeling happy, though still in that miserable world, to see which she had paid so dearly. At length she reached the spot which had beheld her chaste and sinless.

As she approached the convent, she again heard the sound once so sweet in her ears of the bell, calling the sisterhood to choir. Her heart beat quickly, and tears flowed freely from her eyes. The moment she beheld the turret, beneath which stood Mary's shrine, she fell on her knees, and thanked her sweet Patroness most warmly for having drawn her from the depths of vice and misery in which she had voluntarily placed herself. She then approached the convent with faltering steps, though she knew well that no one there could recognize her in her fallen condition, and much changed appearance. But the thoughts of the days of her innocence, and the painful contrast of the past and present, tore her heartstrings, and made her pause to recover strength and determination to proceed.

She at length touches the convent gate. Within that peaceful enclosure she had lived in peace. The signal for the religious to repair to the refectory is given. All the soft calm and tranquillity of her convent life steals upon her, and she almost fancies she has but quitted its routine for a day. It seems as if she has scarce roved beyond the enclosure, that her last fifteen years have been some horrid dream. She wishes to ascertain whether she has been deluded or not. She is among the poor, who, under the convent porch, await to receive the sisters' bounty after their frugal meal. She thanks God he has permitted her to be in the company of his friends. And when the distribution of food takes place, she receives her share from the hands of one in whom *she* recognizes a companion of her youth.

"What makes you tremble so, my child?" asks the nun.

"Oh! I have come some distance, and I am not quite recovered," replies the mendicant. Then, taking courage, she adds, "Pray, tell me, dear sister, is it in this convent that a poor girl, called Beatrice, dwelt, formerly?"

The religious stares at her to see whether she presents any appearance of folly, and then asks,—

"Do you know sister Beatrice, then?"

"Formerly, sister, when she used to adorn our lady's . . . ."

"Blush not so deeply, my child. If you knew sister Beatrice it must have been a great pleasure to you."

"Certainly. But for fifteen years . . . . . "

"Well! for fifteen years?"

The traveller pauses, trembles, and passes her clammy hand across her brow, and then asks,—

"Is it known what has become of sister Beatrice these fifteen years?"

"No one is ignorant of her conduct," replies the astonished sister: "you must indeed have come from a great distance, my poor child, not to have heard of her."

The penitent hangs her head, feeling convinced that her past life is known to all; and she says no more. But the good sister, before retiring, draws the penitent to her, and whispers,—

"Since you formerly knew sister Beatrice, you may just step into the chapel, where you will see her for a few moments."

"I shall see sister Beatrice,?" she echoes aloud; but, thinks she, it must be another sister of the same name: "this cannot be the sister Beatrice I knew?"

"The very same. Our dear sister Beatrice, who for thirty years has been the joy and glory of our house, the same who was brought up in this convent, who for the last seventeen years has been sister Sacristan—the model of a religious, the cherished friend of our Blessed Lady. But, come in, and ask her to pray for you; her prayers are indeed valuable."

The poor sinner, who knows not whether she hears rightly or is under some delusion, advances into the church, throws herself upon her knees on the pavement, and thus makes her way towards our Lady's shrine, where a still more astounding wonder awaits her. She there sees, with admiration, her own person standing before the altar. The figure moves towards her; it has her own features and appearance, not indeed disfigured and withered as they now are, but such as they were fifteen years before, when beautiful, joyful, and pure; she was far from conceiving her sad fall . . . .

The apparition, for such she deems it, approaches her; and with a countenance beaming with goodness, presents her with the same keys which on the fatal night she had laid at our Lady's feet. The figure says to her,—

"Take back the keys, daughter, which you restored to me. In order that your fall should not be known, I have, during the fifteen years you have been absent, myself taken your place. But now that I see you return to my feet in such sentiments of penitence, I know you will never abandon me again. Go now to your cell, and put on your holy habit."

After pronouncing these words in a tender voice, the apparition rises gently in the air, and in the midst of a ray of heavenly light, seems to enter the image over the altar. And thus the poor wandering penitent recognises her dear Mother and constant Protectress. Bathed in delicious tears; overwhelmed, yet relieved, the penitent rushed through the cloister into her cell, feeling she had regained all her strength and health. She found the quiet cell exactly in the same state in which she had left it. Her habit, which she had cast off on that ever-to-be-lamented day, lay on the spot where she had thrown it. She hastily put it on, determined at once to seek the convent director. She again entered the chapel, and knelt to pour forth her gratitude to her dear Benefactress, who smiled on her with heavenly sweetness, for she was rejoicing in heaven at the return of her lost lamb. She then sought the confessional.

The good monk, who during fifteen years had considered sister Beatrice to be most highly favoured by heaven with the gift of perfection, was deeply moved by the sorrowful and penitential avowal made by the real Beatrice of the years of her sad career of vice, and of its wonderful termination; and, considering that our Lady herself desired the scandal to be concealed, wisely determined and told Beatrice not to mention it to any one of the sisters.

By a persevering and austere penance, the more meritorious as it was concealed, Beatrice recovered her innocence before God. She lived many years; and it was not till after her death, which was most edifying, that the wonderful manifestation of our Lady's charity in her regard was made known to the world, by the publication of a manuscript left by the holy penitent to her confessor.*

* This legend has been made the subject of a charming tale by M. Charles Nodier in the *Revue de Paris* (Oct. 22, 1837). He, however, made the seducer a knight, who, being wounded, was taken to the convent, and cured of his own wounds; but in return, inflicts still greater ones on the simple-minded Beatrice. He has also fixed the locality of the event in a convent in the Jura, dedicated to our Lady of the Flowering Thorn. The first portion of the narrative relating to her holy image we have appended to our legend, deeming there may be some degree of authenticity about it; but we give it in the writer's own words, and without being responsible for any of the details.

The Saint.

AFTER some most truthful remarks on the folly of the past age in seeking all its legends and fable from classic mythology, the author just cited continues:—"We shall find many a stirring legend in old dusty moth-eaten books written by simple-minded men; or, at the chimney-corner in some village, far from the haunts of modern society, listening to the tales of the country folk. There you will find those touching and eloquent traditions, whose authority no one will venture to contest, which pass from generation to generation as a pious inheritance from the lips of the elders. These recitals can afford no subject for discussion; they defy the criticism of an exacting reason which contracts the soul, and a disdainful philosophy which withers it; they are not confined to the limits of ordinary occurrences, or even those of possibility, for that which is considered to be impossible at the present day, was doubtless possible formerly, when the world was younger and more innocent than it now is,—was worthy of the miracles God wrought in it, when angels and saints could associate, without much derogation of their heavenly character, with its simple and innocent people, whose life was spent between labour and the practice of good works . . . .

"O, you, my friends, from whom the divine light which illuminated man on the day of his creation has not been withdrawn; you, who still possess a soul to believe, to love, and to feel; you, into whose minds no thoughts of despair of yourselves or your future state ever enter, come and share with me in those enchanting words which revive in our hearts the ages of simplicity and of virtue. But delay not I conjure you! To-morrow, perhaps, will be too late. The spirit of progress has told you that it advances, and the monster takes huge strides indeed. All the ills which writing draws after her, all the evils of printing, her perverse and fruitful sister, menace the destruction of the last asylums of ancient modesty, piety, and innocence, under an escort of gloomy pedants. In a few years, this new world, which the genius of evil will seize upon in its cradle, will be versed in an absurd system of learning, but will be ignorant of God. A few more years, and the small remnant of the children of nature will be as dull and as wicked as their masters. Let us then hasten to listen to these delicious tales of the people, before they have forgotten them; before they have learned to blush at them, and before their chaste poetry, ashamed of her state of innocence shall cover herself with a veil, like Eve, exiled from Paradise.

"For my part, I have resolved never to recount or listen to any other histories than these. The one I am about to relate is drawn from an old biographer, called *Bzovius*, a continuator of *Baronius*, but little known. . . . .

"Not far from the highest point of Jura, on the declivity of its western side, there might be seen fifty years ago, a group of ruins, which once formed part of the monastery of *our Lady of the Flowering Thorn.* It is on the extremity of a narrow and deep defile, but much more sheltered on the northern side, where, thanks to this protection, the rarest flowers of the country flourish. Half a league hence, the opposite extremity shows the remains of an ancient lordly manor-house, which has disappeared with the house of God. All we know is, that it was inhabited by a family renowned in arms, and that the last of these knights, whose name it bears, died at the conquest of his Blessed Lord's tomb in Palestine, without leaving any heir to succeed him. His widow, unconsolable at his loss, would not abandon the spot endeared to her by his memory, but by her pious acts perpetuated her remembrance in the minds of the people far around, by whom she was then and is still known by the name of '*the Saint.*'

"On one of the last days of winter, *the Saint* was walking according to her custom in the long avenue leading to her castle, occupied in heavenly contemplation. She thus reached the thorn bush which then, as now, terminated the avenue, when to her utter astonishment she perceived that one of the thorns was already covered with its spring flowers. She hurried on to the spot, to assure herself whether it was not some remains of snow which caused it to assume this appearance, but she was delighted to see her first impressions confirmed by an immense number of little white starlike flowers with carnation rays. She carefully gathered a branch to suspend in her oratory before a much-venerated image of the Blessed Virgin. Whether this small tribute of love was agreeable to the Mother of Jesus, or that some indefinable feeling of pleasure is reserved for tender hearts in the performance of the least act of affection towards the object of its esteem, never had the lady of the castle experienced more sweet emotions than she did on the evening on which she made her offering. So that she resolved to renew the tribute every day. We can easily believe that she kept this resolution faithfully.

"One day, however, when the care of the poor and the sick had retained her in the village longer than usual, she had to hurry in order to reach her wild flower garden. Night advanced, and it is said she began to regret being out so late, when a pure and brilliant light burst forth over the thorn bush, showing its flowers as clearly as in the day. She stopped for an instant, fearing this unusual light might proceed from bandits, or some other cause she could not divine. But remembering her resolution, she boldly advanced and seized one of the branches, which seemed to drop into her hand, so little effort did it require to break it; she then hastened towards the house without daring to look back.

"During the whole night *the Saint* reflected on this strange phenomenon, without being able to solve it. Anxious to satisfy her mind on the subject, she repaired to the bush the next evening at the same hour, accompanied by a venerable priest, her chaplain, and two attendants. They saw the heavenly light again hovering over the bush, which, as they approached, increased in brilliancy. They then stopped and knelt, out of reverence, at this wondrous sight, and the good priest rising, approached respectfully towards the bush, chanting a hymn of the Church, and pushed it aside without difficulty. The sight which then struck their eyes so astounded them, that they remained for some time motionless, penetrated with gratitude and joy. It was an image of the Blessed Virgin carved with much simplicity in common wood, and coloured with little skill. From this figure proceeded the luminous appearance around. "Hail, Mary! full of grace," at length exclaimed the chaplain, falling on his knees, and from the delicious music which answered his salutation one would have thought that the bush was filled with celestial spirits. He then recited the Litany of Loreto, which the assistants answered, and raising the image from its wooden pedestal carried it with reverence to the castle, where it was destined to occupy a more worthy sanctuary, while the lady and her attendants followed, joining their prayers with those of the priest.

"I need not dilate upon the care taken to surround the image of our Lady with all the elegant and costly materials in the oratory of the lady of the castle. Yet in the morning it was not to be found, and the alarm was great at its sudden disappearance. What secret sin could have deprived the lady of the manor—*the Saint*—of this honoured statue of our Lady?.. Why had our Lady quitted her?... What new resting-place had she chosen?....

"The reader has doubtless devised the solution of this question. The Blessed Mother of God had preferred the modest shelter of the thornbush to the exquisitely carved oratory of the lady of the castle. She had returned to her first abode to enjoy the quiet of its solitude and the fragrance of its flowers. All the inhabitants of the castle returned to the bush in the evening, and found it more brilliantly illumined than on the eve. They fell on their knees in respectful silence.

"'Powerful Queen of Queens,' said *the Saint*, 'since this spot is so favoured by your gracious pleasure, your will shall be obeyed.' And in a short time a splendid chapel, on which all the skill of the first architects of the day was lavished, reared its fretted vaults over our Lady's image. The great and powerful ones of the earth enriched it with their gifts. Kings endowed it with a tabernacle of gold. The miracles worked at this shrine were soon known over the whole Christian world. A great many pious women came and settled in the valley and formed a community of religious. The good widow, moved by divine grace, entered it and was elected superior. She died there after a long life of good deeds, by which she increased the renown of the sanctuary."

Such is, according to the manuscript chronicles of the province, the origin of the foundation of the church and convent of "*Our Lady of the Flowering Thorn.*" This convent, two centuries later, is said to be the scene of the legend of Sister Beatrice.

The Keys of Poictiers.

"Virgo prudentissima."   "Most prudent Virgin."

N the year 1295, Philip the Fair retook Aquitaine from the English by stratagem, unattended by much difficulty, seeing that the people of that country were French, and liked not the English yoke.

The English, naturally loathe to quit this fair province of France, whose warm genial air and rich wines they had found so pleasant, sought every means to regain possession of the territory. But no better plan could they devise than to corrupt one of the garrison, and to engage him to admit them by stealth into a fortified city. Poictiers was the place fixed upon; it was a large, opulent, well-fortified city, seated on high ground, and it was thought that if they could once again firmly station themselves within its walls, they would not so easily be dispossessed of the city.

But the good people of Poictiers were on their guard; the mayor and his officers were loyal and true, the citizens themselves guarded the ramparts, and every evening, having lowered the portcullis, raised the draw-bridges, and well closed and locked the ponderous gates, they bore the keys to the mayor of Poictiers, who always kept them under his pillow during the night.

Treason never acts at ease and exactly as it wishes; it leads man whithersoever it pleases with uncertain steps, masked and sounding the ground as it advances, seeking an entry or issue, and always in doubt as to the security of its path.

The agents who were employed to betray Poictiers, saw at once the impossibility of attacking the mayor; a word or hint would have made him redouble his vigilance. His subordinates were fortunately considered equally honest and incorruptible. After long and ineffectual attempts to shake the fidelity of others, a man was found base enough to sell his trust; it was the secretary to the mayor, commonly called *clerk* in old chronicles, a name given to all men who could write well and were versed in literature. And now begins our legend.

The clerk of the mayor of Poictiers was doubtless a bad man, for rarely is treason undertaken for any but vicious ends. In his bargain with the English he engaged to open one of the city gates for them. He knew well where the keys were kept; but how could he secure them? The slightest movement in taking them from beneath the pillow might awake the mayor. Should he kill him? Oh, no! though a traitor, he could not steep his hands in his patron's blood. He conceived another idea.

Covering his face with a mask, he pretended to have suddenly acquired an increase of patriotism; and one stormy night, knowing that the mayor had passed a laborious day, and was soundly sleeping, he rushed into his room at an early hour in the morning, and hastily rousing him, asked him for the keys of the city, to let out an officer who had been sent for by the king. There was such a tone of sincerity in the clerk's voice and manner, that the mayor suspected no evil; but raising himself, sought for the keys; but to his great astonishment found they were missing.

"Are we betrayed?" cried he, springing from his bed: "I was so wearied, and have slept so soundly, that I did not feel their removal."

In saying these words he had hastily put on a coat, and now rushed into the street, spreading terror and alarm, without remarking the stupified appearance of his clerk, who followed him with trembling limbs, considering whether there could be another traitor in the city besides himself.

The whole city was soon aroused, the citizens seized their arms, and rushed to the ramparts. Thence they discovered the English in small bands, half-concealed, and awaiting evidently for some signal from within. But the gates were all closed and well guarded.

The day dawning, their bands dispersed and disappeared. There was but one apprehension remaining—the keys could not be discovered. Yet was it thought a duty to return thanks to the Almighty for the safety of the city. The mayor, his suite, and the whole population, went to the church of Great St. Mary, to assist at a solemn mass of thanksgiving. This church contained a venerated image of our Blessed Lady, who was honoured as the Patroness of Poictiers. Judge of the astonishment of the multitude in finding the keys which were missing in the hands of the holy image.

"It is our Lady," cried they, "who, foreseeing some treason, has taken care of the keys during the night. It is the Blessed Virgin who has saved Poictiers!"

What tended much to confirm this opinion was, that the mayor, generally so vigilant, had not been disturbed in the night, and that his clerk had fled to the English camp. The circumstances were formally drawn up into a memorial to the king, who thought himself bound to confer special privileges on the church of St. Mary the Great. He accordingly ordered that the keys of the city should in future be confided to the care of its canons; that they should be at liberty to pardon a criminal once a year, and have the administration of justice during the three Rogation days.

Our Lady's Image.

"Virgo Veneranda."   "Venerable Virgin."

THEY who have never visited the towns and villages of a Catholic country, cannot conceive the feeling of delight with which the pious traveller is affected at the sight of those monuments of piety and religious recollection, which, in the shape of crucifixes, images of the Blessed Virgin, and favourite saints, are placed at the angle of streets, in squares, and public places, on bridges, fountains, and obelisks, or between the stalls of a village market or fair. These works of popular art and devotion, formerly existed in great cities also, recalling to the passenger's mind thoughts of the object and end of his earthly pilgrimage. They also served a benevolent purpose, and exercised a civilizing influence over the passions of men. Many a pure spring would have been adulterated but for the presence of its presiding saint. Often has the revengeful spirit of an enemy been appeased, when on the point of immolating his victim, by the sight of a man-god suffering for all mankind. The poor soul of some betrayed girl plunged in deep despair and meditating self-destruction, passes on her way the figure of our Lady of Sorrows, and falling on her knees, obtains comfort and strength from the Mother of

Holy Hope and sweet consolation. Again, in ancient times, cities were but badly lighted, and towns not at all. Piety supplied this deficiency. Each statue or holy image had its little lantern, which gave honour to the saint and light to the locality.

Some pretended philosophers may sneer at these objects of popular devotion. But have they ever considered the benefits of which they have been the source, the evils they have remedied, the griefs they have calmed, and the crimes they have stayed? Among the cities nearest our shores, Antwerp is one which has most fully preserved this mediæval custom, and contains innumerable pious souvenirs of the ages of faith. Paris was formerly equally distinguished. " At the corner of every street," writes the *Abbé Orsini*, "a little image of Mary rose from amidst a heap of flowers, which the pious people of the neighbourhood renewed each morning as soon as the trumpets from the towers of Châtelet announced the break of day. During the night lamps burnt constantly before them, illuminating their little grey niches, and on Saturdays their number was greatly increased. This was the first attempt to light the streets. A poor illumination, perhaps, when compared to our modern gaslights, yet had it one great advantage over ours, for to it was added a pious object, which excited the people to holy reflection. The silver lights of the Madonna's shrines shot forth at intervals like a string of stars from their flowery beds, and seemed to say to those who wandered abroad with ill intent,— 'There watches over this city, wrapt in slumber, an eye that never closes, but which sees through all our hearts—the eye of God.'"

One of these Madonnas, which occupied its little niche at the corner of the streets, Des Ours and Salle-au-Comte, gained great celebrity by an event, the details of which are somewhat obscure, and have given *savants* much room for disputation. It would appear from the popular tradition, that one night, at a very early period, a drunken man left an inn where he had lost all his money, took offence at the innocent image, and struck it several blows with his dagger. Whether, to show her sense of the indignity, our Lady caused blood to flow from her statue, or that the criminal had cut his hand in his daring outrage, the bystanders were amazed to see the holy image covered with blood. They pursued the man; but some persons fearing the popular rage if allowed to vent itself upon its victim, concealed him, and the people to satisfy themselves, made an effigy of the wretch and burnt it before the image, as some expiation for the insult.

In commemoration of this event, an annual procession took place on the 3rd of July, in which an immense effigy fifteen feet high was carried, and afterwards burned in the evening, accompanied by a display of fireworks. This latter part of the ceremony was wisely forbidden by the magistrates in 1745.

The gigantic figures which were burnt in the Rue des Ours, and in many other places, as in Alsatia and Lorraine, have a very different origin from that supposed by some authors, (who derive the custom from pagan times,) and has rather an anti-pagan and entirely Christian meaning.*

* Among these authors is Dulaure in his compilation of mean and obscure pamphlets, to which he has given the title of *Histoire de Paris*, being anything but an historical

Who has not seen a representation of an enormous figure of the human shape, composed of osier work, in which the Druids of Helvetia and of Germany, burnt human victims; a sort of monster idol, which was consumed itself with its holocaust? The apostles of these countries, after having planted that first instrument of civilization, the cross, retained these figures and burnt them, not indeed filled with human bodies, but with branches of trees and other instruments of pagan worship. And in many countries a colossal figure is burnt every year, in commemoration of some person or event, as in the Rue des Ours, on the 3rd of July, within the octave of the feasts of SS. Peter and Paul, and at other places on the 3rd of May, a day consecrated to the triumphs of the cross.

work. He also gives a pagan derivation to the giants carried or drawn in the processions in the towns of Belgium and Flanders. The good people of these countries, however, have retained in their archives and traditions the history of these triumphal giants, as they call them, which refers them to the return of the first crusaders. All bear the name of ancient knights and warriors, except one, which has, I know not for what reason, the name of the Tyrant of Alost. But this is never burnt.

The Precipice.

"Virgo Prædicanda."　　"Renowned Virgin."

ANY saints have lived on earth unknown to men, whose hearts were entirely detached from the world, and who sought only to know and be known to God. Such was one of the patrons of the diocese of Cahors, whose life was so hidden, that even his real name is unknown, and he is venerated under the title given to him by the people—*Amadour*—perhaps from his great love of God and of solitude. He lived in the wild and rugged rocks. We do not intend to give the popular legend concerning him, which is not sufficiently trustworthy. But we state a well-established fact, that in the third century in which he lived, he constructed in one of the rocks, called from him, *Roc-Amadour*, a little sanctuary dedicated to Mary. St. Martial consecrated this chapel, which became a celebrated pilgrimage, and from this humble dwelling hewn out of the rough rock, has the Help of Christians dispensed many a blessing.

In the eighth century, pilgrims from all parts visited it. Roland, the illustrious nephew of Charlemagne, travelling through Quercy, in 778, turned out of the highway to seek the lofty sanctuary of Roc-Amadour. Many persons of distinction followed in the tract of the noble hero of Roncevaux. Rich presents were made to the chapel and placed over and about its simple wooden altar, and soon a body of religious attached themselves to its service, and a town sprung up near it. Several privileges were accorded to the spot by Popes Clement II., Alexander III., Gregory XI., Martin V., Pius II., Clement XII., Pius VI., and Gregory XVI.

During the early wars, the holy image venerated at Roc-Amadour was held in such respect, that they who carried about them the medal on which it was represented were never molested. Sad indeed is it to relate, that the Protestants in 1562, and the revolutionists of 1793, those epochs of destructiveness, profaned this holy spot by their presence and its inevitable consequences. But we will hurry over these terrible scenes. Their violence could not detract one iota of the power or the influence of our sweet Lady, who, as she protected Erard de Brienne during the first crusade in 1217, and the Viscount de Turenne in his engagements in the fourteenth century, still blesses the pious pilgrims who frequent her shrine.

From the innumerable miracles which have been wrought by our Lady of Roc-Amadour, we have selected one simple history.*

* During the invasion of the Saracens, it is related that the banner of our Lady of Roc-Amadour struck the infidels with consternation, so that they fled at its approach. One of the historians of this sanctuary tells us that there exists in its little turret a small bell, which has neither rope nor chain attached to it, but which rings at certain times without the aid of any person. Ferry de Locres attests the same fact. It is considered that on the occasions on which

THE PRECIPICE.

At the commencement of the last century, a man, who, in his early age had made the pilgrimage of Roc-Amadour, was travelling through Auvergne, along a very dangerous road cut out of the rocks and bordered by precipices. He was on horseback. A terrible storm arose. The lightning was so vivid and the thunder increased with such fearful rapidity, that he was obliged to halt and dismount. But as he was in the act of withdrawing his foot from the stirrup it became entangled, and he could not succeed in gaining the ground. In his efforts to disentangle his foot, he struck the spurs into the horse's flank. The animal, which had been frightened by the lightning, on receiving the spur, set off at a furious and headlong gallop along the rocks, leaping over gaps, completely freed from all control.

The terrified traveller bethought him in his need of our Lady of Roc-Amadour; he implored her help with all the earnestness and warmth of one who is about to perish. Scarce was his prayer ended, when he closed his eyes and felt a strange sensation come over him. On his recovery, he discovered that he was in perfect safety and on his feet, while below him at the bottom of an immense precipice, he saw the mangled body of his horse. On looking at his feet, he found that the sole and spur had been torn away, while the upper leather still covered his ancle. The powerful hand which had held him when on the brink of the precipice, had

the bell sounds, it is a signal of some grace having been accorded by the Blessed Virgin, as shortly afterwards pilgrims come to return thanks for favours received on the same day, and in many cases at the same moment that the bell rang.

placed him on an artificial seat in the rock, where he found himself on recovering his senses. The rescued traveller devoutly signed himself with the holy cross, and hastened directly to Roc-Amadour to thank our Lady for his wonderful preservation.

The Chorister of our Lady of Puy.

"Virgo Potens."   "Powerful Virgin."

I. THE HOLY IMAGE.

GREATLY prized by pious Christians is the ancient Church of our Lady of Puy-en-Velay. It has been frequented by pilgrims of every description for many ages. Thither went kings in all their pomp, and beggars in all their poverty; youthful hearts full of ardour, sick hearts full of hope, broken hearts seeking support, mothers, daughters, religious, and warriors. And when the joyous festival of the Annunciation happened to fall on the same day as Good Friday,* there might be seen, as in 1842, as many as fifty thousand pilgrims assembled within the walls of Puy-en-Velay.

They who look upon legends as mere simple popular traditions not worthy of serious attention, fall into a great error, for legends have often a connection with memorable events.

Thus, with regard to this vast assemblage of pilgrims, which the coincidence of the Annunciation and Good Friday falling on the same day drew to Puy, be it known, that Bernard of Thuringia, a holy hermit, in the tenth century, believing himself to be endowed with the gift of

* The Festival of the Annunciation in this case would elsewhere be transferred till after Easter week.—*Trans.*

prophecy, predicted that the world would end in the year in which the festival of the Annunciation of our Lady, ever-blessed prelude to man's redemption, should occur on the same day as that on which this great redemption was consummated. Such a prediction coming from so respected a source, and being very generally spread among the people, caused universal alarm in the year 1842, in which Easter-day fell on the 27th day of March. This terror was particularly apparent through the southern provinces of France. The Church of our Lady of Puy had long been celebrated; crowds of faithful sought its sanctuary as one peculiarly favoured by Mary; there they prayed before one of those venerated images, to which she would seem to impart an especial celebrity, by the manifestation of her favour to those who kneel before them. The Holy See, always in advance in the march of intellect, ever prompt to check superstitious and foolish ideas, calmed the general fear by denying the prophecy, and enriched the Church of Puy with extraordinary indulgences for such years as the Annunciation and Good Friday came on the same day, in the form of a jubilee. Fears were dissipated; the prediction was falsified; for the world was as large as ever on the first day of the year 1843.

The origin of the Church of Puy is thus recorded:—In the ancient language of Auvergne, the word *puy* means a *mountain*.* A Gaulish lady, who had been baptized by St. Evodius, first Bishop of Puy,† was attacked with a dangerous

---

* In Latin *podium*, an elevation or amphitheatre.

† St. Evodius transferred the episcopal see to Puy. He was the seventh successor of St. George the Apostle of Auvergne.

sickness. Believing her end to be at hand, she fancied she heard a supernatural voice, which told her that she would recover her health on the top of a *puy*, or mountain, near her dwelling. She caused herself to be carried there, and when her bed had been placed on the volcanic rock, she fell into a deep sleep. While in this state, she saw a lady of surpassing beauty, surrounded by attendant celestial beings. The sick woman exclaimed, "Who is this gracious and beauteous Queen, who comes to visit me in my sickness?"

"It is the Queen of Heaven, and of us its inhabitants," replied an angel. "She has a desire to consecrate this rock, and wishes you to inform the bishop, her servant, of her will, and in proof of this vision, she has granted you your health: arise, and walk!"

Immediately the vision disappeared, the sick woman awoke, and left her bed perfectly healed. She at once hastened to the bishop and related her vision to him, of the truth of which her presence and cure were a sufficient testimony. St. Evodius ascended the rock, and to his amazement, it being the month of July, beheld its summit covered with snow. While he remained contemplating what this should mean, a stag leaped out of a neighbouring thicket, and with his feet traced out the plan of a church upon the snow, and then fled back to the wood. The bishop had the lines thus marked, surrounded by a palisade, and in a few days laid the stone of the first Cathedral of Puy. Such is the ancient tradition, which dates from the sixth century.

Another circumstance tended to render this foundation still more illustrious. Some children of the Cross, who, before the first crusade, were loath to die before having made the pilgrimage of Palestine, returned to Puy, bringing with them a famous image of the Blessed Virgin. It was under the dynasty of our first kings. Touching relations and wondrous events were told of the statue. It was black, and was undoubtedly one of the most ancient figures of the Holy Mother of God.*

* We will here give the description of this image by Faujas de St. Fond in his "*Recherches sur les Volcans éteints du Vivarais et du Velay.*" The author was permitted to examine the statue minutely; and though of the modern philosophic school, he declares it to be the most ancient one in France.

"It is placed over a Roman altar, surmounted by a canopy. Both our Lady and her child are black. She is covered with a large mantle of cloth of gold, covered with precious stones and other enrichments. Her feet are covered with shoes of the same stuff, and her head is adorned with a crown, of antique form, somewhat like an ancient helmet. Another crown of richer work and material is suspended over the figure. Rows of small pearls hang from the back of the head like hair; the eyes are painted, and have small demi-spheric pieces of glass or crystal, which give them great lustre. The image is about two feet and a half high. Our Lady is seated in the manner of the ancient divinities of Egypt. The execution of the work is rude, and such as might be expected from the hands of primitive workmen. Its material is cedar-wood, covered with small bands of linen, pasted over the wood in a very skilful manner, according to the Egyptian fashion."

From his examination of it, St. Fond declared it to be an Egyptian statue. He wrote in 1777.

Many wonderful miracles have been wrought by the intercession of our Lady of Puy. Her shrine has been visited by Popes Urban II. and Gelasius II., and by Louis VII., Philip Augustus, St. Louis, Philip the Bold, Philip the Fair, Charles VI., Charles VII., Louis XI., Francis I., kings of France, and many other princes. What must not have been the effect of the example of so

We give the following account of the image of our Lady of Puy, without, however, vouching for the authenticity of the details.

When the shepherds who had come to adore the Child of Bethlehem left the stable, they retired, says the holy text, praising God and spreading through the mountains the wonders of that sacred night on which the Saviour of the world was born. These happy tidings reached a tribe of Arabs on the confines of Egypt, who came to see our Lady and her Divine Infant. On their return they carved her image, representing her seated with her Holy Child on her lap. This figure they attached to one of the columns of the Kaaba, and placed her in the number of their divinities. This fact is mentioned by Arabian historians. El Azhraki relates that the figure of the Virgin Mary, with the young Aïssa (Jesus) upon her knees, was sculptured as a divinity against one of the columns of the Kaaba (or sacred dwelling), and that it was to be seen there at the time of Mahomet.

This same tribe of Arabs who first adored Jesus in his Mother's arms, when they heard of the massacre of the Innocents, rose in a body, says El Azhraki, and made war against King Herod, which did not subside till some time in the reign of his son.

Now, this is said to be the ancient image venerated at Puy, and, as may well be conceived, is the object of Mary's great complacence. When this

many eminent personages in increasing the popular devotion to this ancient image of the Mother of Jesus, which is said to have been brought from a little temple of the Arabs, who were the first to honour Mary, and had carved her figure after the Egyptian manner.

holy representation of our Lady had been placed in the chapel erected by St. Evodius, numerous habitations were erected around it, which soon formed the town of Puy.

Besides the graces which have been obtained by votaries at her shrine, our dear Lady has blessed the surrounding country. Holy saints and zealous missionaries have arisen under her shadow, and it was before her that the pious Adhemar de Monteil, Bishop of Puy, vowed to join himself with Godfrey de Bouillon in the first crusade. And when, at the close of the second crusade, France was infested with bands of robbers, who covered the highways, robbing travellers, burning castles, and pillaging villages, it was under the banner of our Lady of Puy that the bishops established the Confraternity of Knights of the Blessed Virgin, one of the noblest branches of that ancient order of knight-errantry, whose mission was to pursue bandits, succour the oppressed, and, clearing the country from invaders, to restore peace and happiness.*

---

* The church of our Lady of Puy had many privileges. Its canons were allowed to wear mitres. Kings and dauphins of France were honorary canons from their birth. The treasury of the church was very rich. One of its most precious possessions was a magnificently illuminated copy of the New Testament, presented in 835 by Theodolphus, Bishop of Orleans, to our Lady of Puy, as a thanksgiving for his deliverance from the prison of Angers, on Palm Sunday, by Louis the Gracious. This manuscript, in a very good state of preservation, may be still seen among the archives of the bishopric of Puy.

II. THE YOUNG CHORISTER.

The event we are about to relate is extracted from a large collection of wondrous legends. A few years only have elapsed since it possessed an intense interest, from the extraordinary revelations concerning the present Jews in Asia, which were made public in the official interrogatories (translated from the Arabic) concerning the murder of Father Thomas and his servant, at Damascus, on the 5th of February, 1840. But to our legend.

Among the choristers who assisted at the offices in our Lady's Church at Puy, in 1325, was an amiable youth, cherished by all the city for his mildness, docility, and tender devotion to our Lady, as well as for his sweet clear voice. Never was this voice so brilliant and thrilling as on those festivals dear to the children of Mary, when its sharp clear tones rose on high and reverberated along the aisles of the ancient cathedral. So marvellously brilliant was his sweet voice at the midnight mass of one Christmas, that the principal people of the city resolved to surprise him with some mark of their esteem on the following morning. But when they approached his parents' dwelling for this purpose, they found it filled, not with joyous feelings, but with deep despair; for they had lost their son. He had been seen to enter the crowd on emerging from the cathedral after mass, but no one had either seen or heard of him since.

Search was made in vain. Citizens and clergy, fathers and sons, magistrates and nobles, sent and went to seek him in all directions. They all returned unsuccessful. Every trace of the boy was as completely lost as if, says the legend, "he had been invisibly taken up to heaven."

Never was Christmas time spent so drearily in the city of Puy.

What had become of the sweet singing-boy? A Jew, whose passion had been roused at hearing the Christmas carol, announcing the birth of Jesus, sung by the Christian youth in tones of such exultant joy—a Jew, whose rabbis had asserted that to kill a Christian was a good act, and no murder, had seized the child at the corner of a dark deserted street, gagged him, carried him to his dwelling, and there secretly and quietly murdered him, believing he was performing a religious and praiseworthy action. The body was easily disposed of without risk of discovery.

The fanatic, flushed with the success of his first immolation, determined on sacrificing another little infidel (as he called the Christians) at Easter tide. He again sought for a victim from the body of choristers.

Knowing there would be a procession on Palm Sunday, he left his house, and lingered about the cathedral. The sacred banners and veiled cross soon met his view. Piously the faithful followed, bearing their blessed palms, and joining in the loud *Hosanna*. Little thought the murderer that his death-knell sounded.

As the procession passed him at the foot of the steps, which rise before the western door of the cathedral, a great confusion ensued; for the long-lost chorister appeared and took his place among his companions. He had been taken from the tomb by a powerful hand, he said, and appeared to tell them the manner of his death, and to stay the murderous hand of his destroyer, who sought another victim. He then related the circumstances of his murder; and, pointing out the terrified Jew, denounced him as the culprit.

The people ran to the Jew's house, which they soon demolished, and having discovered the body of the chorister, which was uncorrupted, they carried and laid it before the image of our Lady in the cathedral. The Jew's sentence was soon pronounced. He was stoned to death by the populace.

Did this extraordinary occurrence rest on the mere testimony of good simple people; if it were a mere legend unsupported by any authority, a narration of some credulous chronicler, many readers might think they showed a ready wit in proclaiming it to be "a mere fiction,"—a very easy mode of rejecting any wonderful occurrence. But King Charles the Fair, who came to Puy as our Lady's pilgrim, had a correct account of the facts drawn up and certified; and with the advice of his council, drove the Jews out of Puy. In addition, he granted a diploma to the choristers, by which they were entitled to try such Jews as were found attempting to enter the city. And on several occasions did the youths assemble and give their judgment on such cases as were brought before them, which sentences none could set aside.

Our Lady the Deliverer.*

"Virgo clemens."   "Clement Virgin."

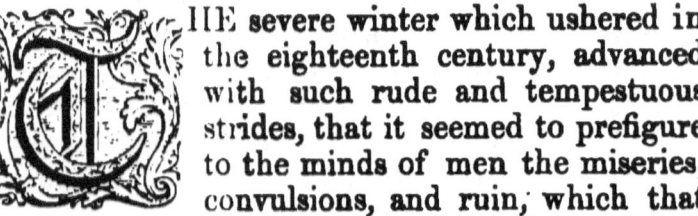HE severe winter which ushered in the eighteenth century, advanced with such rude and tempestuous strides, that it seemed to prefigure to the minds of men the miseries, convulsions, and ruin, which that century of troubles carried in its womb. Calamities of divers kinds afflicted the earth; and the sea, swept by tempests, covered the shores with the sad wrecks of its fury.

But, in spite of unruly waves and boisterous winds, commerce, ever venturesome in pursuit of wealth, and which, according to the Dutch proverb, would go and scorch its sails in the flames of hell if it could hope to establish there a depôt for its merchandise, was sending her ships over the seas of the world. A merchant ship from Havre, fatigued by its long course, heavily laden, and carrying many guns, was returning from Lisbon, on the 12th of February, 1700, through a most tempestuous sea, running many risks, but reckoning on her good equipment to reach the port in safety.

A Norman sailor, who was on board, could not avert his eyes from a point on the horizon, where

* Notre Dame de la Déliverande.

he kept his sight fixed on a speck, which kept increasing as the ship neared.

"If our Lady the Deliverer comes not to our aid," said he, at length, to a passenger, "we shall pass a terrible night."

"What title is this you give to our Lady?" asked the passenger.

"You must certainly be a Portuguese, or a native of some outlandish place, not to have heard of this celebrated pilgrimage," replied the sailor: "it takes its origin, they say, from the time of the first apostles of the country. For more than six hundred years, a miraculous image of our Lady had been venerated in the country between Caen and Bayeux, when the rude men of the north came and ravaged France. Although we are certainly descended from these Normans, I hope we bear no resemblance to them in impiety. The Church, at least as it formerly did, does not now pray to be delivered from us.* Our Lady's chapel was destroyed by these barbarians, and its sacred image buried beneath its ruins. The pilgrimage became a sad spot for those who remembered it, and who had often there invoked the assistance of our Lady the Deliverer, whose powerful aid was sought by distressed mariners at sea. Two centuries passed away * * * *

"The remains of the chapel had been used in the erection of cottages, and the land had been cultivated, so that the precise spot on which it had stood was forgotten. Nobody had ever been able to discover the holy image. But now our dear Lady took compassion on the people who had become Christians. It was during the reign of

* "A furore Normanorum, libera nos Domine." Litany used in France in the ninth and tenth centuries.

Henry I. of France, when our Duke William set out for the conquest of England. Thus has the circumstance been told me,—

"But see," said the narrator, interrupting his discourse, "how the darkness increases. The sky seems covered with a black mantle. It is not yet mid-day, and we can scarce see before us."

"And this February rain is most bitterly cold," said the passenger: "it seems to me that our ship has got into a bad sea. We are running, as you will soon see, across the reefs of the isle of Ouessant."

The sailor made the sign of the cross. The passenger did the same, with a sigh.

"May our Lady the Deliverer be our pilot!" continued the Norman: "we shall stand in great need of her assistance" * * *

"Well, I was telling you how she took compassion on the poor people, and wished to restore her pilgrimage. The shepherd of a neighbouring lord discovered a very singular occurrence. Every day he saw one of his sheep leave the flock, and wander abroad without any molestation on the part of the dogs. He found that the animal went into a small meadow, where the grass was finer and fresher than anywhere else; but, to his surprise, he saw that instead of browsing there, he turned up the earth with his feet. For several days this sheep took no nourishment,—which, however, did not prevent its being one of the fattest of the flock. When tired with its labour, the sheep lay down on the spot until evening, when it returned to the fold at the shepherd's call. These facts were mentioned to Baudoin, the lord of the manor, who was much astonished, and came to the spot, accompanied by his friends, to ascertain the truth of the story. He then ordered his labourers to dig up the soil on the spot where the sheep had barely scratched to the depth of a foot; when, to the delight of all assembled, after an hour's labour, they discovered the venerable image of our Lady the Deliverer. It was transported, amid the rejoicings of all the neighbouring people, to the great church at Bayeux. But what followed will doubtless appear more strange to you; for the next morning the statue had disappeared; and on seeking for it, it was found in the precise spot where it had been discovered on the preceding day. This circumstance seemed to show that the ancient chapel had stood on this ground, and that it was our Lady's desire that it should be rebuilt in the same place. This was accordingly done. Henceforth the pilgrimage was revived, and has continued uninterrupted to the present day. During which time, our Lady the Deliverer has worked many astonishing cures and wonders."

At this moment, an order from the captain interrupted the narrative. The sailor was called to his work. The passengers themselves laboured at the pumps, for the ship was filling from several parts. Premature night brought an increase of the terrors with which a tempest at Cape Finisterre is ever attended. We might draw upon our imagination for a description of the storm, but we prefer not to interrupt the simple narrative of the legend by our own words.

The sailors had said their night prayers, and were chanting the "*Ave Maris Stella*" in their rough, but plaintive melody. The winds and the waves replied in sounds of fury. A long and terrible night ensued; no sun appeared on the next morning; but some faint gleams of light, which they were glad to call day, burst upon the shattered vessel; for, carried along by the raging waters, the ship had lost all her rigging and sails; her cannon, rudder, and compass, were gone. Hurried along by the winds, she was about to capsize, when the Norman sailor cried out,—

"We are all lost, unless we implore the all-powerful aid of our Lady the Deliverer!"

All the sailors instantly uncovered their heads, and kneeling, as well as they could, made a vow to make a pilgrimage to her sanctuary.

The passenger from Lisbon saw, with sadness, that the captain and his two brothers stood unmoved and uncovered during this outburst of religious feeling. Charles Ferret and his brothers were, alas! members of the cold sect of Calvin. Yet were these men possessed of some religious sentiments. Unhappy in being born of parents out of the Church of Christ, they were happy in the possession of good hearts and right understanding, untainted by the obstinacy of heresy. She, who showers down such favours on the children of men, let fall some ray of light into the hearts of these men, darkened by an erroneous faith.

"If the holy Virgin can hear us," said Charles Ferret, falling on his knees, "I also heartily invoke her aid." His younger brother imitated his example. Instantly there came a calm; the winds subsided; every heart beat with emotion, while the shattered vessel gained its position, and floated safely on the tranquil sea.

"O, Lady, our Deliverer! I am yours for ever," cried the youngest brother.

The second brother, however, still remained unmoved. His senior reproaching him, he replied:

"I see in what has happened the goodness of our God, who comes to our assistance; but I am not prepared to abjure my religion."

"A Protestant who enters the Church renounces nothing," said the Portuguese, "but detestable errors. They who formed the cold sect to which you belong, have taken from you every succour which the mercy of God has supplied to those in danger, and left you nothing in their place."

"Behold with your own eyes, my unhappy brother," cried out the captain; and he pointed to the top of the first mast, left uninjured, around which a soft light was seen to play, and in it the figure of a heavenly Virgin was distinctly seen. She held in her hands an infant, whose outstretched hands extending over the ocean, seemed to call upon it to be calm. The second brother, touched by this marvel, could doubt no longer, but declared his belief in the intercession of Mary. Meanwhile the ship, though deprived of her principal powers of motion, calmly floated into the port of Havre.

The first act of the brothers on their landing was to proceed to the nearest church, and there abjure their errors. They afterwards placed themselves at the head of the pilgrimage of the ship's crew and passengers to the chapel of our Lady the Deliverer, to thank her for her miraculous intervention, and to have masses of thanksgiving offered at her shrine.

The Pilgrim of our Lady of Hal.

"Virgo Fidelis."   "Faithful Virgin."

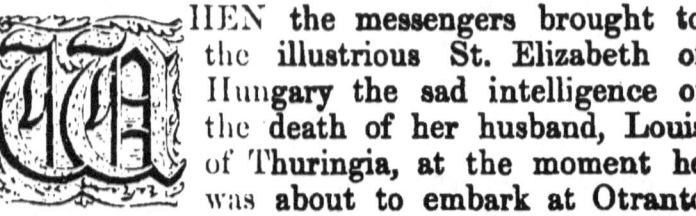HEN the messengers brought to the illustrious St. Elizabeth of Hungary the sad intelligence of the death of her husband, Louis of Thuringia, at the moment he was about to embark at Otranto for the Holy Land, they presented to her four precious images of the Blessed Virgin. The good princess shared these treasures with her beloved daughter, Sophia of Thuringia, wife of Henry, the magnanimous Duke of Brabant, and one of them was sent to the village of Hal, near Brussels. This image was two feet high, carved in wood, darkened by age, but perfect and well carved. The Holy Virgin held her Divine Son on her right arm, and bore a lily in her left hand. It was placed, in 1267, in a beautiful chapel, since changed into a splendid church, which attracts such numbers of pilgrims; and the miracles which our Lady worked at this shrine were so celebrated, that in course of time the simple village of Hal became a large bustling town, encircled with walls and entered by great gates.

During the pains and trials with which the path of this life is so abundantly strewn, suffering hearts, whom the spirit of doubt has not withered, love to take refuge in such sanctuaries wherein the mercies of God are most abundantly dispensed. So many favours did our Lady of Hal show to her devout clients, that they, with grateful hearts, spread far abroad the fame of her wondrous power. Her praises formed the subject of conversation of a party of honest people of Epernay, in Champagne, on an evening of May, in the year of our Lord 1405. Europe, at that period, was neither prosperous nor happy. France, delivered into the hands of faction by the folly of Charles VI., and still infested by the English, seemed to hasten to its ruin. A pilgrim, one of the party, who had just arrived from Hal, recounted how he had passed through Hainault, and how that beautiful country, the noble inheritance of the unfortunate Jacqueline of Bavaria, was also the battle-field of two parties, who fought with fury. But in these times the people cared not much about politics; they were only interested in the material results of the schemes of the day, and spoke of them only as they were affected by them. They far preferred to the wiles of diplomacy, accounts of pilgrimages, and simple narratives of such consoling works as raised their hopes and excited their religious feelings. Thus did the good traveller obtain an attentive hearing while he set forth the history and miracles of our dear Lady of Hal. He recounted the most striking wonders which the sweet Virgin Mary had performed for those who loved her and her Divine Son; and terminated his recital, by describing the adventure of the falconer, whose history had been recently carved in stone in the Church of Hal; for in those days the people were instructed by works of art rather than by books. Thus did he relate it :—

"Dearly do the nobles of Hainault love the sport of falconry, and richly would they pay for a well-trained falcon. Now, it unfortunately happened, that the falcon of a gentleman who lived near Hal, which was much prized by its master, flew away. The negligent or stupid falconer, trembled, with some reason, when his lord asked for the bird. He told him that it was lost; upon which the gentleman flew into a violent passion, and declared, that if he did not find the falcon in five weeks, he should pay for it with his head. This was very hard; but then, every lord possessed of a fortified castle exercised sovereign and almost despotic rights over his vassals. The five weeks passed in deep anguish, but no falcon appeared. The poor man had spent the time in searching everywhere, in tracking the woods, in wasting his breath in calls for the lost bird, but all in vain. At length he obtained a respite of another month: but this delay was of no avail. Sentence was then pronounced, and the wretched man, condemned to be hung, was led out to execution, where his eyes were bound by the charitable hangman, that the culprit might not see the preparations for his death.

The falconer, in deep distress, felt that his last hour had arrived, unless rescued from death by a superhuman power. He wept in silence. But suddenly he struck his forehead and reproached himself with having neglected the powerful assistance of the Help of Christians—our Blessed Lady of Hal. He slipped out of the hangman's hands, knelt down and prayed with that fervour which ever accompanies the prayer of the dying man:

and he prayed with confidence; so that in a few minutes was heard the tinkling of the little silver bells which are attached to falcons, and in two seconds afterwards, the bird itself alighted on the shoulder of the condemned.

"So runs the tale," said the pilgrim. "The falconer was pardoned, and in gratitude for Her intervention, he caused, with the assistance of his friends, his figure with his eyes bandaged and the falcon on his shoulder to be carved in the Church of our Lady of Hal; and in commemoration of the same event, Charles the Bold gave a silver falcon to this church."

The good pilgrim related many more favours obtained by the intercession of the Virgin Mary, and told how the illustrious Duke of Burgundy, Phillip the Hardy, insisted in his last illness on being carried in pilgrimage to our Lady of Hal, where he died on the 27th of April, in the year 1404.

Among the number of those who listened with eager attention to this narrative, was a native of Epernay, called John Sampenoy, a handsome young man twenty-eight years of age, very devout to the Blessed Virgin, and greatly esteemed by his fellow-citizens.

"I am to be married in two months," said he, "and to prepare for the holy union, I will go and visit our Lady of Hal."

The next day he set out after mass, having taken leave of his affianced, and received due instructions from a holy monk to avoid joining strangers on the road. This he faithfully promised to do. But as he was between Rheims and Laon, trudging alone at an easy pace, as men do who have a long distance to go, he was met by two men who seemed in a great hurry, and who, judging his object from his dress, asked whither he bent his steps.

"To our Lady of Hal," he replied.

"Well," said the others, "we are going to the same town, and it will be company for you if we walk by your side."

The pilgrim dreamt not of evil coming from men on their way to our Lady's shrine. His companions slackened their pace, and conducted themselves pretty orderly until they arrived at Avesnes; although it must be confessed that the good John Sampenoy thought them great babblers, and too fond of the cup for pious pilgrims. As they passed through the gate of Avesnes, the guard stationed there arrested them. Our pilgrim was surprised at being included in the arrest, the more so when he heard their names pronounced to be Nicholas Barrois and Peter Normand, two notorious highway robbers. He immediately accounted for his being in their company, declared himself to be John Sampenoy, and told them his birthplace, and the pious object of his journey. But his consternation was heightened by hearing the robbers, doubtless through love of doing harm, declare that he had spoken falsely, and that he was one of their gang; whereupon John was sent to prison with them.

Prisons are bad enough in our days, but they were much worse then. The two robbers rallied their unfortunate companion without any mercy, then fell asleep like men accustomed to many and various lodgings. John, however, could not close his eyes. The next day he beheld fully the terrible position in which he was placed. He was led outside the city to the gibbet which had been erected for the guilty robbers.

To everything he could say as to his innocence, the judges replied, that he must be more guilty than the others for persisting in denying what was charged against him. The good monk, however, who was called to prepare him for death, declared before God, that he believed him to be perfectly innocent.

"Holy Father," replied the provost, "be assured he is a great scoundrel, and has even tried to deceive you. As the worst of the three, he shall be hung last."

John Sampenoy wept bitterly. The two robbers, who knew they had no pardon or mercy to hope for, and determined to die like true brigands, demanded drink, ridiculed the religious who offered them the consolations of religion, and determined as far as they could to make the poor pilgrim share their fate. These villains then mounted the scaffold, and died like true sons of Satan as they were.

After they had been executed, John was made to mount the fatal platform. He conjured the assistants to believe that he was innocent and a true pilgrim of our Lady of Hal, and begged them to pray to her for his happy passage into eternity, as his only hope was in her. The monk then knelt, the people imitated him, and they sung the "*Salve Regina*," and after John had been hung, slowly chanted the "*De profundis.*"

In an hour nearly all the people had dispersed, and John's body gave no signs of life. Yet there lingered a few pious women near the scaffold, who believing John to be innocent, could not think that our Lady would abandon her pilgrim. They had observed that the body hung quietly and had not made the contortions which the others had done, but seemed suspended in the air by some invisible power.

At this moment a gentleman rode hastily into town. He was well known and much esteemed by all for his virtues and good deeds—he was Lord John de Selles. He sought the provost, and said,—

"I come to beg the life of the pilgrim, for whose innocence I pledge my word."

"If he were innocent, you should have been here an hour sooner, for I cannot now grant you his life. His body you are welcome to," was the reply.

Lord de Selles said nothing, but hurrying to the place of execution, had John's body cut down, when, to the great amazement and joy of the people, he fell on his knees and thanked his liberator.

"It is not to me you ought to return your thanks," said John de Selles, "but to the Lady who sent me here, and whom you will see at Hal. When there, say an *Ave* for me."

Not only in Hainaut, but in Champagne, whither John Sampenoy returned to his wedding, is this history preserved among the people in all its details, which Justus Lipsius, the great and powerful writer of the sixteenth century, has recorded with the greatest faith in its truth, and in testimony of his own gratitude to our Blessed Lady, he offered a silver pen at her shrine.

We annex a few further details and anecdotes:—

During the religious troubles, when "the

beggars,"* sacrilegious enemies of faith and art, pillaged churches, violated sanctuaries, and burnt images, Oliver Van der Tympel, their commander at Brussels, resolved one day to attempt an attack upon Hal. He approached the city on the night of the 10th July, 1580, with a troop of "beggars," who vainly dreamt they should have an easy prey. But, says the legend, our Lady sleeps not; the citizens of Hal were aroused and ran to defend the ramparts. A man named Zuick mounted a ladder placed against the wall, boasting that "in a quarter of an hour he would cut off the nose of the little woman of Hal." "And I," said his companion, Risselman, "will carry her to Brussels, where I will burn her in the great square." As he finished these words, he received a wound in the breast and fell dead; while another bullet shot off the nose of the other. When the "beggars" had been repulsed, his comrades jeeringly asked him if he would not like to go and look for his nose at Hal?

In memory of the defeat of these villains, a procession annually moved along the ramparts on the 10th of July. In the evening the people constructed little mounds in front of their dwellings and placed grotesque figures on them, which they called Mynheer Oliver Van de Tympel.

Our next incident is of an impertinent fellow somewhat like Zuick. This man came to Hal in 1624, on the day of the great procession, urged by curiosity rather than devotion. He was stationed at a citizen's window, and when the miraculous image passed, he cried out jeeringly, "Ha! ha! here she comes, the little woman of

* A name adopted by the Huguenots themselves. See the "Legends of the Commandments of God," p. 22.

Hal, who cannot walk; she is obliged to be carried." As he said these words, the master of the house discharged his gun (as is customary on such occasions) in honour of the *fête*, when the barrel burst, and without hurting any one else, a part of the steel cut open the blasphemer's mouth and so wounded his tongue, that he remained dumb from that time.

A citizen of Bruges, kept prisoner by the Turks at the end of Charles the Fifth's expedition, was most cruelly treated and loaded with a chain weighing sixty pounds. One evening, while praying to the Blessed Virgin, he remarked that the prison door was left open, and throwing his chain over his shoulder and clearing the prison, found means of embarking, and reached his country safely. In gratitude to our Lady, he carried his chains in the great procession of Hal.

A good woman of Binche, on going to church on Easter Sunday, 1419, left her child in the cradle well wrapped up in several bandages (according to ancient custom of the peasants). An hour after a neighbour entering to get a light, the door not being locked, the poor woman being too poor to fear robbers, she perceived to her horror that the child was strangled in its cradle. Having great devotion to our Lady of Hal, she instantly vowed the child to her should she recover. She cut the band and the little innocent recovered. Men whose hearts are hardened by incredulity may doubt this; but, thank God! all hearts are not reduced to a state of ossification.

Many other children have been restored to life by our Lady of Hal. We will give the most celebrated instances mentioned by Justus Lipsius. Stephen Morel, of the town of St. Hilary, near

Cambray, had a son who died at birth and was buried without being baptized. Firmiana, his mother, was miserable at her child being deprived of Christian burial and the hope of heaven; she undertook a pilgrimage to Hal, and returned with the firm belief that her son was not dead. She caused his grave to be opened, when the body was discovered to be fresh and limp, although it had been several days under ground. A physician was called in, and the child carried to the church, where it showed undoubted signs of life. The good priest baptized and vowed him to the Blessed Virgin. But he died in an hour, and seemed to have received life only to admit of his being christened. It was then interred in sacred ground, and in her grief, the mother could console herself with the certainty of her child's bliss.

Let the algebraist philosophers laugh at these records; we can laugh at them in return, and what is more, *pray for them.*

The great festival of our Lady of Hal is kept on the first Sunday in September. A grand procession takes place, which is joined by twelve of the most ancient confraternities of the neighbouring towns (who bring in rotation a new rich robe for our Lady's image, which they have the privilege of carrying), and by many others of less celebrity.

Mary of Flanders.

"Speculum justitiæ."   "Mirror of justice."

O N Easter-day, 1071, Count Robert-le-Frison, of Flanders, held a council at Courtray. He was surrounded by Baudouin of Ghent, Bouchard of Comines, Gerrard of Lille, Varner of Oldenburgh, Varner of Courtray, and Gratian of Ecloo, all devoted friends, who accompanied him later on his expedition to the Holy Land. They had also aided him in the conquest of Flanders, and he had just gained by their assistance, and a fortunate circumstance, the battle of Cassel, in which he had defeated King Phillip I.

This victory had also crushed the party of Richilda, called the wicked countess, who still governed Hainaut.

The council then were in high spirits, though not entirely satisfied. They blamed Robert for having generously given Richilda her liberty without any conditions. He was advised to beware of Phillip, who could easily recruit his army, and to seek an alliance with the emperor.

After having patiently listened to the council of his friends, Robert went to consult what he called his *oracle*. This was no other than his daughter Mary, a young princess, of a most pious and learned disposition, who, although only sixteen years of age, had just given him a great proof of filial tenderness. For, on the eve of the battle of Cassel, uneasy about his success, she had made a vow, while praying before the altar of our Lady of Courtray, whom she deeply loved, to devote herself to the religious life among the pious daughters of the Blessed Virgin, if by Her intercession her father obtained the victory. The whole of the time of the battle had been spent by her in prayer; and after her petition had been granted, she had put off her noble costume, and assumed the white robe of Virgins, who dedicate themselves to the service of their Divine Spouse. She saw no one, but lived in the most secluded manner. Her father alone had obtained from her a promise that she would stay a short time with him before entering the cloister for ever.

Robert, as we have said, now went to consult his beloved daughter.

"My dear child," said he, "I am reproached for having set free the Countess Richilda."

"The widow of your brother!"

"You it was who counselled me so to do, my daughter!"

"It was the Blessed Virgin, the Mother of Mercy and Mirror of Justice, father, who has been our counsellor. Be generous towards your enemies, and you will diminish their number. Goodness finds its reward here. When Richilda was your captive, she alone was the object of compassion; now she is free, you are blessed for it. What matter the narrow views of your council? There is no good policy but Christian policy, which is loyal and generous."

"With such sentiments, Mary, why will you abandon the world?"

"To serve you more completely, father! I will constantly pray to God for you. Prayer is powerful. Now, I ask you three things: one regards myself; two are respecting yourself. First, allow me to retire to the Abbey of Missines, where I shall fulfil my dearest vows, and where you—but you alone—may sometimes see me. Then make peace with the empire, for Phillip will return; and give liberty to your captive, Eustace of Boulogne."

"He must at least pay a heavy ransom."

"You must free him without ransom. It will be advantageous for you that he should be your debtor. He is brother to the Bishop of Paris, one of the wisest of the king's counsellors. Obtain friends, father; they are a prince's best treasure."

Robert-le-Frison paused an instant, then said:

"But, daughter, the emperor is irritated against me."

"You have been generous towards Richilda and Eustace, like a noble Christian. Do not then doubt the much-maligned emperor, but hasten to anticipate him. Let your ambassadors set out this day. You can easily pretend to send through them your homage to the chief of the empire for your countdom of Alost."

"Your counsel, my daughter, shall be implicitly obeyed. But as to the ransom of Eustace of Boulogne?"

"Before three months you will receive it. And now, let me beg of you, father, to grant me a fortnight's absolute retreat and seclusion in the Abbey of Missines."

Robert said nothing. Mary took his rough

hand, kissed it gently, and letting fall her veil, retired.

Heaving a deep sigh, the count sought his prisoner.

"Eustace of Boulogne," said he, "you are free!"

"On what ransom?" asked the astonished captive.

"Your friendship!"

Eustace looked steadfastly at him, then warmly grasping his hand, replied:

"In life and death."

Robert, already well paid, continued. "Here are your arms and steed, your esquires await you; go in peace."

Six days after this event, towards the decline of day, the emperor, Henry IV., gloomy and irritated by the reverses caused by his crimes, rode out in the environs of Cologne, where he held his court. He was accompanied by two esquires only. Suddenly a lady clothed in white appeared before him. She rode a cream-coloured horse, and wore a purple head-dress. Seizing the bridle of the emperor's horse, she said,—

"Prince, you shall triumph when your cause is just. Now, turn your eyes towards Flanders; her warriors are brave. Take care, lest you repulse the powerful Count Robert, the conqueror of Cassel, who comes to ask for peace."

"Count Robert!" cried the emperor,—"one of my enemies!"

"You have reason, prince, to diminish their number."

Saying these words with great emphasis, the white lady disappeared in a neighbouring thicket. Stupefaction was displayed on the emperor's countenance. On recovering, he followed on the track of what he considered an apparition; but could discover nothing. The lady had vanished. "It is the guardian angel of our house," said he. The two knights were not less surprised than the emperor. As they entered Cologne he enjoined strict secrecy on them.

Next morning, the envoys of Count Robert approached the city. They feared lest the emperor, violent as they knew him to be, should retain them as prisoners. But a vision appeared to them also, as attested by old historians, on the authority of Baudouin of Tournay, who accompanied them.

On nearing the city at break of day, their progress was suddenly arrested by the appearance of a white lady with a blue velvet head-dress.

"I know who you are, whence you come, and whither you go," said she. "Messengers of the Count of Flanders, have confidence in your cause. The emperor will not dare to give you an unfavourable reception, but will even answer you propitiously. Know also that Robert-le-Frison will overcome his enemies, and that his children will reign in Flanders."

After having uttered these words, the lady disappeared in the wood, as she had done on the previous day; and the count's deputies falling on their knees, half-frightened, but still hopeful of the divine intervention, spent a quarter of an hour in prayer.

"Surely," said they, "this must be our Lady of Courtray!"

They continued their journey in good spirits. The emperor received them mildly. Having done homage for the countdom of Alost, they asked for peace and alliance. The emperor bade them to be assured of his good intentions.

They returned full of joy, recounting their mysterious vision to everyone, which the old chronicles call, " the strange adventure of the Lady who appeared near Cologne to the ambassadors of Robert-le-Frison, Count of Flanders." The people believed with them that it was an apparition of our Blessed Lady. The good news did not reach Robert, however, without a corresponding share of misfortune. He learnt that King Phillip, unable to support the indignity of his defeat at Cassel, had assembled his army, convoked all his vassals, and at the head of a large army, had besieged, taken, and sacked the town of St. Omer. But, as usual, these accounts were exaggerated. The Count of Flanders called together his warriors. Although unable immediately to meet the imposing force of Philip, he commenced to fortify the Flemish towns which the king came to lay waste. He thought of his daughter Mary, who had inspired him with hope, and went to see her at the Abbey of Messines.

In the meanwhile, Eustace of Boulogne was called upon to join the banner of the French king, whose vassal he was, and he had no alternative but to break his oath or march against the Flemish. One morning, Eustace was sadly thinking over his position, when he saw a sealed packet of letters lying on his table. He asked his pages who brought them, but no one could answer his question. Uneasy at this strange occurrence, he besought his brother Godfrey, Bishop of Paris, who accompanied the king, to come into his chamber, to be present at the opening of the packet and to read the letters to him. When the prelate understood the nature of his brother's obligations to the Count of Flanders, he said: "Whether these letters be true, or only a means of enabling you to pay your ransom and put an end to these odious wars, let us take them to the king."

On hearing their contents, which tended to show, that if King Philip ventured further in Flanders, or even remained much longer at St. Omer, he was in peril of being betrayed, seized, and conducted to his enemy the emperor, the king, naturally of a timid disposition, was much alarmed. Eustace of Boulogne took care to seek rather to increase than allay his fears, so that the next day Philip and his army were on their way back to Paris, and never again appeared in Flanders.

The exact truth was never known respecting these letters. When Robert-le-Frison heard of Philip's departure, to mark his appreciation of Eustace's services, he gave him the forest of Bethloo. He soon overthrew the little opposition which remained in the power of Richilda and her son Badouin to make, and by the intervention of the Bishop of Liege, was solemnly crowned Count of Flanders, and left his rights undisputed to his children.

Mary of Flanders became Abbess of Messines, which she rebuilt, for Richilda of Hainaut, in her furious wars with Flanders, had nearly destroyed it. But this pious princess did not die there, for, accompanying her father in his voyage to the Holy Land, she expired, it is said, at Jerusalem, in 1085.

It was only after her death that the exact amount of the generous devotion and services for her father was discovered. She saved Flanders, by inspiring her parent to be generous to his enemies, and two small head-dresses of purple and blue velvet being found in her cell, gave rise to a belief that it was she who had appeared before the emperor and her father's envoys in so mysterious a manner. The people, however, still believed that it was no other than *our Lady of Courtray* herself.

The Scholar's Vision.

"Sedes sapientiæ." "Seat of wisdom."

HE University of Padua, which had enjoyed a reputation for learning for thirty years, was amusing itself in 1220 with a little German scholar, who was that year the butt of his companions and victim of his masters; in fact, the common "fag." He came from the Danube, and his name was Albert de Groot. Born at Lawingen, a small town in Suabia, little known at the present day, he was of good origin. But he had neither pride nor vanity; and how could he, the poor, timid, dull, clumsy boy, without a word to say for himself, be vain? His appearance was so much against him, that his pitiless companions nicknamed him *the ass*. The Paduans italianized his name (joining his country to it) into *Groto Tedesco*, thence into *Grotesco, Groteschino,* and added many other epithets less flattering. To complete the ridiculous figure of the poor youth, though *great* by name, he was so *small* of stature, that, at fifteen years of age, he was not taller than a boy of ten. All these misfortunes combined, tended to render the life of the little scholar one, indeed, full of thorns. He felt, too, more sensibly his ill-treatment than might be supposed; and often would he have

listened to the inspirations of despair, if his mind and heart had not been thoroughly impressed by a pious mother with an ardent piety, a deep humility, and a tender devotion to the Blessed Virgin.

Though he felt it hard to be called *the ass*, on account of his want of talents, bad memory, and other deficiencies, he still said to himself, sadly, that he, no doubt, merited the appellation; and that the learning, which he wished so ardently to possess, was not attainable by him. Having attended the lectures of the blessed Jourdain, of Saxony, who had just been elected general of the Dominicans, he was so moved and delighted by the sacred orator, that he was led to entertain a hope that God might call him into that holy order, if not to shine among the illustrious men who were its glory—however much he desired it—at least to save his soul in humbly following its rule. He accordingly petitioned to be admitted into the Dominican convent. His request was favourably received by the new general, who was his countryman; and he was admitted to the habit, and allowed to continue his studies.

Alas! he here also found trials he had hoped to escape. His dull mind was long in comprehending the different rules and customs of the house; and though there was more charity among the Dominican novices than the university students, he still felt that he was looked upon as the lowest in the house in point of intellect. His humble piety sustained him for some time; he did not easily lose courage; he always hoped that he should at some time overcome these obstacles, and break the shackles of his mind. He pronounced his vows, and became a monk; still he remained a dull scholar.

After two years' patient labour, he began to lose confidence, and thought he had, perhaps, been deceived, or yielded to a sensation of pride in entering an order, whose mission it was to preach to the world, to carry the gospel to every people, and, consequently, to shine brightly, as well by its excellence in every science, as by its eminence in virtue. He considered within himself that he never should be able to attain to any powerful use of logic, or the command of language, and he said to himself, "I am now vowed to God's service; I know that He is good, that He will not require of me more than I am able to perform; He will not ask me, when I appear before Him, whether I have preached eloquently, but whether I have lived well; not whether I have been learned, but whether I have been innocent; not whether I have written fine works, but whether I have performed good actions. I know I am the most useless of his servants. But, blessed be his holy will! He wants not my aid! I might weakly plead the august cause of the holy Church, propagate the Catholic faith, or combat heresy. I forget that God rises up whom he pleases, that vanity must not tempt his wisdom, though he chose for the founders of His Church twelve poor fishermen. May His holy will be done! I will then depart from this holy house, which I should never have entered, and where I know that I am but a burthen. Like the solitaries, I will retire into the wilderness, and occupy myself with my own salvation only. God resists my aspirations for wisdom, but when I am alone with Him, He will not reject the love which I will unceasingly offer Him."

As these feelings increased, the little monk thought that his imagination was brightening, and that his reasoning faculties were improving. He, however, rejected these thoughts as a temptation, and continued in his original resolution of leaving the monastery.

His timidity prevented him from communicating this project to any one; he fancied that they would receive it with raillery, as they did everything else which he uttered. His only confidant was the Blessed Virgin. He passed a novena before her altar. He implored her assistance, and begged her to obtain for him a knowledge of the holy will of God, to which he desired most ardently to conform.

On the evening of the day fixed upon for his departure, he prayed more fervently than ever. He waited till all the fathers had retired to rest; then, placing himself under the guidance of Mary, left his cell, and reached noiselessly the convent walls; and, planting a ladder against them, knelt for the last time, to pray God that the step he was about to take might not be displeasing to Him, assuring Him that although he was about to leave the holy house in which he had plighted his vows, his heart was still, and ever would be, devoted to His holy service.

As he was about to rise and mount the ladder, a most extraordinary spectacle presented itself to his eyes. Was he dreaming? Or was some miraculous favour accorded him? This last is the opinion of the cotemporary writers, who have recorded the fact. He saw, at a short distance before him, and about to approach him, four ladies of majestic appearance. A bright light surrounded them; their graceful dignity and mild demeanour inspired him at the same time with respect and confidence. The first two placed themselves at the foot of the ladder, as if to prevent his mounting. But they had no need of opposing him, for he had again fallen down on his knees, and prostrated himself before these celestial messengers, as he justly imagined them to be.

The third lady, approaching him mildly, asked him how he could thus despair in the task he had before him? and how he could bring himself to fly ignominiously, and expose himself to the great dangers which would surround him in the world. The scholar answered, without rising, and humbly exposed his incapacity for learning, which prevented him from carrying out his desires.

"The reason is, you seek from your weak human understanding the gifts which come from God alone. You have also, in the Queen of the Universe, a protectress who loves you, for she knows that you are her faithful servant. Never have you petitioned her for the gift of knowledge, as if you knew not that she is, as of all virtues, the seat of wisdom. She now comes to you in her goodness; ask what you want of her with confidence. We will aid you with our intercession."

The delighted scholar, recognizing in the fourth lady the Blessed Virgin, whose sweet smile assuages all pains, was encouraged to ask her for the favour he had so much at heart. Hitherto he had prayed only for the graces which lead to salvation. He was now struck with the feeling that the only reason for his wishing for science was to consecrate it to the glory of God; and, therefore, relying on the favour of his sweet Patroness, he earnestly sought of her the gift of wisdom. "Wisdom is great and varied, my son," replied the fourth Lady: "would you know everything,—do you not remember our first father, who was offered unbounded knowledge by the fallen spirit?"

"Oh! no, most holy Virgin," cried Albert, in alarm: "I ask only for such knowledge as it may please God to bestow on me. I regret the dangerous conceit of wishing to fathom the mysteries of heaven. I desire, with the bounds of faith, to possess the science of philosophy or of nature.

"Human science," said the gracious lady, "is vain, and beset with dangers; you had better have asked for the gift of theology, which would have opened to your understanding so much of the sacred mysteries of faith as it is fitting for man to know. But your request shall not be denied. Only take care lest this philosophy you desire sow in you the seeds of pride. You will possess it for a long time; you will be tried by the great labours it will call forth from you, and by the hasty judgments men will pass upon you. Be faithful; suffer not your heart to be puffed up with knowledge; and I promise you that this science you ask *shall be withdrawn from you on the day in which it is likely to become dangerous to you.*"

The apparition then disappeared.

Albert instantly felt himself another being, and remained an hour in prayer of thanksgiving; yet, fearing he had made a bad choice, he demanded, most fervently, the grace of humility—his safe guide and anchor.

He put down the ladder, and returned to his cell, but slept not.

Next day there was a general stupefaction in the classes. Albert was the theme of universal astonishment; a ready and subtle intelligence had eclipsed his dulness. Nothing stopped his progress; he overcame every difficulty. The most abstruse problems were to him as clear as day. All he heard and read became instantly fixed and arranged in his memory. In a year, he not only surpassed his fellow-students, but even confused his professors. Great was the general astonishment. It was said, that by some miracle the *ass* had been metamorphosed into a *philosopher*. Nor were they mistaken, though the humble scholar had kept the vision a secret confined to his own breast. In a short time he became Doctor of Philosophy, the teaching of which was confided to him. And so completely did he discharge this duty, that he obtained the name of "*the* philosopher," as being alone worthy of that title.

And he worthily maintained his position of Christian philosopher; ever full of charity, a lover of his cell, inaccessible to the seductions of the world and its glories, dividing his loved solitude between meditation, prayer, and study, by which he advanced with giant strides along the paths of learning. He never left his monastery but to attend sermons. Those of St. Anthony of Padua, who lived then, charmed and delighted him most. He studied the natural sciences, and found every object of creation a step in the ladder whereby his soul reached God. He swerved little from the routine he had set himself, and wandered not into the other paths of erudition. Still he sometimes visited the edifice which the Paduans still call Titus Levy's house, and deciphered the inscriptions it contains.

When he had attained his thirtieth year, he had so universal a knowledge of everything connected with philosophy and natural science, that he could argue and discuss (according to the state of science at that period) on every subject of which a knowledge could possibly be obtained —*de omni re scibili*. The Dominican order considered fit to exhibit to the world this prodigy of learning formed within its cloisters. He was sent to Cologne to teach philosophy and divinity, for he studied the latter science with ardour, but with less success. At Cologne, Hildesheim, Fribourg, Ratesbon, and Strasbourg, he dazzled Germany with his talents; being, however, as much admired for his humility and modesty as for the wonderful depth of his knowledge and the immensity of his intellect. He always resided in the houses belonging to his order, and would always chose the meanest cell, and live the same as the lowest brother in the order.

Jourdain of Saxony dying in 1236, Albert was elected Vicar-General of the Order of St. Dominic, the duties of which office he administered for two years with evident blessing; so that when the General Chapter assembled at Bologna, to elect a General, in 1238, they unanimously conferred that dignity on Albert; but he resisted the honour with such humble perseverance, that they gave way to his entreaties. Raymond, of Pennafort, who was then elected in his place, being absent at Barcelona, Albert hastened thither to place the seals of office in his hands, and then returned to his dear little cell at Cologne. There he again taught in the school; and such was his success, and the great number of eminent men who attended his lectures, that he was sent to Paris.

The University of Paris (called simply the *school of Paris* before the time of St. Louis), said to have been founded by Charlemagne, had been reconstituted by Louis the Young, and encouraged by the many privileges of Philip Augustus. Men of the first talent eagerly sought its professorships. The scholars of the university were counted by thousands, and formed a large undisciplined body dispersed about the city, and often troublesome to the public peace. The kings considered it a duty to encourage learning, and St. Louis, who then reigned, loved to see his people instructed and enlightened, well knowing that ignorance, and bad teaching, still more dangerous perhaps, are the great enemies of religion, morality, and also necessarily of the happiness of mankind.

As soon as the little monk of Cologne, whose small stature and modest bearing contrasted strongly with his immense learning, made his appearance in the schools, all Paris were enthusiastic in his praise. The wits called him Albert the Little, on account of his stature; while his friends named him Albert the Great, for his merit, little thinking that they only translated his name. The French people, who are not fond of two consonants, and who have changed for their convenience Alberic into Aubry, Albinus into Aubin, and of Clodoald and Theobald, make Cloud and Thibaut, paid no respect to the patronymic of Albert; with them he was plain "Master Aubert."

So immense was the concourse of persons who crowded to hear the professor, that he was obliged to give his lectures in an open square, which has ever since retained his name. It is *Place Maubert*.

This took place in 1245, when Thomas Aquinas was the most distinguished of Albert's scholars, and already showed marks of that astounding theological genius, which his master foresaw, and by which he attained to such a knowledge of divine truths, as to be justly regarded as one of the brightest lights of the Church.*

On his return to Cologne, Albert was elected provincial of Germany, which office he held for three years, without suffering it to interfere with his public lectures.

About the same time he received a commission similar in its object to the society of the Holy Infancy, lately established by a saintly prelate. The Poles, who were then barbarians, had the horrid custom of putting deformed infants to death; they also killed such as were difficult to bring up, and even old people who were a burthen to their friends. The Holy See, ever alive to the calls of charity, charged Albert to go and endeavour to put a stop to these savage customs. He accomplished this difficult charge with great success. The Pope would have given him a bishopric as a mark of his gratitude, but he could not overcome the humble resistance of Albert. It was not till 1260, that he was obliged by his superiors to accept of the bishopric of Ratisbon. He administered this see for four years with great fervour, when he obtained permission from Urban IV. to return to his little cell at Cologne, where he would never allow himself to be treated other-

* St. Thomas was so timid and reserved, that he had a difficulty in expressing himself at the schools. Whence, as well as on account of his great size, his companions called him *the dumb bull*. But on one occasion, on which he overcame some difficulty which had puzzled his companions, Albert said to them, "You call him *the dumb bull*, but the time will come when he will so *roar* with learning, that the whole world shall resound with his *bellowing*."

wise than as the least of the brothers. There he employed his time in study, lecturing, and expounding the scriptures.

Despite his love of retirement, his submission to the head of the Church caused him to take many long journeys. The objects of these were to preach the crusade through Germany; to assist and speak at the Council of Lyons, in 1274; and to take part in overcoming the difficulties of the Holy See.

His language was the universal theme of admiration; but never to the age of seventy-five years had he listened to the least whisper of vanity, when one day in his chair at Cologne, seeing his immense auditory electrified by his discourse, he raised his head with a feeling of self-satisfaction. She who had ever protected him came to his aid— he seemed to see her;—and stopping suddenly in the midst of a fine period, left the pulpit without finishing it. He had lost his memory! The gift of knowledge left him at the moment when it was about to become a subject of vanity to him. He felt he had fallen into the state of dulness he was first in at Padua. He understood the warning, and instantly prepared for death, which he received most piously two years later, on the 15th of November, 1282. St. Thomas Aquinas, his beloved disciple, had preceded him to his reward by eight years, eight months, and eight days.*

* Albert the Great was beatified by Gregory XV. in 1622. He was dining at Cologne on the 7th of March, 1274, "when suddenly," says the old legend, "he burst into tears; and turning to the religious, said, sadly, 'Brother Thomas Aquinas, my dear son in Jesus Christ, he who was the light of the Church, is at this moment leaving the world.'"

The Three Knights of St. John.

"Causa nostræ lætitiæ."   "Cause of our joy."

OULQUES of Anjou, the fourth Christian King of Jerusalem, held with a wavering hand the weighty sceptre of Godfrey of Bouillon. He had, however, fortified Bersabee, a city on the limits of his kingdom, and confided the custody of it to those brave soldiers of the cross—those devoted men, whom the strength of Christian charity had converted into Hospitallers of the Holy City, and had become armed monks in 1104, for the defence of the holy sepulchre and Christian pilgrims. Religious knights, they carried the cross at the hilts of their swords; wore hair shirts under their coats of mail, and their great figures are indelibly fixed in our chronicles and are carved in our churches. They were called the Knights of St. John of Jerusalem.

Four leagues from Bersabee was situated the first stronghold of the Saracens, Ascalon, then occupied by a large army with whom daily skirmishes, combats, ambuscades, and surprises, had to be encountered.

In the year 1131, the epoch at which the events we are about to narrate took place, there were among the crusaders at Bersabee three knights of great renown, brothers, of the house of Eppe, who, at the command of the Holy See, had quitted their delightful seat two leagues from Laon, to come to the assistance of the Christians in the East, and had distinguished themselves by surprising feats of arms. Their proved courage, fervent faith, their ardour, and their well-known valour, frequently obtained for them these distinctions, which are eagerly sought for by men of courage; the advanced post in a battle—the favour of repelling a formidable attack—the honour of commanding a dangerous sally.

One day the sentinels on the watch-tower of the Christian garrison suddenly sounded an alarm, spreading dismay in Bersabee. A large detachment of Saracens had left Ascalon and were rapidly advancing towards the town. The three knights were immediately charged with the care of a sally to intercept and cut off the enemy, so as to prevent them from laying siege to the town, which of all things was most dreaded by the Christians in that country, situated as they were, as encamped pilgrims. The encounter was prompt, and, as is the custom of the Orientals, impetuous. But the Franks, as they are called in the East, did not shrink before the scimitars of the heathens. But, after sustaining the first shock, they charged, and becoming the assailants, drove the Saracens to the gates of Ascalon. With men whom Islamism keeps in a wild state, war has no other tactics but perfidy and stratagems. The crusaders, carried on by their ardour, traversed a ravine in which an ambush was concealed, and from which, as they passed, there rushed forth a fresh reinforcement of Saracens, who attacked them from behind. Human strength, despite valiant hearts, is circumscribed. At the end of an unequal contest, the three knights stood alone over the corpses of their massacred companions, and almost before they were aware of their position, found themselves prisoners, disarmed and tied with cords, and thus ignominiously led into Ascalon. The infidels, furious at the dear price they had paid for their victory, overwhelmed them with insults, and would have taken their lives, but that they expected a heavy ransom for such noble knights.

No one, however, remained on the field to tell the Christians at Bersabee of the fate of the three knights, and it was therefore concluded that they had perished with the rest.

Skirmishes still being of daily occurrence, it was not considered prudent to leave the prisoners at Ascalon. An officer, who was going for a reinforcement from Cairo, deemed the best present he could offer the sultan would be three noble Christian warriors. Admiring their handsome features, their imposing stature, and wondrous strength, and delighted with the recital of their great deeds of arms, the sultan felt flattered by so noble a present. He received them most graciously, and his dragoman announced to them, that it was in their power to make their condition much better than it had ever been.

The knights understood the hint, but answered not.

A week was allowed to pass, during which time the captives were surrounded by every luxury, and were even scarcely subjected to any surveillance. After which time, the sultan, throwing off all disguise, told them he was prepared to admit them into the number of his favourites, and to give them the highest position in his army, if they would renounce Christianity and embrace the doctrines of Mahomed. Here arose a war more formidable to a simple warrior, than that carried on with lance, axe, or sword; a combat of simple intelligence against all-powerful brute force. The knights drew back at this proposal, and all crossed themselves. They were neither theologians or disputants, but they had a firm faith and deep sense of honour. They replied, that as Christians and knights, their hearts, as well as arms, were devoted to the service of Jesus Christ; that conquering or conquered, triumphing or fallen, they hoped never to forfeit their God or their honour.

This reply astonished the sultan, who ordered the knights to be reconducted from his presence, while at the same time he resolved to try other means to shake their constancy. For several successive days he exhausted all his arts in vain. The three brother knights were resolute in their faith.

They were then treated with less indulgence, and the most skilful men in Cairo were sent by the sultan to win them over. But they also failed in their purpose. Maddened by the obstinate coolness of the knights, these men easily obtained that they should be placed in the vilest dungeons of the prison, that their food should be of the worst description, and that they should be loaded with chains. Thus the captivity of the Knights of St. John became daily more intolerable. In this state they endured a slow martyrdom of two years' duration. Their courage and cheerfulness did not, however, forsake them. When men expected to find them gloomy and sad, they found them singing or chaunting some holy hymn. When brought before the sultan, as they were at long intervals, they appeared with serene brows and smiling visages.

The infidel was puzzled by this enigma; this wonderful perseverence of the followers of Christ astounded him; and the more the knights refused his offers, the greater was his desire to win to his cause such devoted men. He knew that they opposed to him, and the wiles of Satan, prayer—the most powerful of the Christian arms. The knights frequently and fervently besought of God the grace He so willingly accords of ever loving and serving Him. They asked this gift by the name so terrible to the enemy of mankind. They implored the intercession of our Common Mother, who never abandons her children. Children of Mary, knights of Christ, captives for His cause, and living in the fear of God, they suffered with patience, when the sultan determined to make one more, and last, effort to gain them to his service.

He had a daughter called Ismeria. She was young and beautiful, and was famed for her learning and wit. Often had he conversed with her of his Christian captives, and complained of their continued resistance of his favour.

"Father," said she, "I think the wise men you employed to persuade them have not acted prudently. If I might venture to ask for an interview with them, I think I might make some impression on them." She said this from curiosity to see the noble knights, in whose praise she had heard so much spoken.

"Well, daughter," replied the sultan, "I grant your request. To-morrow you shall see the prisoners. You shall be conducted to their prison.

May your efforts be crowned with success; you will achieve the greatest triumph in bringing them into the service of the Prophet. I am not apprehensive of your winning the heart of one of these noble knights, for I should, indeed, be proud of such a son-in-law."

The princess went the next morning to the prison most tastefully arrayed. She had learned some French from an European slave. Careful not to inform them of the mission on which her father had sent her, she announced to them that she had long wished to see them, from the noble deeds she had heard related of them, and from a desire to save them; for seeing they were not ransomed, and continued firm in the Christian faith, the people demanded that they should be put to death.

They replied that the messengers charged by them with the commission to announce their captivity in France had doubtless met with some accident on the way, so that their relatives must believe them to be dead, and that they should not be able to get their ransom unless one of them were permitted to go to Europe.

This, however, was not what the sultan wanted. They added, that as to denying their faith, they trusted too much in the goodness of God to fear he would allow them to dishonour Him and their knighthood. They then thanked the princess for her kind sympathy and attention, and expressed the great pleasure it gave them to hear her speak their own language.

Ismeria, touched with compassion for men with such noble sentiments, then commenced her task of bringing them over to the religion of her father, which would be the only means of ensuring their safety. She spoke with such simple candour, that the knights, on their part, became moved with pity for the poor girl, whose soul was a slave to such fatal errors. After having asked her whether any person in her suite understood French, and heard her reply in the negative, they said that, with her permission, they would explain to her the nature and hopes of the Christian religion.

The princess not only consented to this proposal, but even manifested a lively curiosity to know the real truths of Christianity from men so noble and sincere. Such a desire was doubtless the first grace manifested to her. The eldest of the knights then related to her what he had learned from the Church, of the creation of man, his fall, and its consequence; the promised redemption, its accomplishment by our Blessed Saviour, his passion and death; the reconciliation of God with man, and the exaltation of woman-kind through the Blessed Virgin Mary. He explained the Trinity and Unity of God, and the other sacred mysteries of religion, and then spoke of the eternal recompense promised to the elect. The clearness and beauty of his words astonished his brothers, who were neither clerks nor preachers. In their humility they thought not of the saying of our Blessed Lord: "When you shall bear testimony of me, do not meditate before how you shall answer. For I will give you a mouth and wisdom, which all your adversaries shall not be able to resist and gainsay."

The princess was deeply affected by this discourse, and promised to return the next day. She delighted her father by informing him that she hoped that a favourable result would attend her conferences, if she were allowed to continue them. In the night she had a dream, in which she fancied she saw our Blessed Lady watching over her. This tended much to assure her of the truth of the Christian faith. The subject of the second day's interview was the Blessed Virgin Mary, the fountain of grace. The knights gave such a glowing description of their sweet Protectress, and narrated such beautiful legends of her, that the princess, desirous of honouring this heavenly Queen, begged the knights to make a figure of our Lady. The brothers were not artists; but, anxious to please, promised they would do their best if they were provided with a piece of wood and tools.

In an hour everything was ready, and they began by invoking her assistance whose figure they wished to represent. They worked for several days to bring the block of wood into a little shape. But what was their astonishment on awaking one morning to find the image perfectly completed in the highest style of art! This beautiful image had surely been the work of angels during the night. Protestants may say that one of the knights was *perhaps* a somnambulist, and that he worked at his task during the night! Well, this will only be a different form of the miracle.

The good knights impatiently waited for the appearance of the princess. On seeing the figure of the Mother of God, she fell on her knees in ecstasy before it; and her delight became still greater on perceiving that the statue resembled, in every particular, the vision with which she had been favoured. She tenderly kissed the feet of the image, and the captives called it *our Lady of*

Liesse,* on account of the joy it caused in their prison.

In the following night the princess had a second vision. She seemed to see our Blessed Lady in the same form as the image, who told her to deliver the Christian knights, and fly with them to France, where, after having spent a holy and pure life, she should receive an imperishable crown of glory in heaven. The princess hesitated not about what she should do. At daybreak she went to the knights, told them of her vision, and promised to perform all it had enjoined. The knights, struck with delight and admiration, fell on their knees, and returned thanks to God and our Blessed Lady for their delivery; and faithfully promised, on the honour of their knighthood, to take the princess, at the peril of their lives, with them to France, and place her where she should most desire.

The next night was fixed upon for their departure.

As soon as her attendants had retired, Ismeria collected her jewels and precious stones, and went to the prison. The guards were asleep; she entered with precaution, struck off the captives' chains, and, accompanied by the knights who carried in triumph their dearest treasure, the image of our *Lady of Liesse*, gained the city gates, which to their joy they found open. On reaching the borders of the Nile, the little troop had an evidence of the visible protection of Mary. By the faint light of the stars they perceived a boat, with a single rower in it, making towards them.

* An old French word, signifying joy—probably from the Latin *lætitia.—Trans*.

He offered to ferry them over the river; and when he had done so, to their great astonishment, the man and his little bark disappeared. For this intervention of their Divine Protectress, they returned their hearty thanks.

Here we pause to make a sacrifice to the scruples of our times, ere we relate a still more wonderful miracle. But if it be not true, how shall we explain the various monuments which relate to it? It has been shown that Homer never lived, because there remain no other traces of him but his works. But the history of the fact we are about to record has been written on stone and marble; and its truth has been acknowledged for centuries. Still we say to our readers they are free to disbelieve in this case; if human prudence believes itself to be gifted with sufficient light, it may doubt such things as are not of faith. Having said this, with the reader's indulgence, we will pursue our narrative.

The princess and the three knights hastened onwards till daybreak. Their fatigue, the fear of pursuit, or some unpleasant encounter, induced them to seek shelter and repose in a wood of palm-trees. Despite her uneasiness and the thought of her father, whom she loved, Ismeria soon fell asleep by the side of the holy image. The knights proposed to keep watch in turn, but in vain did the first watcher combat sleep; he was soon laid by the side of his companions. Never could they, or Ismeria, give any account of the time that elapsed during their repose. What was their astonishment on waking to find themselves surrounded not by palm-trees, but by such as grow in the north of France; to see between the branches glimpses of spires and turrets different from those of Egypt, and to breathe a cooler air than that of Africa. They rubbed their eyes, believing themselves still under the influence of a dream, for often had they dreamt of their dear country. But the princess reassured them of the reality of their position by the strange emotions which the air and climate of the north, and the heavens covered with clouds unknown to Egypt, caused in her. They found the image a few paces from them, near to a fountain, of which they seemed to have some recollection. Soon a shepherd passed near them driving his flock. He was dressed in the European costume. The knights calling him, he came, and replied in their own language. They fancied they had seen him before. They asked in what country they were?

"You are," said the shepherd, "in Laon, near the borders of Champagne. This wood and fountain are in the domains of three noble knights of Eppe, who went to the Holy Land under our Lady's banner." The shepherd here made the sign of the cross, then continued: "We are told that it is now three years since the knights went to God. But from your appearance, gentlemen, it would seem that you came from the crusade. Perhaps you can tell us something of our poor masters, for though this lady is evidently a foreigner, I see by the cross you bear you are good Christians."

The shepherd here seeing the image of *our Lady of Liesse*, fell on his knees before it, much struck at its beauty. The knights, who had hitherto been kept silent by their surprise, and the emotions which were rising in their breasts, imitated him; and shedding sweet tears of gratitude, thanked our Lady, most fervently, for this new and astounding mark of protection. Their sufferings, and the length of their beards, had so disguised them, that they could not easily be recognised. But as soon as they declared who they were, the shepherd hastened to spread abroad the news of so wonderful a return. All the villagers eagerly repaired to the fountain, where they found their noble lords, and conducted them and the princess with great rejoicings to the castle of Marchais, one of the mansions belonging to the knights. Their mother, who still lived, nearly died of joy at the sight of her three lost sons returned to gladden her widowhood. She cordially welcomed the Egyptian princess, who had been the instrument employed by the Almighty to set them free. She undertook to prepare her for holy baptism. It was also determined to erect on the spot to which it had been so wonderfully translated, a church for the image of *our Lady of Liesse*. Ismeria earnestly begged to be allowed to devote her jewels and precious stones towards this great work of thanksgiving.

As soon as she had been baptized, she sent a message to her father, to announce to him the wonders Mary had wrought in her behalf, to assure him of her safety and happiness, and to entreat him to become a Christian.

The church of our *Lady of Liesse* was immediately founded. To satisfy the devotion of the people, who eagerly crowded from all parts to see and venerate this now miraculous image, it was placed in a temporary chapel, near the fountain, until the church was finished. The Bishop of Laon, Bartholomew de Vir, a most holy prelate, baptized the Egyptian princess, the eldest of the knights of Eppe being her godfather. She received the name of Mary at the holy font; and her piety increased so rapidly, that she shortly afterwards begged to be received into a convent, to spend her days in holy chastity, and devote herself entirely to the service of the Almighty.

The church destined for the holy image was completed; and shortly afterwards, a town called Liesse surrounded it, and it became a celebrated pilgrimage. We cannot here undertake the task of enumerating the acts of power and goodness by which our Lady has rendered this shrine so famous. Here has She healed many a wound, relieved many a heart, and sustained many feeble souls. The waters of the fountain have cured the disorders of those who have confidently used them, relying on the powerful assistance of Mary. Let the incredulous smile at this assertion. Perhaps they may one day be happy to have recourse to them. May Mary pardon and assist them!

At the outbreak of the revolution in 1793, the treasury of our Lady's church at Liesse was very great. This was plundered by the "friends of liberty, toleration, and respect for the rights of property;" but the richest gift of all, the intercession and favour of Mary, still remains in her sanctuary.*

* In 1851, an English lady of title presented a large silver lamp to the church of our Lady of Liesse, to burn day and night before the blessed Sacrament, in thanksgiving for the cure of her son.—*Trans.*

The Oak of Hildesheim.

"Vas spirituale."   "Spiritual vessel."

ALBERT Krantz, the sober and learned historian of old Saxony, relates the following circumstance.

The emperor, Louis the Gentle, was a prince endowed with many good and religious gifts. He was very devout to the Blessed Virgin. Favoured with a grace common to the saints, he never lost sight of the presence of God. Everything to him was a sign of His omnipresence; he saw it in the waves of the sea, the silent forest, the brilliant day-break, a glorious sunset, the perfume of the flowers, a calm night, a good action, or pious thought.

One day, as he was hunting in a forest in Saxony, the pursuit of a wild boar led him some distance from his court who accompanied him. He lost the trace of his prey in a close thicket, and when he stopped, he found himself in the midst of a vast solitude under a magnificent oak. On admiring this fine work of God, he felt his heart touched; desiring to say his prayers there, he desired his chaplain, the only person of his suite who had been able to follow him, to attach to the trunk a small image of the Blessed Virgin, which he held in great veneration, and caused always to be borne near his person.

He then knelt down with his chaplain and recited the rosary.

In so calm and deep a solitude, these devout men were soon absorbed in prayer and lost to all sense of the external world, when the sound of horns aroused and reminded them of their situation, and the uneasiness which must have seized their followers. Louis immediately sounded his horn in reply, and mounting his horse, hastened to join them, accompanied by his chaplain. The latter in his hurry forgot the image, which he left attached to the oak. The rest of the day being spent in various duties, his neglect did not occur to him until he was about to say mass the next morning. Then knowing that the emperor would miss the image from its accustomed place during the mass, he hastened to the oak. He easily recognized it, but the image was not to be seen.

Uneasy and distressed, he sought all around for it in vain. He felt sure that no one would be so wicked as to remove or steal a sacred image, which was well known to be an object of devotion to the emperor. After some further search, he discovered it on another and still larger oak.

He endeavoured to detach it, but, to his surprise, all his efforts to remove it were useless. It seemed so firmly fixed, as to defy all human strength to displace it.

Surprised at so extraordinary a circumstance, the chaplain returned to the emperor and informed him of what had taken place. Louis the Gentle hastened with his court to the spot, and there witnessed the prodigy. He caused a church

154   THE OAK OF HILDESHEIM.

to be built hard by, and many miracles rendering it famous, dwellings were erected for the pilgrims, which afterwards increasing, formed a town, and in course of time was converted into an important city and the seat of a bishopric. Such is the origin of the city of Hildesheim.

The Wooden Candlestick.

"Vas honorabile."   "Honourable vessel."

THE lamps and candles burnt in our churches, the flowers which decocorate our altars, the incense which smokes before our tabernacles, are not, as some frivolous persons may imagine, unmeaning accessories to public prayer; they are pious symbols which elevate our minds to God. The flame of the candles is the emblem of the ardent desires of God's glory which should animate us; flowers teach us the sweet scent of the Christian virtues; and like incense, should our prayers ascend towards heaven.

The temples devoted to the cold forms of Protestantism are devoid of all these accessories. They imitate not the Catholic Church in consecrating to the service of the Almighty, in his churches, the most beautiful gifts of Divine Providence, flowers, perfume, and the highest productions of art.

In many legends we find flowers to be most dear to our Blessed Lady. The houses in which a little taper is burnt before her images never fail to draw down the benediction of heaven upon their inhabitants. We see in the lives of the saints, how grateful, and so to speak sensible, our Blessed Lady is to those who render her these little services which good children pay their mother. Mary sends her heavenly favours to those of her children who dedicate the first flowers which bud in their little gardens to her shrine, and crown her figure with simple garlands. Often the flowers thus offered are not suffered to fade; and the taper presented by a poor child burns more slowly than that given by her rich neighbour.

The good brother Cesarius, who has given us the *Legend of Sister Beatrice*, relates that there was in the twelfth century, near Groningen, a very poor convent, in which holy women dedicated themselves to God, under the patronage of our Blessed Lady. Their chapel was exceedingly plain and unadorned. It was built of wood, a village carpenter had made the altar, tabernacle, and even the candlesticks. A small brass lamp hung before the Holy One, who reposed on the altar of this humble sanctuary.

But the sisters possessed a rich treasure in a long venerated image of their dear patroness, called *Our Lady of Jesse*. Innumerable were the pious legends connected with it. Brought from Palestine, it was said to have been carved in cedarwood by the angels themselves. This the holy sisterhood believed. They were also told, that one day, while the venerable priest who said mass knelt at the words of the creed, ET HOMO FACTUS EST, the little child Jesus took the crown from off his head and placed it on that of his mother. Thus she alone wore a crown.

On a great festival of our Blessed Lady, the religious went to hear mass poorer than usual, for they had no oil, and but two wax candles burnt on the altar, while another supplied the place of the lamp placed before it on a wooden candlestick. The sister sacristan left alone in the chapel, put out the two lights on the altar, after which, considering that the third light would not burn till morning, she, with a sorrowful heart, extinguished it also, and left the chapel.

Half an hour afterwards, two carpenters came to examine some portion of the chapel which they were going to repair in the morning. On leaving, they told the porteress that it was imprudent to leave the candle burning on the wooden candlestick, which it might ignite, and thus threaten the destruction of the chapel.

The porteress repeated this to the sacristan. She, astonished, went to the chapel and again extinguished the candle. The porteress being uneasy about the matter, went again later to see whether it was out, and found it still burning!

This astounding fact was soon communicated to the whole of the pious sisterhood. They called in the venerable priest who had said the mass, who pronounced it to be a miracle of our Blessed Lady. He advised them not to extinguish the light. "For," said he, "whatever is under the protection of the Blessed Virgin is well guarded."

Cesar d'Heisterbach adds, that this candle burnt for a year without being consumed; that then the good religious received assistance and kept their miraculous taper as a sacred relic.

Now, is this wax candle burning for a year an allegory of some secret and ingenious charity?

or is it a miracle of the goodness of Mary? Whatever others may think of it, we are delighted to believe that the charitable hand who furnished the wax was that of our *Lady of Jesse.*

The Holy House.

"Vas insigne devotionis."   "Vessel of singular devotion."

HRISTIAN Europe, in the spring of the year 1291, was in a state of fearful distress. Daily was intelligence of a disastrous character received. We were hourly losing ground in Palestine. Despite the great feats of arms of Godfrey of Bouillon, of Baudoin his noble brother, and their valiant successors; despite the brave and mighty efforts of St. Louis, the only place which remained in the possession of the Christians was St. John d'Acre, the ancient Ptolemaïs. The empire of Constantinople, conquered at such great peril, by Baudoin of Flanders, also slipped from the hands of the Latin Church, while the Catholics of old Europe made war upon one another, and exhausted forces which might have been worthily and advantageously employed in the service of the cross in Palestine. England and Flanders were leagued against France; Italy was distracted by the wars of the Guelphs and the Ghibelines; north and south, east and west, petty quarrels and miserable feuds usurped the place of the grand cause of religion, which then, as now, and at every time, was that of humanity.

Europe blessed without seconding the pontificate of Nicolas IV., who governed the Church with great wisdom, encouraged the arts and sciences, founded the university of Montpellier, diffused learning, and vainly endeavoured to reconcile Christian princes, whose dissensions tended much to shorten his life. He saw with grief the infidels take advantage of the discords which weakened the children of the Church, to destroy everything which the heroes of the cross had founded.

During this time there occurred a most memorable and wonderful event, which we are now about to record.

Some honest and simple peasants, who went every morning to cut wood in the forest of Mount Tersato, in Dalmatia, were much astounded on the morning of the 10th of May, 1291, to find there (in a little meadow surrounded by trees, which they had left on the preceding evening bare and desolate) a small house, which seemed to have risen out of the earth, or to have dropped from heaven, for there it was, without any appearance of labour, placed on the grass, having no foundations in the earth.

The good people rubbed their eyes, scarcely believing their sight, and approached the building timidly, with doubts wavering between the expectation of a miracle or of some work of enchantment. What could this strange edifice be? and how could it have been conveyed to this spot in one compact mass in the course of one night?

The house was forty feet long, twenty-five high, and twenty broad. The stones, old cement, and other materials of which it was composed, were different from those of the country, both in form, substance, and arrangement.

After an humble prayer, the woodmen entered the building, fortifying themselves by the sign of the cross. It had two doors, one at the west and the other on the north side; on the west was a small window rather elevated, and facing it a chimney; in the centre was a small altar. There were remains of paintings on the walls representing some of the mysteries of our redemption. At the back rose an image in cedar-wood four feet high. It was a figure of the Blessed Virgin, blackened by time or the smoke of the candles, " and upon its head was a crown of precious stones; the hair, being divided after the manner of the Nazarenes, hung down over the neck. It was clothed in a golden garment, fastened by a large girdle in the fashion of that country, and over this was thrown a sky-blue mantle, which reached the ground. The child Jesus, with his face full of grace and majesty, was placed on his mother's left arm clothed in his little tunic, with flowing hair, giving his blessing with his right hand and holding in his left a golden globe representing the earth."*

The woodmen again fell on their knees and betook themselves to prayer. Once more they asked themselves and one another what could this house be? It was some sanctuary. But why did it contain a chimney? How could it rest on the ground without any foundations? Over the western window they saw an ancient crucifix. In the eastern wall they perceived a cupboard, on opening which they discovered an earthen vessel and a wooden bowl. All this tended still more to mystify them. Struck at the same time with veneration and joy, for which

* Louis Richeome. *The Pilgrim of Loreto*, chap. vii.

they could not account, they hastily descended to the village and announced to their neighbours this wonderful event. One of them who had a sick child found him cured. The whole population soon ascended to the miraculous chapel. The aged and infirm dragged their wearied limbs thither; the sick recovered their health there; minds troubled by evil spirits became calm at its sight; afflicted hearts received consolation. Every mouth sent forth hymns of joy, every voice recited the praises of God, every lip expressed the liveliest thanks to the Mother of Mercies.

The pilgrimage commenced this day was never to cease. Huts were hastily erected near the chapel. The woodmen in turn watched every night in expectation of some new wonder, and they all declared that during the silence of midnight they heard delicious strains in the air—the sweet symphonies of angelic choirs.

Count Frangipani, the governor of the country, in concert with the prelates, sent priests to serve this rustic chapel. They could not divine its origin any more than the woodmen. In considering, however, the manner of its sudden appearance, they could but recognize a great miracle, of which they expected to be enlightened by the Almighty. They forgot not that our Saviour had said, he who has faith shall remove mountains. They remembered that this promise had been fulfilled to the letter in the person of St. Gregory Thaumaturgus. This great saint was expounding our mysteries to a pagan priest seeking the truth, who demanded of him, in the name of Jesus Christ, some material miracle. "For example," said he, " cause this mountain to change its place."

Gregory, full of faith, and firm in his confidence in God, unhesitatingly commanded the rock to move from the left to the right side of the road. It did so.* Thus, without doubt, by the faith of a saint, the hands of angels, or the will of the Almighty, had this chapel been removed to Mount Tersato.

A week passed away, when Europe resounded with the news of a great disaster. In the preceding month of April, the Saracens † had taken St. John d'Acre, so that one hundred and ninety two years after its glorious conquest by Godfrey of Bouillon, the Christians, driven out on all sides, did not possess a single town in Palestine.

Philip the Fair reigned in France, Edward I. in England, Alphonse X. in Castille, Alphonse III. in Portugal, Charles II. in Sicily, and Gradenigo was Doge of Venice.

None of these princes answered the appeal of the Sovereign Pontiff, who was deeply afflicted at the sight of the Holy Land again falling into the hands of the infidels. The degenerate princes, who ruled at this period, absorbed in their own quarrels, entirely forgot their brethren in the east.

Then, as it were, to palliate this apathy, certain captious writers began to consider the crusades in a new point of view, and to condemn these holy wars, so full of true grandeur, so fruitful in acts of heroism, and the source of so many elements of European civilization.

---

* Narrated by St. Jerome, St. Basil, St. Gregory of Nisa, and other biographers of St. Gregory Thaumaturgus.

† The *Saracens* so called themselves, pretending to be the *sons* of Abraham by *Sara*, and not by Agar the bond-woman.

The capture of St. John d'Acre was the more afflicting to Christian hearts, as it had thus become almost impossible to obtain a safe passage to the holy places of Palestine. For more than ten years previous to this period, their pilgrimage had been attended by many perils. It was no easy task to reach Jerusalem; and hard were the conditions upon which the pilgrim could pay his devotions at our Lord's sepulchre. The crib of Bethlehem was still more difficult of access.

As to the holy house of Nazareth, that sacred mansion which the recollection of so many mysteries tended to exalt, that revered abode of the Blessed Virgin and St. Joseph; where the angel Gabriel had announced to her that she had been chosen by the Almighty for the Mother of His Divine Son, where the word had been made flesh, in His immense love for the unfortunate children of Eve; where Jesus our Saviour had lived till His thirtieth year,—that sacred spot, called, from time immemorial, "the Holy House," situated in a country inhabited by the most ferocious people, was inaccessible to a great many pilgrims. The few Christians who were enabled to reach it did so by purchasing the protection of some Saracen chief, and travelling with an escort of enemies.

About this time, two pilgrims, travelling to Palestine, reached the foot of Mount Tersato, where they heard of the capture of St. John d'Acre. One of them, an old man, had previously made the tour of the Holy Land, and was now conducting his son thither. "Let us continue on our way, as we have made a vow to accomplish this pilgrimage; and I hope, with the assistance of God, we shall be able to kiss our Saviour's crib at Bethlehem, and His tomb at Jerusalem. But

I fear, alas! that we shall not be able to reach Nazareth, and that, less happy than your father, you will not be able to adore your Saviour on the spot on which he became man. Oh!" continued the aged pilgrim, "this holy house is always present in my mind, and every day I seem to see it; I am carried to it in spirit; I remain absorbed in it, as I was on the blessed day on which I first entered it on my knees."

While thus lamenting, he was attracted by the religious aspect of the crowds who ascended the mountain. He heard that a wonderful chapel had lately appeared there, and could not suffer his son to leave the place without taking him to see it, and offering up his prayers therein with him.

The two pilgrims ascended the mount. On approaching the chapel, the old man was struck motionless and speechless with surprise. On recovering himself, he hastily entered the building, and prostrated himself in adoration.

He had recognised, in the midst of this Dalmatian wood, in this mysterious sanctuary, the most holy house of Nazareth, the sacred dwelling of the Blessed Virgin, the venerated abode where she had so long lived the model of virgins, wives, mothers, and of all the saints, Mother of God and Queen of angels, and in which *the word was made flesh*. By the window, says a pious tradition, the angel Gabriel had passed to salute the handmaid of the Lord. The cupboard had been used by the Blessed Virgin. Every portion of it, in fact, recalled the remembrance of the holy family.

When he had recovered his voice, the aged pilgrim explained his sensations to his astonished hearers; and from this time no one entered the sacred house, except on his knees.

Already had the truth of this translation been revealed to many pious personages. A prelate of that country, Bishop Alexander, who dwelt at St. George's, had been for some years confined to his bed by paralysis. He saw in a vision the Blessed Virgin, who told him of the translation of her house, and promised to restore him to health if he caused himself to be carried thither. Though this wonderful cure took place, still many refused to believe the identity of the Holy House.

To confirm the belief of the faithful, however, some Christian prisoners, who had disembarked on the shores of the Adriatic, on their return from Palestine, where they had been redeemed, related that on the morning of the 10th of May (the day on which the house appeared at Tersato), fear and wonder took possession of the people of Nazareth, on finding that the house of the Blessed Virgin had suddenly disappeared, that no one had seen it move, and that nothing but its foundations were now visible, level with the ground.

Such of the prisoners who had visited Nazareth, upon hearing of the wonderful arrival of a strange house at Tersato, went thither, and testified to its identity with the house they had seen at Nazareth.

Other testimonies accumulated to such a degree that doubt was no longer possible. Yet the Church is slow to confirm the truth of extraordinary events. Four commissioners were selected to go to Galilee. Being well supplied with means, they soon reached Nazareth, where all their observations tended to confirm, without the shadow of a doubt, the truth of the translation of the Holy House thence to Tersato.

The dimensions of the house at Loreto, with the one recently broken from its foundations at Nazareth, accorded with the nicest precision. Each presented to view the same stone and materials, and a similar mode of construction; and it was evident that the house had been cut off level with the ground, as it were by a scythe.* The entire disappearance of the Holy House of Nazareth, and the appearance of the strange sanctuary on the same day, the 10th of May, dissipated at once the doubts of many of the incredulous.

Still, notwithstanding all these proofs, and the abundant graces which Mary daily dispensed in her earthly abode, these wonders so disturbed the weak understanding of poor human nature, that many even now entertained doubts and objections to their authenticity. But, as if heaven determined to convince the incredulous, and again demonstrate to the world that the removal of mountains is easy to the hand that first founded them, a new prodigy took place. During the night of the 10th of December, 1294, the *Holy House* suddenly disappeared from Mount Tersato, and was found on the same day in the marches of Ancona, near Recanati, in a forest of laurels, belonging to a widow named Laureta; happy woman, whose name was hence-

---

* There still remained at Nazareth on one side of the foundations of the house a small chamber cut out of the rock. This room still bears the name of the Blessed Virgin's house, because it formed part of her dwelling. The Franciscans consider this grotto to have formed our Lady's oratory. Near to it is discovered the ruins of the church, built over the Holy House by the Empress St. Helena, and which was visited by St. Jerome and St. Paula. I am not aware of its having been remarked elsewhere that the Holy House, so dear to St. Jerome, was translated to his native land, Dalmatia.

forth to be perpetuated in the sanctuary of our Blessed Lady of Loreto. This occurred under the pontificate of St. Celestine V.

Great was the astonishment of the people on discovering, in the midst of the wood, this ancient chapel firmly resting on the ground without foundations. The shepherds of the place related that, in their night watch, they had seen a great light in the heavens, and they now thought it must have been the angels carrying this sacred dwelling.

In the states of the Church itself, the very centre of faith, great disputes were held concerning this miracle, which was then the general subject of discussion. Among those who denied it were not only philosophers and logicians, but also many bands of robbers, who were interested in not believing anything about it.

These brigands, not admitting the sanctity of the house of Loreto, posted themselves with hardihood in the forest, where they robbed the pilgrims of all ranks who came from every part to see and worship in the Holy House.

Sixteen commissioners, consisting of gentlemen and men of learning, had been sent to Nazareth to examine the state of our Lady's house there, when a new miracle took place. For, after a sojourn of eight months in the laurel forest, the holy house (so regretted by the Dalmatians, who flocked there in pilgrimage, and who, to preserve the memory of its first translation, had erected a model of it on the spot on which it had stood)* was again transported a third time, and going

---

* The following hymn is sung daily in this church by

nearer to Recanati, took up its position on a hill belonging to two brothers, about a mile distant from its former position.

The two brothers, engaging in a quarrel concerning the right of possession of the Holy House, it was again, four months later, miraculously removed a short distance further on the public road, where it still remains.

This miracle, four times repeated in the sight of innumerable witnesses, confirmed by the *procès verbal* of the sixteen commissioners who had re-

the Father Minor Observantines, who have the care of it.—*Trans.*

> Huc cum domo advenisti,
> Ut qua pia Mater Christi,
>   Dispensares gratiam.
> Nazarethum tibi ortus
> Sed Tersatum primum portus,
>   Petenti hanc patriam.
> Ædem quidem hinc tulisti,
> Attamen tu permansisti,
>   Regina Clementiæ.
> Nobis inde gratulamur,
> Digni quod hic habeamur,
>   Maternæ præsentiæ.
>   Amen.

Here thy sacred house thou broughtest,
Holy Mother when thou soughtest
   To dispense thy heavenly grace.
Nazareth thy birth illumined,
But Tersato thee assumed,
   Seeking for a resting-place.
Here thy house no more resideth,
But thy presence still abideth,
   Queen of heavenly mercy fair.
Oh! may grateful love possess us,
That thou still doth deign to bless us
   With thy fond maternal care.
         Amen.

turned from the Holy Land, has been discussed, and its truth maintained in a learned treatise, by Benedict XIV., one of the most holy and learned pontiffs who ever sat on the papal throne.

In its last position, the Holy House was placed beyond the reach of dispute; its identity being recognized by the people, it was resolved, that besides erecting chapels on the spots where it had previously stood, a magnificent church should be raised over the sacred building itself. An attempt was made to encase it in marble, but the workmen found the ancient walls protected by the divine hand, for it was impossible to make the marble adhere to them. A space was therefore left between the venerated walls and their rich enclosure.

The most celebrated artists of the fifteenth and sixteenth centuries exhausted their talents in architecture and sculpture in the decoration of the four walls which enclose without touching the Holy House. They are composed of white Carara marble, and are covered with bas-reliefs representing scenes in the life of the Blessed Virgin, and the translation of her sacred abode from Nazareth to Loreto. Statues fill twenty niches formed between double columns.

The interior of the Holy House can alone be seen, and it remains exactly in its original state, with the fragments of painting executed in Palestine. Our Lady's figure appears in several places bearing her Divine Child in her arms. St. Catherine and other saints are also pourtrayed, with St. Louis of France, who reckoned among the happiest of his life the day he spent in the Holy House at Nazareth—the 12th March, 1252—nearly forty years before its translation.

The ground has been covered with white and red marble, and many and severe are the prohibitions to pilgrims to take the least particle of the holy walls. A stone is shown which had been stolen, but the robber was so tormented with remorse that he brought it back, and it was replaced. The Portuguese Bishop of Coimbra, who assisted at the Council of Trent, obtained a brief, authorizing him to remove one of the stones to enrich a church which he was erecting in honour of our Lady of Loreto. But he experienced such difficulties and delays in its transport, that he conceived it to be a sign of the unwillingness of our Lady to part with it, and accordingly he returned with it to the sacred dwelling, into which it was borne in solemn procession.

It would take up too much space to enumerate all the rich offerings made to the shrine of Loreto before the revolutions which broke forth at the close of the last century, and which were signalized by the outrageous public robberies, dignified by the name of the rights of war.* Louis XIII. presented to our Lady of Loreto a triple crown of gold, and Anne of Austria, the figure of an angel of silver, bearing in its arms the dauphin, in gold, as a thank-offering for the birth of Louis XIV. The Queen of England, wife of the unfortunate James II., sent an angel of gold to Loreto. Twelve golden candlesticks were sent by other princes, besides twenty-eight

* In 1797, the army of the French republic having taken possession of Loreto, the Holy Image of our Lady was taken to Paris, and placed in the Louvre. On Napoleon's attaining the rank of First Consul, he sent it back to the sanctuary with great honours.

others of silver gilt, innumerable lamps, precious stuffs, stones, jewels, and other valuable presents. Italian noblemen were equally liberal with foreign princes, and endowed Loreto with so much territory, that an important city was soon formed around the sanctuary. In 1586, Sixtus V. erected a bishopric there, and the same Pope caused the following inscription to be carved on the façade of the Church of Loreto: DEIPARÆ DOMUS UBI VERBUM CARO FACTUM EST.*

The altar, it is said, occupies the same spot as that on which the Blessed Virgin stood when the angel announced to her the Incarnation of our Lord.

If it would detain us too long to enumerate the many presents offered to our Blessed Lady at this sanctuary, how much greater time would it occupy to relate the innumerable graces which She has there dispensed? Many of these will be found in the Annals to the Holy House, to which we must refer the reader.

We therefore conclude this simple narrative with an enumeration of the learned men who have attested the truths of these facts, which are recorded in the public acts of Fiume, Recanati, and Loreto; the *procès verbal* of the sixteen commissioners who went into the Holy Land; the bulls of the Sovereign Pontiffs, Benedict XII., Urban V., Martin V., Eugene IV., Nicholas V., Calistus IV., Pius II., and their successors, particularly the learned Benedict XIV. and Leo X. Tursellinus has written the History of the Holy House, in five books, and among its other nume-

---

* "*This is the house of the Mother of God in which the Word was made flesh.*"

rous illustrators will be found the names of Paul Rinalducio, Francis Prior, Baptist of Mantua, Erasmus, Albert Leander, Canisius, Antony Muret, Bruzen de la Martiniere, and even Leland and others.

The Indian's Cloak.

"Rosa Mystica."   "Mystical Rose."

HEN the hand of God arrested the hordes of Attila before the walls of Paris, he chose for his instrument a young, unknown girl, St. Genevieve. In the midst of human distress, the Almighty thus effects the greatest results by means the most humble and insignificant, wishing in his bounty to confound our pride. When, later, He took pity on France, on the point of falling entirely into the power of a foreign invader, he sent to oppose their mighty hosts, from the extremity of the country, from a little village in Champagne, a timid peasant girl, of mean birth, uneducated and unassisted, but by His aid Joan of Arc triumphed.

He thus shows that heaven needs not human help to change the fate of earthly interests, and when He sometimes deigns to choose from among us an instrument for his designs, He confounds our pride by selecting them from the most humble.

Shortly after the Mexican continent had received the faith, our Blessed Lady, in her exhaustless love, desired to bestow upon the newly-converted countries some evidence of her favour. She herself chose the spot for her sanctuary, and her own hand endowed it with an image, most powerful in attracting the hearts of pilgrims. But she chose for her confidant, neither the renowned conquerors, or powerful princes, or rich nobles, but a poor unknown Indian.

In 1531, ten years after Cortez had added the flower of Mexico to the crown of Charles V., there lived amid the huts of Quantitlan, two leagues from Mexico, a young Indian, lately converted to the Christian faith, whose name was John Diegue. He was married to a female of his tribe, also a Christian, and they lived with his uncle Bernadine, who had been a father to him, in that calm and sweet happiness which God grants to his servants. John Diegue never failed on every Saturday to visit Mexico. He there heard mass in St. James's Church, and offered himself with pure devotion to our Blessed Lady's service. In this journey, so dear to him, he had to pass a celebrated hill called Mount Tepejacao. Before the conquest, the Mexicans worshipped on this mount a goddess, whom they invoked as the mother of the gods. This idolatrous worship had of course disappeared with the spread of Christianity.

Every time John passed the hill, he thought of the old goddess, and to show his devotion to the true Mother of God, whom he tenderly loved, he always said an Hail, Mary, and sang in his native tongue the praises of the Blessed Virgin.

As he was about to pass the mount, on Saturday, the 9th December, 1531, he was surprised to hear, mingling with his rude chant, melodious singing, which he took at first for the warbling of birds, but it was more expressive. His curiosity was awakened; he endeavoured to find out whence this divine melody proceeded, and perceived, resting on the hill, a shining cloud. From the brilliancy of the colours which darted from it, it bore the appearance at some distance of a rich flower-bed. This spectacle astounded him, and he fell on his knees in awe, on hearing his own name pronounced by a voice in the cloud.

The accents of this voice were so enticing, that after a while he had the courage to climb the hill. On reaching its summit, he perceived a throne of great splendour, on which sat a lady of incomparable beauty. Majesty shone around her, and from her garments proceeded rays of dazzling splendour.

So ardent was the faith of the young savage, that this apparition did not excite in him any fear or bewilderment. He understood that he had the happiness to contemplate a part of the glory which surrounds the Mother of God in eternal bliss. And why should not such a vision be the recompense of those rare souls who live in the constant contemplation of heavenly things?

The Queen whom he saw on the throne, addressing him with maternal tenderness, asked him whither he went.

"I am going to hear mass at our Lady's altar," said he.

"Your devotion, my son, is agreeable to me," replied the Lady, "for I am that Virgin whom you so love. Your humble heart pleases me, and I make you the confidant of my desire to have an altar raised to me on this hill, from which I will dispense my favours to all who seek them, and where the Christians shall ever find a mother! Go, announce my wish to the bishop."

The Bishop of Mexico, at that time, was John of Zummarraga, a pious and learned Franciscan, who was held in great repute. John Diegue, full of joy, hastened to the good prelate, and fulfilled his mission with so much ingenuousness, as to leave no doubt on the prelate's mind of the truth of his statement. Still, so extraordinary was the event, that the bishop, fearing to act in so important a matter with anything approaching levity or haste, and deeming it possible that the Indian might have been misled by some illusion or dream, said to him mildly: "What you have related to me is really so strange, that I can hardly bring myself to credit it on your sole authority," and he sent him away.

The poor man retired sadly confused, and not understanding why the bishop would not credit what he assured him he had seen with his own eyes. He, however, went and heard mass, and afterwards set out on his return home.

On reaching the hill, he again heard the same music, and beheld the same appearances of majesty and the same throne. It surely could not be an error of his senses. The heavenly Lady was also there. She spoke to him kindly, and asked him whether he had fulfilled his message. He told her that his word had been doubted, and humbly acknowledging his unworthiness to be entrusted with such a mission, he timidly suggested to our Lady to choose a person less obscure and ignorant to make known her wishes. Mary, however, reassured him, and told him to go to the bishop's house the next day.

The Indian said nothing to his uncle and aunt, but on the Sunday set out for Mexico. He again called on the bishop, and renewed his request.

The prelate received him kindly, but still refused to give implicit credence to his narration.

"I know what I will do," thought the Indian to himself; "to-morrow I will bring my uncle Bernardine."

And he went quietly and heard mass.

Again, on his return this day, as he passed Mount Tepejacac, where he had seen our Lady, she was awaiting his arrival, and listened with compassion to the continued rejection of his mission.

"To-morrow," said she, "I will give you a sign."

He entered his hut more joyously that day, without, however, for a moment abandoning his design of taking his uncle with him on the morrow, "who," thought he, "will be able to speak better than I can." But in the night his dear uncle was seized with a sudden and dangerous illness, and far from being able to take him, the youth was obliged to remain at his side to administer to his wants. His pious occupation entirely banished from his mind his intended visit to Mexico. It was not till Tuesday morning that the exceeding dangerous state of his uncle obliged him to leave him to seek a priest to administer spiritual consolation.

On coming in sight of the hill, John Diegue suddenly remembered his neglect. He feared to receive the blame he merited, and turned into another road. But on his way stood our Blessed Lady.

"Why have you changed your ordinary route, my child?" she asked.

"Ah! Holy Virgin, pardon me for having neglected your commands," he replied, falling on his knees; "it was my uncle's illness which kept me at home."

"Do not disturb yourself on that account," said the Blessed Virgin; "your uncle is healed at this instant. You will, therefore, go to the bishop with an easy mind. You shall take him a sign. Go," added she, "to the spot where you first saw me, and gather a bouquet of flowers."

Another might have hesitated at this order. It was not the season for flowers, and on the spot indicated, there grew nothing but briars. But the Indian obeyed without hesitation, and reached a parterre of flowers. He chose the most beautiful, and brought them to Mary, who instantly formed them into an exquisite bouquet, which she gave him to present to the bishop.

The Indian was fearful of spoiling the flowers before he reached the house. He wore a coarse cloak; this he took off, spread out, and placed the bouquet in it. But so great was the perfume which exhaled from the flowers, that it betrayed him. As soon as he entered the bishop's house, the servants asked him how he got those exquisite flowers which he carried with such mystery? But the Indian would not reveal his secret. One of the servants, more curious than his fellows, opened the cloak, and uttered a cry of delight at so rare and beautiful a sight. Another, still bolder, attempted to seize them, but, to his astonishment, found they were painted.

The bishop speedily heard of this new wonder, and hastened to meet John Diegue, now convinced that he had an extraordinary mission. The Indian then opened his rustic cloak, which he had hitherto firmly held. When, to the great astonishment of the prelate and his suite, and to the stupefaction of the Indian himself, the cloak, instead of flowers, presented to the view a beautiful painting representing our Blessed Lady, in the most exquisite colours and most artistically finished.

The Indian stood with his arms extended, wrapped in astonishment. The bishop and his attendants fell on their knees, and after having venerated this miraculous picture, placed it in his chapel, until a more fitting and public position could be given to it in a new church.

At daybreak the next day, 13th December, the Bishop of Mexico walked in procession with the clergy and people to the privileged hill; John Diegue, who led the way, was about to point out the precise spot where the Blessed Virgin had first appeared to him. He hesitated for a moment, when a spring of water sprung up near him. This fountain, near which was founded the Church of our Lady of Guadelope, has never ceased to flow, and its waters have operated many wonderful cures.

The name of our Lady of Guadelope was given to the effigy so miraculously painted on the Indian's cloak, in memory of another celebrated image, venerated from time immemorial in the village of Guadelope, in Estremadura, the native place of the conquerors of Mexico.

The uncle of John Diegue, who was cured the same moment that the promise was made, arrived at the spot. Many other miracles took place. A town was soon formed round the new sanctuary, which, on account of the increase of pilgrims, had to be rebuilt on a larger scale, and is the great and beautiful church which we admire at the present day. It was consecrated in 1709. The image of our Lady of Guadelope is in the transept. It has often been copied, and the most celebrated of these copies is at Rome, in the Church of St. Nicolas, *in carcere Tulliano*. Her festival is kept on the 12th December, the day on which the same powerful hand, who called creation out of nothing, and who loves to confound our pride by the humility of his instruments, drew this exquisite portrait of the Blessed Virgin on the poor Indian's cloak.

The Jew's Child.

"Turris Davidica." "Tower of David."

E call those ages of which we know little, barbarous; and we disdain to acquire any knowledge of them, in order that we may the more easily condemn them. In those days there were, however, public schools, into which the children of the poor were admitted with no less generosity than in our own days. Those ages produced writers and artists the most varied and the most talented. They have everywhere left numerous monuments of their piety and their taste. As early as the sixth century there existed public schools in France of the same description as we now have.

In the year 527, under the reign of the sons of Clovis, there was a very popular school at Bourges, where rich and poor scholars mingled and studied together. At the same time, that species of charity, which moderns call "toleration," was in full vogue, and which, by the way, never flourishes in its truest sense so well as in Catholic states. Jews and pagans lived in peace amidst a Christian population, whose prayers and example produced the happiest effects upon them. The children of the Jews were received at this school, and from this custom arose the following occurrence.

A Jew workman had a son of between ten and twelve years of age, who went to school with the other children of the neighbourhood. He did his best to learn what he was taught. After having spent some hours in reading, writing, and arithmetic, he amused himself with his school-fellows. Some of these would at times enter a church, and kneel before the image of the Blessed Virgin—called our Lady of Bourges—which may still be seen in that city. The little Jew followed their example, and honoured her whom he heard called the Mother of God.

His father, who was constantly engaged in his business, and was naturally of a taciturn disposition, did not make any inquiries as to how his son spent his time; and thus the little Jew became a Christian in everything but the essential of baptism.

One Easter-day was appointed for the first communion of many of his playmates. They were all dressed in new clothes, and went joyously to their church. The young Jew followed them, heard mass, and modestly walked with them to the altar rails, and received the holy Eucharist.

Before leaving the church, he went with the others to return thanks before our Lady's image.

The long absence of the child was this day remarked by his father, who asked him on his return where he had been?

We know not his calling, but he was engaged at the time near a large fire. The child simply recounted that he had followed his companions to the church, and received the holy sacrament with them.

Without being a zealous follower of the old law, the Jew was influenced by the fanaticism and hatred of Christianity common to so many of his sect. His rage was excited by the act of his son; and seizing him, he threw him into the fire, and heaped more fuel on it to increase its heat.

All this was done in a moment.

The Jew's wife, hearing a cry, rushed to the spot, and asked for her child. The Jew made no answer, nor gave any sign. Accustomed to his surly humours, she sought over the house for her son. Not finding him, she returned to the workshop, when the faggots flew assunder, and she fancied she saw her poor boy's form in the fire!

Her screams of anguish brought the neighbours to the spot. They also saw the child, who seemed most wonderfully to be seated with a smiling face in the midst of the fire. They seized the tongs, and having removed the burning embers, drew out the child, who, to their surprise, was not burnt or injured in the least. . . . . In answer to their inquiries, he said, " I have been preserved by the Lady who stands over the altar, and who came and shielded me from the flames."

All knew that he meant our Lady of Bourges. The populace, hearing of the circumstance, became so infuriated, that they cried out for instant punishment of the unnatural father, who was condemned to the death he had chosen his son; and without reflecting on their unauthorised deed, they committed him to the flames. The mother and child became Christians.

Evagius, the historian, whose exactitude is unimpeachable, relates a somewhat similar occurrence. It took place in Constantinople, and at about the same time.

" The son of a Jew, who was a glassblower,

seeing his comrades go to church after school to finish the remains of the consecrated hosts, as was the custom at that time, followed them, and eat also of the sacred bread. His father, hearing of this, was seized with frenzy, and threw his child into the furnace, where his glass was melting.

"His wife, in ignorance of her husband's crime, sought her child for three days, when she was startled by cries from the midst of the furnace, whence her son came forth safe and unhurt. He told her that a Lady, in purple clothing, had appeared to him, and rendered the flames around him harmless.

"Every one in the city, as in that of Bourges, recognised in this Lady the Blessed Virgin. The Jew's family embraced the Christian religion; but he himself, remaining obstinate, was ordered to be put to death by the Emperor Justinian."

May the glorious daughter of David take pity on the Jewish race now on earth, and bring them to recognise the divinity of her dear Son, our only Lord and Saviour Jesus Christ!

The Siege of Guelders.

"Turris eburnea."   "Tower of ivory."

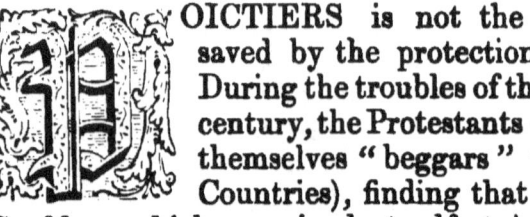OICTIERS is not the only city saved by the protection of Mary. During the troubles of the sixteenth century, the Protestants (who called themselves "beggars" in the Low Countries), finding that the city of Guelders, which remained steadfast in the faith, had lost its little garrison, which was called off to another point menaced by the enemy, and that there were neither troops nor amunition in the place, came one night and laid siege to the town.

On their awaking in the morning, the honest townsmen beheld their homes assailed by a horde of armed ruffians. Cannons threatened each gate, and general consternation spread among the people.

The governor and the magistrates saw well from the ramparts that they could not hold out for two days.

The "beggars" knew this, and ordered the gates to be opened to them, unless they wished the town to be pillaged.

"If they enter," said the governor, "even without opposition, we shall be deprived of our greatest blessing—religion; our churches will be profaned, and our religious and clergy insulted. Still I cannot recommend you to have recourse to arms; we are too few and too weak."

"But," said a magistrate, "if God is with us, what shall we care for those who are against us? Yesterday we honoured, by a procession, our Lady of Carmel, the Patroness of our city; she has protected others in the time of need, let us have recourse to her in our present necessity."

All assented to this advice; and the governor, magistrates, and citizens instantly proceeded in procession to the Carmelite church. The "beggars" were in delight, thinking they were coming to capitulate. But, far from thinking of it, the good people of Guelders, kneeling before our Lady's image, felt their confidence in her increase. The governor, taking the keys of the city, advanced towards the altar, and deposited them at the foot of the image. Then kneeling before it, he prayed thus aloud:

"O Holy Virgin, Mother of the God of armies, shield of the Church, whose faithful children we have the happiness to be. You are our only defence, our only strength, our only hope and refuge. Do not forget that our enemies are also yours.

"You know their designs. If they prevail here, they will outrage your sanctuary, insult your image, profane your temples, and proscribe your worship. You will not suffer this, O powerful Queen! The keys of the city are under your care. You will defend us! For God, the ruler of all men, can refuse you nothing!"

As he finished his prayer, the weather, in an instant, became so foggy, that it seemed as if the night had come on prematurely. It was impossible to perceive objects a yard before one. The good people understood this; a rain, nay, rather a deluge, fell in torrents, accompanied by such tempestuous wind, that no one could stir out. The river overflowed, and turned the meadows into lakes.

The storm lasted three hours, after which the weather becoming pure and serene, the people of Guelders left the church, and went to the ramparts. The town was surrounded by a deep ditch; the "beggars" had decamped, leaving their cannon and baggage behind them.

The city became possessed of this booty. The enemies' banners were offered to our Lady of Carmel, with other trophies. It was said that the fugitives, who dared not return, saw a figure in the air, and flaming swords, which drove them away. In memory of their deliverance, the people of Guelders established an annual procession on the anniversary, which terminates in the Carmelite church by a solemn act of thanksgiving to the Blessed Virgin Mary.

Our Lady of the Hermits.[*]

"Domus aurea."   "House of gold."

"I HAVE been to our *Lady's of the Hermits*, which is a two days' journey distant from Mount St. Gothard. I felt penetrated with a deep respect for this holy place. In the centre of the great church, there is a chapel much venerated, and said to have been consecrated by Jesus Christ. This miracle is vouched for by a bull of the Sovereign Pontiff, Leo VIII., and is further attested by several bishops; and I can assure you that I have never been so moved by so tender devotion, or seen so holy a chapel, if I except that of our Lady of Loreto."

So wrote St. Charles Boromeo in the sixteenth century, of the celebrated pilgrimage of Einsiedeln, or *our Lady of the Hermits*, which still attracts Catholic pilgrims to the Swiss mountains. Many wonderful legends illustrate the origin of this august sanctuary. Minds devoid of faith may doubt these pious traditions. But they cannot so easily dispose of the many miracles which are daily wrought by the Blessed Virgin in her noble church of Einsiedeln, which are confirmed by the testimony of twenty thousand pilgrims, who yearly

[*] Notre Dame des Ermites.

visit this venerated spot, where, even at the present day, one hundred and fifty thousand annually partake of the Holy Communion. In the ninth century, a scion of the noble family of Hohenzollern, called Meinrad, embraced a religious life. He had been piously educated in the Abbey of Richenau. In his cloister he found not the retirement and tranquillity he sought, on account of his high rank being known to the inmates. He therefore sought, and obtained, permission to retire to Mount Ezel, near lake Zurich. He there spent seven years in sweet solitude. But the reputation of his sanctity increasing, he was visited by so many persons that he became alarmed; and in 837, "he fled to a vast forest, near a fountain, to which he took only an image of the Blessed Virgin, before which he spent his hours of prayer. Such was the origin of the convent of Einsiedeln.* The oratory of Meinrad is now the church; his cell, the vast abbey; his fountain still slakes the thirst of the weary pilgrims; and the image, which was the object of his veneration, is the same that for ten centuries has drawn Christendom to its feet to obtain succour at her hands."

According to another tradition, the wonderful image of our Lady of the Hermits, which is three feet high, carved in wood, blackened by time and the smoke of the lamps, was given to a pious solitary, by the Princess Hildegarde, daughter of Louis, King of Germany, and grand-daughter of Louis the Meek of France. The same princess also built a small chapel for the good hermit.

He lived there in peace and happiness for twenty-six years, when, on the 21st of January, 863, the

* The word Einsiedeln, or Einsidlen, means a hermitage.

weather being bitterly cold, two men came to seek shelter in his cell. Meinrad received them kindly. But these men were robbers, who, expecting to find some booty, murdered the solitary in the night. All they could find was a hair shirt. They fled precipitately, thinking at least no one would discover their crime. But they were deceived. Meinrad, like the fathers of the desert, had friends among the birds of the air. Two ravens, the companions of his solitude, who shared his meals, following the murderers, menaced them with their cries, as far as Zurich, where the inn-keeper, perceiving this singular circumstance, and suspecting something evil, delivered them over to justice, when they confessed their crime, and were put to death. The same inn still bears the sign of "*the two faithful ravens;*" they also form the arms of the abbey, and the religious always keep and feed two of these birds in the monastery.

The body of Meinrad was conveyed to Richenau, where God manifested the sanctity of his servant by many miracles. Forty-four years after his death, Benno, son of the King of the Burgundians, went to visit the cell and little chapel of St. Meinrad. He there felt such sweet emotions, that he exclaimed, "This is the place of my repose;" and took up his dwelling in the cell. Some of his companions joined him, built other cells, and lived together in the exercises of piety, until the arrival of St. Ebernard, who came to share their retreat. He employed his riches in building a monastery and church, and adopting the rule of St. Benedict, became first abbot. At his invitation, St. Conrad, Bishop of Constance, came to consecrate the church in the year 949. St. Ulric, Bishop of Augsburg, accompanied him. Little did the prelates imagine the wonderful event which was to take place, as we are told by the pious legendaries.

In constructing the new church, they had left Meinrad's little chapel in the centre.

On the eve of the dedication, the holy Bishop Conrad rose at midnight to pray. On a sudden he saw the mysterious consecration of this privileged sanctuary take place, by angels, as St. Charles says, in "a most miraculous manner." Delighted, he remained for some time in ecstasy at the sight, and when on the morrow, everything being prepared, they sought for St. Conrad, he told them of the miraculous consecration. But so strange did the fact appear, that they refused to believe him, and were about to proceed with the consecration, when a voice from heaven declared thrice, that the chapel had been consecrated.* Such is the ancient tradition.

The church of our Lady of the Hermits soon acquired great celebrity. The Emperor Otho I. conferred on the Abbot of Einsiedeln the title of prince. Sovereign pontiffs, emperors, kings, prelates, and noblemen, vied with each other in enriching and granting privileges to the abbey. The church and other portions of the monastic buildings were decorated in the highest style of art. Populous hamlets sprung up round the abbey. The body of St. Meinrad was translated hither in 1039. Other precious relics were en-

* All the chroniclers of the abbey speak of this event. Some other churches, as St. Denis, near Paris, and Rheims cathedral, have the same tradition of being consecrated by the divine interposition. St. Thomas Aquinas makes allusion to these exceptions, where he writes in his *Summa:* "*Quædam templa dicuntur angelico ministerio consecrata:*" —"Some churches are said to have been consecrated by angelic ministry."

closed in many altars. The gifts of crowned heads to the abbey formed a splendid treasury; and although the revolution which closed the last century with such horrors laid waste the abbey, it is still, as wrote a French traveller a short time since, one of the most beautiful edifices in Switzerland.

We must say a few words respecting the fountain of St. Meinrad, which flows before the church, and which has worked many cures. It decorates the space in front of the western towers. Fourteen beautiful marble columns, each of which has its jet, support this fountain; they are dedicated to our Blessed Lord, his Holy Mother, and the twelve apostles.

It is well known that the people easily adopt pious legends. The good folk of Switzerland and Germany imagine that a particular blessing is gained by those who drink of the fourteen jets of this fountain; so that they never fail on leaving church to make the round of the fountain, and many forgetting where they began (as the columns are all alike), go round twice, to assure themselves of the blessing, which causes some innocent merriment to the bystanders. Others, to make more sure, place their large hats against the pillar they commence with, and so find it when they have made the circuit.

Many volumes might be filled with accounts of the miracles wrought at Einsiedeln. We cannot refrain from recounting one which took place in the present century, and which we take from a little work entirely devoted to the glory of Mary.

The district schoolmaster of a canton in Lucerne had a child called Placid, who, at the age of eight months, was seized with terrible convulsions, the consequences of which were most deplorable. The poor boy reached the age, when it is usual for children to rejoice their parents' heart by pronouncing their first accents; but he remained dumb. How great was the grief of the parents, when, at the age of four, he was still not only speechless, but idiotic, manifesting no feelings of love for those around him. The most skilful physicians were in vain applied to; they pronounced the case to be hopeless.

The parents were happily endowed with good religious sentiments and love for the Mother of God. They addressed themselves to our Lady of Einsiedeln, made a vow to go in pilgrimage to her sanctuary, and offer a silver tongue to her shrine, if the little Placid should, by her intercession, obtain the gifts of speech and reason.

The father then set out for Einsiedeln, which he reached on the 18th of October, 1818. He threw himself at the feet of the Blessed Virgin, and with all the earnestness of his soul, besought her to take compassion on his son, promising that if, on his recovery and advance in years, he showed a disposition for study, he would devote him to the work of the sacred ministry of the altar. Such ardent prayers met with their reward. A delightful surprise awaited the father on his return. Let him relate it in his own words:

"I had just reached my home," says he, in his declaration, "when, as usual, my two eldest children came forth and threw themselves into my arms for my caresses; but what was my joy, when suddenly the poor dumb idiot child, the object of my pilgrimage, my dear Placid, leaving his little chair (from which he had never yet risen without aid), came to me, and stretching out his little arms, said thrice distinctly, 'Papa, papa, papa!' Tears came into my eyes at this proof of the goodness of God, who had heard my prayer, and I most heartily a thousand times thanked Him and the glorious Mother of my Saviour, for their having granted my petition."

From this moment the little child changed his habits, nay, almost his nature. He was then four years and a half old, and he immediately made up for lost time by his application to study, in which he so soon surpassed his fellows, that his father, considering it right to keep the promise he had made to our Lady, sent him to her Abbey of Einsiedeln. He became a monk, and is now (as we hear) labouring for his own and neighbours' salvation in one of the houses of the order in Switzerland.

The Choir Boy of our Lady of Chartres.

"Domus aurea."   "House of gold."

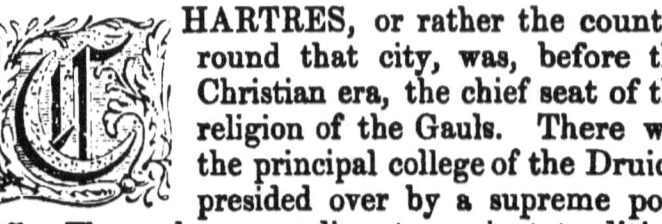HARTRES, or rather the country round that city, was, before the Christian era, the chief seat of the religion of the Gauls. There was the principal college of the Druids, presided over by a supreme pontiff. There also, according to ancient tradition, in a large grotto, protected by a group of aged oak-trees, the Druids erected an altar to "the Virgin, who should bring forth a son."*

Without staying to consider what degree of confidence is due to this ancient tradition, we will place before our readers the description of the image in this chapel, borrowed from a manuscript in the possession of the Chapter of Chartres.

"The grottos or crypts of the Cathedral of Chartres are very considerable, and form the spot on which the Druids, the ancient priests of Gaul, offered their sacrifices, held their assemblies, and which served as an asylum for the first Christians in times of persecution. For this reason, these crypts are still called the 'holy places.'

"Here the Druids raised upon an altar the figure

* *Virgini parituræ*. Isis was anciently honoured in many places as the predestined mother of a future liberator.

of the Virgin Mother, two hundred years before her birth. This image was two feet and a half high, and carved in the wood of the pear-tree. It represented a woman seated on a throne, holding a child upon her knees. Her robe was a plain tunic falling to the feet. Over this was a mantle like an ancient chasuble gathered up over the arms. On her head was placed a crown, whose ornaments resembled the oak-leaf. From the back of the crown, a veil fell over the shoulders, leaving the face open. The countenance was oval, regular, and pleasing, being most gracious and modest. The child wore a plain tunic, and his head and feet were bare. His right hand was extended in the act of blessing, and in his left he held a globe.

"We must not omit to mention a singular circumstance; it is, that the eyes of the child are open, while those of the mother are closed. This difference was not accidental, says the tradition. The Druids, it continues, represented the Virgin Mother with her eyes shut, to show that they were still in the dark when this statue was made, also that she whom it represented was not yet born. They had, however, represented the child with its eyes open, to show that they believed him to be ever living and existing from all eternity, and which would lead us to imagine that they had some notions of the mystery of the redemption."

This image is said to have been honoured in the crypt which is under the present cathedral, when the first apostles came to announce the gospel in Chartres. They who have not seen this crypt may form some idea of its extent, when they know that it contained thirteen chapels. The first Christians therein celebrated the sacred mysteries during the bloody reigns of the persecutors. They found strength in Mary, and this strength has never failed the city of Chartres, which is so ardently devoted to her. Charles the Bald gave the church one of the richest presents possible for king to give. It was a linen garment, said by constant tradition to have been worn by our Blessed Lady. This holy relic, long kept at Constantinople, was sent to Charlemagne by the Empress Irena; and many miracles had been wrought by merely touching the garment.

Among the various circumstances we might mention before proceeding with the narrative of the Choir Boy, we will content ourselves with the defeat of Rollo. He came with his Normans to pillage Chartres. Bishop Vantelme, having no means of resistance, trusted that our Lady herself would defend the city she so loved. After invoking her aid, he went forth at the head of his clergy and his people, attired in his pontifical habit, carrying with him our Lady's tunic. As he approached, he beheld the Normans, seized with fear, fly in disorder, dragging their chief with them. The good bishop then intoned the *Magnificat*.

Chartres was several times saved in this way in many instances, which may be seen in the history of the city.

In 1568, the Huguenots laid siege to Chartres. They had a design against our Lady.* Thus their first attack was directed against a gate, above which was enthroned her figure with the inscrip-

---

* A legend states that a former king of Chartres, dying without children, left his kingdom to our Lady; hence the people call her Queen of Chartres.

tion, *Carnutum Tutela—Patroness of Chartres.*
To this spot they pointed their cannons. But,
wonderful to relate, not one shot touched either
the image or the gate; to commemorate which,
a chapel was afterwards erected on the spot.
They were obliged to renew the attack elsewhere,
and finally to raise the siege. Since that time a
figure of the Blessed Virgin surmounts and protects every gate in the city.

We might relate a hundred similar anecdotes,
but we must hasten on with our promised narrative.

In the year 1116, under the reign of Philip I.,
and during the height of the crusades, the city of
Chartres being governed by Geoffrey, its sixty-first
bishop, on the evening of the 31st of October, a
grand procession took place in the subterranean
church of Chartres, singing the praises of our Lady,
Queen of All Saints, whose festival they were to
celebrate on the morrow. The bishop assisted.
The pious faithful sung with great warmth and
earnestness. The priests and religious each bore
a little taper. The bishop, with mitre and crozier,
blessed the people at each station, surrounded by
the little choir boys, who appeared like a troop of
angels.

Among these children was one scarcely ten years
old, who seemed to be the most devout. Son of a
poor widow, he was her riches and her joy. He
might be said to have divided his heart into three
portions,—one he gave to God, another to our
Blessed Lady, and the third to his mother. Of
each he was a fervent lover, and never did any
ceremony in honour of Mary take place at which
her little child was not present. He indeed was
never perfectly happy except when in church, for

then he was in the actual presence of the most beloved objects of his heart. And when in the street a stranger accosted him and asked who he was, he ever replied, with a charming pride, "*I am the Choir Boy of our Lady of Chartres.*"

Nor could his mother be happy while he was out of her sight. Thus, she too spent a great portion of her time in the church. Her fond eyes followed him, whether he served at mass, carried the holy water, bore the incense, or formed one of the groups round the good bishop when he officiated.

On the occasion, then, to which we have referred, imagine the distress of the mother at not seeing her child on the procession returning to make the second tour of the church—see it increase when it again moved round without him. What could have become of him? Nothing she imagined could have kept him away for more than a quarter of an hour. At the close of the office, the faithful retired. The mother in agony rushed into the sacristy, asking every one if he had seen her son; but no one had remarked his absence until now.

She returned into the crypt with the sacristans, who now shared her solicitude. The other choir boys followed, then the priests and religious, and finally, the good bishop himself. Every one loved the little fellow, and were alarmed at his absence. They all wished to be the first to find him. Could he have fainted, or been taken ill, or fallen asleep with fatigue on some tomb? for many martyrs had their tombs there. But their search was vain; every nook and corner was visited without any result. They called on him, but heard no reply, save the echoes of their own voices. He must either have left the church unperceived, or been carried off by some one, or perhaps have fallen into the deep well which was behind the Druids' altar, called the well of the Saints-Forts. On hearing these suspicions, the poor mother ran to the well with a torch. No sooner had she bent down with her light, than she sent forth one of those cries of maternal anguish, which rend every heart that hears them. She was instantly surrounded by the crowd. She had seen a surplice at the bottom of the well! By the uncertain light, the others declared they could see nothing. But could a mother's eye be deceived? By desire of the bishop, one of the most active of the attendants carefully descended the well, and there he found the poor boy drowned, stiff and inanimate, struck by the withering hand of death.

All the bystanders remained in deep grief around the mother, no one attempting to console her. She seemed to be struck with so wild a grief, that she almost frightened them. Her feelings were, however, attended by a sense of incredulity; for she could not believe that her dear child was really snatched from her.

No sooner had the attendant placed the body on the ground, than the mother eagerly seized it in her arms and flew to the altar of our Blessed Lady, at whose feet she laid it, falling on her knees and exclaiming in heart-broken accents—

"Behold him, Holy Virgin, this poor child whom we have lost! He is no longer mine! He belongs to you, O Lady of Chartres. I gave him to you living, and now I give him to you dead. You know how he loved you, sweet Lady; you were his protectress, and you will not permit him to remain in this state."

The tears of the attendants mingled with those of the faithful widow. Everybody knelt and joined in her prayer. One only, however, hoped that a child who had been drowned for an hour could recover. This was the holy prelate. He shared with the mother the hope that the child would be restored to life. And in the event, faith repulsed death—the child opened his eyes. His companions ran to the altar and helped him down, and his own voice joined with them in returning thanks for his miraculous recovery.

After this act of thanksgiving and joy, the boy was besieged by scores of questioners. In answer, he replied, that, having had the imprudence to pass behind the altar, and not thinking of the well, he had fallen into it. Being astonished to see that he had not received the least blow or wound in his fall, but still had been deprived of life for an hour, they asked him whether he had felt or heard anything. "I felt nothing," said he, "but a feeling of intense happiness—I saw nothing but the angels who passed about me—I heard nothing but their harmonious voices, who answered, in the words of the Church to the salutation of the Lord Bishop, when he said *Pax vobis*. They also replied to the *Dominus vobiscum* of the archpriest."

Such is the extraordinary adventure of the Choir Boy of our Lady of Chartres. Bishop Geoffrey was so struck at the marvellous circumstance related by the boy, that in order to preserve the memory of it, he established the following custom —always retained in the Cathedral of Chartres since the year 1116—that whenever the bishop or priest chants the *Pax vobis* or *Dominus vobiscum*, at the mass or offices of the Church, the choir do not answer *Et cum spiritu tuo*, but a pause is made, during which they believe the angels sing it, and that the Almighty hears them.

Our Lady Help of Mariners.*

"Fœderis arca."   "Ark of the covenant."

TOWARDS the end of the twelfth century, or the beginning of the thirteenth, a Marseilles fisherman being surprised at sea by a tempest, tried in vain to regain the port, and was in danger of being lost. He was alone in his boat, which sprang a leak, while the wind was adverse, and his rudder was lost. He now felt, with beating heart, that nothing less than a miracle could save him; that he must bid adieu to every hope of again beholding his native land and dear family. Agitated by these thoughts, he raised his eyes to the rock (de la Garde), which rises like a sentinel of granite upon the mountain, which overlooks the sea, port, and city of Marseilles. On the summit of this rock he fancied he saw an aerial figure, whose transparent form could be traced in the deep obscurity which at this instant enveloped the earth and sky. He also imagined that the figure held out its hand to him in an encouraging manner.

From the instant that he felt himself to be on the eve of perishing, the fisherman had never ceased to invoke the "Star of the Sea," who is ever ready to aid poor mariners in their distress.

* Notre Dame de la Garde—Our Lady of Safeguard.

He therefore firmly believed that she had come to his assistance. He fell on his knees, and leaving his bark to her guidance, he sang, with all his might, the *Ave Maris Stella;* the deep tones of his voice rising above the roaring of the waves.

The boat, as if drawn by a powerful hand, darted through the waters, and reached the foot of the mountain.

The rescued fisherman sprang on land, and eagerly mounted the steep declivity of the mountain, till he reached the top; but he saw nothing. He then fell on his knees, and returned thanks to his Protectress. On reaching his hut, he related his adventure to his family, who had been praying for his safety.

All who heard the event wondered how it was possible for him to reach the shore alive; and no one doubted that he owed his life to the miraculous interposition of our Blessed Lady. Other seamen related how they had several times seen, at the summit of Mount la Garde, a sweet apparition, which they could hardly describe; but on its appearance, the tempests calmed, and they were delivered from danger. They could not give any other interpretation to these events than that our Blessed Lady had chosen this rock as the spot whence she loved to come to the help of distressed mariners.

A chapel was therefore erected on this point in 1218, and was enriched with an image of the Blessed Virgin, which was called our Lady of Safeguard, or Help of Mariners. The spot was much frequented by pilgrims. Other traditions give an earlier origin to this chapel; but they rest on doubtful authority.

One fact, however, cannot be denied; that since the year 1218, our Lady of Help has always been the Protectress of Marseilles, and the refuge of distressed mariners. No one dreams of embarking on the shortest voyage without placing himself under her protection; no one undertakes a long journey without visiting her chapel. It is but three years ago that the public journals recorded an event, one of the thousands which might be adduced concerning this sanctuary.

A ship, long tossed about by the tempest, was about to perish, when the seamen, seeing that all their own efforts were useless, threw themselves on their knees, and fervently implored the aid of our Lady of Help, their only hope; the passengers imitated them, and even the steersman left the wheel.

At the same moment that every eye was turned upwards, a most extraordinary spectacle or vision presented itself to the view. They all saw, dimly, a figure at the wheel, which seized it and directed the vessel's course. All remained kneeling, while they felt that the ship, by a miraculous power, was gliding through the waves at an extraordinarily rapid rate. Soon they heard the silver tones of the bell of our Lady of Help, which had been presented to the chapel by the seamen. This well-known signal convinced them of their safety. Shortly afterwards the ship triumphantly entered the port, and the crew disembarked in safety. Following the first impulses of their hearts, the twenty-nine persons, who were on board, went barefooted, with their clothes still dripping with wet, to the chapel on the rock, to chant the *Magnificat*, amid tears of gratitude.

The numerous *ex-votos* which adorn the chapel of our Lady Help of Mariners, and the rich plate and precious stones which fill her treasury, are striking testimonials of benefits received through her powerful patronage.

The revolution of 1793 robbed her of her diamonds and other jewels, and her image of massive silver gilt. But faith soon repaired the wrongs committed by impiety; and after some time, a silver image, and other splendid presents, were supplied by pious and faithful persons, who made it a duty to expiate the crimes of others, and to make restitution for thieves.

But it is not seamen alone who experience the powerful patronage of our Lady of Help. The city of Marseilles invokes her in all its necessities. Every year, at Corpus Christi, her sacred image is brought down from her chapel on the mount, and carried in procession through the streets, resting for one night in the ancient church of St. Martin; and the people, who love her dearly, who surround her sweet figure with flowers and other humble offerings of affection, are never weary of exposing to you their simple faith. Thus the fishermen, who, barefooted, carry her image on a richly-decorated stand, will tell you that the farther they carry it from her beloved chapel, the heavier it becomes, and its weight lessens as they approach her sanctuary on their return. The people will also assure you that they have good reason not to leave her image for more than one or two days at most in the city on her annual visit; for if it were not taken back after that time, it would return by itself.

There exist everywhere among the masses powerful ideas, which show the earnest longing in the heart of the natural man for some definite faith, and the consciousness of an immaterial and spiritual world. They, whose only commerce with religious matters is for the purpose of criticism, place these popular traditions in their list of superstitions. They are not so, however; they are simple opinions, often imaginary, rarely offensive, and which the Church never adopts nor rejects, but enlightens and purifies.

But what will our opponents say of what took place during the visitation of the cholera in 1832? The whole populace of a great city, the largest in France next to Paris, can attest the truth of events which have taken place thus recently.

This pestilence, which in thirty days seized 30,000 victims in the capital, had spread desolation over the city of Marseilles. In the small streets, so thickly inhabited by the mass of the population, there was not a house without its sick; and then, be it remembered, the sick were the dying. The people assembled in the public squares; clamours rose from a hundred thousand mouths, demanding that our Lady of Help should be carried in procession. The next day the clergy, vested in purple—the penitential robes of the Church—the soldiers of the garrison, all the seamen in the port, the tradespeople, and all the men and women who were untouched by the pestilential breath of the cholera, ascended the mount, and brought our Blessed Lady's image down to the city, amid tears and lamentations.

She was borne through all the populous streets. All the sick saluted her from their windows, or, if unable to rise, from their beds. The children offered her flowers and pious canticles; the mothers, flowers and tears. The *cortège* paused for an instant before every house (and there were many such), of which all the inhabitants were sick. The day before had scarce been long enough to inter the bodies of the dead; on this day not a single funeral took place. The cholera had fled at the progress of the Health of the Sick—the Consoler of the Afflicted. Nor did it reappear; they whom the physicians' skill had abandoned were restored to health; and for many weeks might be seen, crowding the mountain chapel, among those saved from shipwreck, many who had been snatched from the jaws of the grave.*

Such miracles have, however, been at all times vouchsafed to those who have the faith to ask them of the all-powerful Mother of God.

* Another renowned image of the Blessed Virgin Mary is venerated near Boulogne, under the title of *Notre Dame de la garde*.

"The Hour of Death."

"Janua cœli."   "Gate of Heaven."

An aged man, a poor Capucin friar, called Felix Cantalice, lay, expecting his last hour, stretched on a hard mattress, which he, however, thought too soft for him. It was at Rome, on the 18th of May, 1587. Although he had led a saintly life from his childhood, the good old man was not without some fears at restoring his soul into the hands of his God. His lips repeated constantly the name of Mary—that holy name which imparts such strength to the dying Christian. On this occasion we are told that she appeared visibly to her servant, holding in her arms her child Jesus. Godescard mentions this fact without entering into any details, but the legends add that the Blessed Virgin placed her Son in the holy man's arms, whose soul was filled with immense joy. They also add, that while he tasted the bliss of heaven, before he had broken the ties of earth, he saw the enemy of mankind in a corner of the room, who, not daring to approach nearer, exerted his utmost power to cause the saint to entertain a feeling of pride. But Felix said to him, "Go, you can do nothing here, for I am with my judge, whom I know will deal mercifully with me." Such was the happy end of this servant of Mary.

The following narrative is taken from the Golden Legend.

There was a clerk, who had a great devotion to the Blessed Virgin, was most assiduous in his duty to her, and invoked her often during the day, saying:

"Hail, Mother of God! Hail, spotless Virgin! Hail, joy of angels! Hail, Mother of eternal light! Hail, Mother of God, whom all creatures praise, be for ever our Protectress."

Falling dangerously ill, and seeing death approach, he was seized with a great fear. The Blessed Virgin appeared to him, and said,

"Why have you such fear, my son; you, who have rendered me such constant homage? Be of good heart, for you shall soon share with me the joys of paradise."

But it is not only at the terrible hour of death that Christian hearts have recognised the power of the name of Mary invoked in their necessities. Hear what happened to a preaching friar of Lyons in the year 1501. "This monk was on his way to Orleans. Having arrived at Gien, he embarked on the Loire, to render his journey more pleasant. On account of an inundation, the tempestuous state of the weather, and the ignorance of the sailors, the bark could not be brought to shore. It remained in the middle of the river, carried about whithersoever the winds pleased. It soon began to fill with water so rapidly that all the passengers thought themselves lost. The friar, seeing that nothing was to be hoped for from human aid, placed all his confidence in the Blessed

Virgin, to whom he addressed his most earnest supplications. Our Lady came to his assistance and saved him, while the whole of his fellow-passengers perished in the waters. He is still living," continues the narrator, "and is ever exhorting his brethren to devotion to that Blessed Virgin to whom he owes his life."

Our next legend comes from the same source.

A man, who was steeped in crime, yet preserved, in the midst of his disorders, some devotion to the Blessed Virgin, fell dangerously ill, and losing his senses before he had time to recollect himself, felt great terror at the thought of appearing so unprepared before his Judge. Trembling at this idea, he became unconscious of all around him, and seemed to appear at the dread tribunal. Satan was there before him. "Heaven," said he, "will find nothing in this man which belongs to it. He is mine on many grounds." And he enumerated, with complacency, the bad actions of the culprit.

The man was covered with confusion. The Judge said to him, "You are allowed to speak in your defence."

But the poor soul remained silent.

The demon then said, "This soul has belonged to me for thirty years, and he has obeyed me as a slave does his master."

The man still kept a painful silence.

"He is mine," said the evil one, "for if he has ever done any good actions, they are certainly lost in the multitude of his iniquities."

The Supreme Judge would not, however, immediately condemn the poor soul, but granted him a respite of eight days to enable him to defend himself if he could.

The man, as he retired in the most desponding mood, met a beautiful, but grave person, who asked him the cause of his grief. "Suffer not yourself to be thus overcome with fear," said the good spirit, or angel; "I will assist you."

"Who are you?" asked the man.

"I am called Truth," answered the spirit.

A little farther, another angel, called Justice, promised to aid him.

The eighth day came. Satan was again at the tribunal, and took up the accusation.

The angel of Truth said, "when this man sinned, his soul, which is here, never consented to the evil."

The demon was now silent.

Upon the second count, that he had led a vicious life for thirty years, the angel of Justice replied:

"This soul has never for one day ceased to revolt interiorly against the unworthy master who dragged him on."

Satan replied not.

But, at the third allegation, that his bad actions infinitely surpassed in number his good ones, no one appeared in the sinner's defence.

"Let his actions be weighed," said the Judge.

The two angels then urged him as his only chance to have recourse to the Blessed Virgin, Mother of Mercy, who sat at the Judge's right hand.

"Implore her aid," said they; "she alone can save you."

The poor soul earnestly followed this advice; and Mary, leaving her seat, placed her hand on the side of the scale, bearing his good works. The demon dragged down the other side with all his might, but in vain; the hand of Mary was all-powerful, and the sinner was freed. The transport of joy so overwhelmed him, that he awoke; for this terrible vision was but a dream. But receiving it as a salutary warning from his holy Protectress, he changed his life, did penance for his sins, and died many years afterwards in sincere sentiments of piety.

The Rock of Bétharram.

"Stella Matutina."   "Morning Star."

 PHENOMENON, which has never been explained, often takes place with miraculous images of our Lady, which have been found in an extraordinary manner, with especial circumstances, calculated to astonish our weak understanding. Such a phenomenon was manifested in the cases of the Holy Image of Liesse, which could not be removed from the fountain by which it was placed; and in that of our Lady the Deliverer, which, having been taken into a church, was brought back in the night by an unknown power to the locality of its ancient sanctuary.

The same wondrous events took place in the following legends.

At Nogent-sur-Seine, in Champagne, there exists a figure of the Blessed Virgin, so beautiful, that it is generally known by the name of our Fair Lady. This famous image formerly attracted so large a concourse of pilgrims, that it was deemed necessary to erect a large chapel in place of the little oratory four feet square, a kind of isolated niche, in which she had smiled upon her clients from time immemorial.

The chapel was built of large size and beautiful

architecture, and to it was the image transported. But on the next morning it was found again in its little niche, where it was considered to be the wish of our Lady that it should remain, which was accordingly done.

Near the town of Lestelle (which at the period we write of did not bear that name), a league from the castle of Coarraze, where Henry IV. passed his infancy, and four leagues from Paris, in the early part of the eleventh century, some young shepherds perceived, a little before break of day, upon the summit of a rock which was called Betharram, a shining light, for which they could not account. This light had the appearance of a star fallen from heaven and fixed on the point of the rock. They dared not approach it, but they told their friends what they had seen, and their neighbours resolved to pass the next night in the fields in the hopes of seeing the same prodigy.

The star again appeared, and the people having recited a prayer, began to ascend the mount. On nearing its summit, their astonishment was great at seeing a beautiful image of the Blessed Virgin, placed in a natural niche at the top of the rock, from which proceeded a dazzling light. They were seized with great respect for this wonderful image, and wishing to expose it to the veneration of their neighbours and families, carried it barefooted with canticles of joy, and placed it in a small oratory outside the village.

The report of this miraculous discovery soon brought the people of the neighbouring towns to offer their homage to the image of Mary.

The shepherds were continuing their watch over their flocks, when, towards the middle of the night, they were astonished at seeing the star again appear on the mountain. They had now courage to ascend and see its cause, when, to their still greater surprise, they found the image in its rocky niche.

This wonder excited no less interest than the former. The good people believing that it was on the Rock of Betharram that Mary desired to be honoured, felt themselves called upon to erect a small chapel on the spot. But the accomplishment of their design was far from being easy. The rock was so hard, that they were unable to cut it; they therefore took the image again, but this time they placed it in their parish church. The doors were closed and a guard placed round the church during the night. But in the morning the image had disappeared, and was again found on the rock, surrounded by the shepherds singing the *Ave Maria*.

It was then determined to erect a small edifice on the summit of the rock. The people of the surrounding country eagerly lent their assistance, and a chapel was soon built, and a pilgrimage formed at the spot selected by the Blessed Virgin herself for her sanctuary.

Plundered by the self-styled reformers of the sixteenth century, and the infidel revolutionists of the nineteenth, the chapel of our Lady of Betharram still exists, and from it does our sweet Mother of Mercy dispense her favours to all who invoke her powerful aid.

The Poor Sick Woman.

"Salus infirmorum."   "Health of the sick."

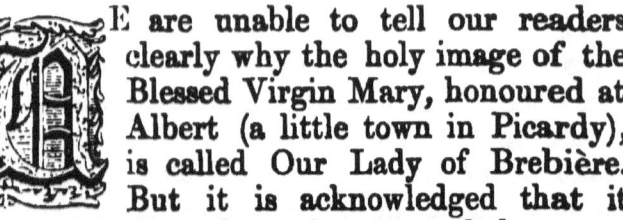 We are unable to tell our readers clearly why the holy image of the Blessed Virgin Mary, honoured at Albert (a little town in Picardy), is called Our Lady of Brebière. But it is acknowledged that it dates its origin from the early ages, and the many miracles which have been worked in its sanctuary are recorded in monuments, which can leave no doubt of their authenticity on the mind of the devout reader.

If the many votive offerings which cover the walls of this sanctuary are insufficient to bear testimony to the pains and ills she has cured, the tears she has dried up, the benefits she has bestowed, we refer to the minute documents which have been drawn up in legal form, concerning recent events, which were accomplished before thousands of spectators.

We have selected one of these events, which we take from the pastoral of the Bishop of Amiens, published the 20th of March, 1787. No one then attempted to contest in the least detail the miraculous cures which the bishop's letter announced.

Everybody in the deanery of Albert knew poor Magdalen Roussell, of the parish of Warloi. In

1786 she was fifty-nine years old, of which number she had been thirty-five afflicted with disease.

At the age of twenty she was attacked with a serious epilepsy, which threw her into terrible convulsions. The origin of this disease could not be discovered. Its attacks were accompanied by most trying symptoms: she fell into convulsions about twenty times a day. The common people, not being able to understand the state of her disease, generally declared that Magdalen Roussell was possessed.

The Marquis of Gouffier, who had been told of these circumstances, wishing to give her an opportunity of having the best medical assistance, sent for the sick woman to his seat at Heilly, and put her into the hands of the most skilful physicians of the day. During four months she took two hundred potions. After which, the doctors finding her disease incurable, sent her back to her parents, giving her certain medicines, which she continued to take for some months. They had, it is true, at times been able to give some little relief to the patient, but her disease had not been, and they said could not be, eradicated from the system. Shortly after her return home, her disorder got much worse, and, like a river overflowing its banks, spread desolation over her frame.

Magdalen Roussell thus led a life of torture. Her body was covered with sores and ulcers; she carried one arm in a sling, and being unable to work, lived on the alms of her neighbours. Everywhere she was repulsed, some regarding her as an object of disgust, and others dreaded her contact, lest she should communicate her disease to them.

One day, in the year 1786, her desolate situation having been rendered more galling by the bitter words of her neighbours, she went to expose her sorrows, and to weep at the feet of her parish priest. She knew well that the poor and afflicted meet with regard and compassion from the ministers of Jesus Christ. The good priest's door is ever open to them, he ever greets them with a smile, his ears are ever eager to hear their troubles, his mouth to give them comfort, and his purse to afford them relief.

The rector, therefore, received her with cheerfulness, saying, "We will cure you, my poor child," and then he told her what follows.

"A youth of the parish of Vaux, near Corbie, being a cripple from infancy, was hardly able to drag himself along, much less walk and being but sixteen years old, was on the point of death, when he was earnestly recommended to the care of our Blessed Lady of Brebière. He was carried in pilgrimage to her shrine, where he was suddenly cured, to the great astonishment and delight of the assistants, and then walked home, the bells of his village church pealing forth joyously to receive him.

"You must expect your cure also, my daughter," continued the good priest, "from her who is the health of the sick. You must make a devout novena to the Blessed Virgin. During this novena, approach often to the all-fortifying sacraments of the Church. You can do so, for your sufferings and the way you bear them, expiate the faults you may fall into. Begin then to day. It is the 14th of May; I will send you to Albert on the 23rd."

Magdalen Roussell, consoled, took confidence.

Full of love to our Blessed Lady, she made her novena with a simple, devoted heart, asking for her cure, provided only it should be pleasing to God to grant it. She would equally joyously receive her cure or her death at his holy hands.

After having faithfully fulfilled the religious duties imposed upon her, the sick woman, accompanied by a companion, set out for Albert, on the 23rd of May. She happily reached her destination, heard mass, and received the holy communion at our Lady of Brebière's altar, and then prostrating herself before her holy image, begged our dear Lady to take compassion on her, and obtain for her either the cure of her malady or a happy death.

At this instant she had twenty-four ulcers on her body, which was terribly emaciated by thirty-nine years of suffering. She seemed to feel at first that the second part of her prayer was heard and that she was going to die. Her sight became clouded, a cold sweat covered her body, accompanied by strange sensations. She employed the little strength left her in beseeching God's pardon and mercy, and a happy passage into eternity, when, on a sudden, the pains left her, and feeling her strength return, she said to her companion, " God has cured me; thanks to our Blessed Lady." She indeed returned home in sound health, for on examining her body, it was found that the ulcers had disappeared, and she never had a return of them, but remains in health, a living witness of the power of Mary.

The pastoral letter from which we have gleaned these facts concludes with the following words:

" If persons with irreligious prejudices prefer to discredit the truth of this event, and if others, through sectarian bigotry, refuse to believe that graces are obtained from our Lord through the intercession of our Lady and the saints, or treat as superstitious the reverence shown by us to pious images, how can we better answer them than in the words of our Divine Redeemer himself, as recorded in St. Matthew (c. xi. v. 21).

"'Woe to thee, Corozain! woe to thee, Bethsaida! for if in Tyre and Sidon had been wrought the miracles that have been wrought in you, they had long ago done penance in sackcloth and ashes. But, I say unto you, it shall be more tolerable for Tyre and Sidon in the day of judgment than for you.'

"But if we must thus rebuke the incredulous, how consoling is it to us, that the pious faith of all true Christians enables us to continue in the words of our Redeemer:

"'I bless thee, O Father, Sovereign Lord of heaven and earth, because thou hast hid these things from the wise and prudent of the world, and hast revealed them to little ones.'"

The Demoniac.

"Refugium peccatorum."   "Refuge of sinners."

THEY who search the records of the different pilgrimages of the Blessed Virgin will find that many of her images have been discovered on oaks: and all the legends and popular traditions encircle them with some wondrous mystery. Some may rest on doubtful authority, but others present incontestable proofs; and we should not reject a tradition merely on the ground of our not being able to unravel the mystery.

Our Lady of the Thorn is a celebrated pilgrimage near Chalons-sur-Marne. The holy image there venerated was discovered in the year 1400, by some shepherds, in a thorn-bush. Our Lady of the Oak, near Bar-sur-Seine, was found in an oak, also by country people. Many other images of the Blessed Virgin have been given to the Christian world by equally humble means; and often is it found that in the sanctuaries which they have graced has the Mother of Mercy granted her choicest favours.

Our Lady of Montaigu (or the peak) surmounts a hill, as its name denotes, situated in Belgium. Justus Lipsius has written the wondrous history of this image; and the record of the numerous miracles obtained at this sanctuary filled three goodly volumes in the last century.

The church of Montaigu, rebuilt with splendour by the Archduke Albert and Isabella his wife, in the early part of the seventeenth century, still possesses a rich treasury; and its venerated image occupies a silver niche, studded with precious stones. Discovered by a shepherd on an oak, from which it is said he could not detach it, this sweet image was preserved at first in a small rustic oratory, built round the oak, which served for niche and canopy. The "beggars" (or Huguenots), however, during the troubles of the Reformation, demolished this chapel; but the image, concealed by a pious woman, was preserved. At the "religious peace," as it is called in that country, it was again conveyed with joy to Montaigu, where the archduke erected for its reception the beautiful church we still see there.

The aged oak was cut down, and portions of it sent to various parts of the world; but a large portion of the trunk was preserved under the altar. We have culled one out of the innumerable miracles wrought at this sanctuary, and recorded by Justus Lipsius.

A good family of Lille, which still exists, and occupies an honourable position in the city, was sorely afflicted in one of its members—a daughter—who was possessed, it is said, by many demons.

At the present day, when so little pains are taken to observe the precept of St. Paul, to fight against the spirits of darkness, or invisible tempters, one is mocked at for speaking seriously of a person being possessed; and learned men decide that the possessed were mad.

But our asylums never cure these kind of mad

people, for whose relief the exorcisms of the church can effect more than all medicine.*

The demoniac of Lille was a young woman of eighteen years of age, named Catherine Dubus. How she became possessed is uncertain. The external appearances are alone known with certainty.

When the fearful hosts who kept possession of this woman agitated and troubled her, she could scarcely be held down and kept quiet by six powerful men. Her invisible enemies led her to the water side and to precipices, where a slip would be fatal to her, and dashed her against walls, as if they wished to get rid of her. They had so corrupted her senses as to make her seek noisome or poisonous substances for food; she even eat sand and stones. Had she been a poor girl, many might have been eager to pronounce it an imposition, for the sake of procuring money. But the parents of Catherine Dubus were possessed of a comfortable independence, and were above suspicion of this kind.

She was taken by her parents to the sanctuary of Montaigu, then recently erected. She was exorcised before our Lady's image. During the awful ceremony, which was to deliver this poor soul, the possessed was seen to vomit needles, stones, nails, sulphur, and other substances. She pronounced strange words, revealed unknown events, and said extraordinary things above human knowledge to comprehend. Flames were seen to

* Such has been acknowledged by many eminent medical men, especially by M. Moreau, of Tours, physician of Bicetre (a large lunatic asylum near Paris), who was ordered by the French Government to make a report on mad-houses in 1842. See his opinions frankly given in the *Revue Independante*.

issue from her mouth, and then disappear. The assistants declared that they saw demons leap out of her, and they were men not easily deceived. That such was the case there could be no doubt, for Catherine Dubus returned home, with her grateful parents, entirely dispossessed and healed. Nor did she ever have any relapse.

Legend of the Lord of Crequy.

"Consolatrix afflictorum."   "Consoler of the afflicted."

LOUIS the Young, King of France, having, at the command of St. Bernard, engaged in the crusade, in 1147, no brave man could hesitate to follow his banner. Dukes and counts, barons and knights, all the young nobles assembled with their vassals, and an army of eighty thousand men were soon on the move towards the Holy Land.

Among the knights who then took the cross, "vowing to defend the tomb of Jesus Christ," Sir Raoul de Crequy was conspicuous as well by his illustrious name and noble origin, as by his handsome person and military air. His father, Gerard, Count of Ternoy, was still living. He had shone amid the staff of Godfrey of Bouillon, and his spirit seemed revived in his young son Raoul.

In this very year, and about six months before the time we write of, Raoul de Crequy had married a Breton lady of sweet and amiable disposition. She was *enceinte* when the baron enrolled himself under the banner of the cross without her consent, *which was contrary to use and to custom*. She was so afflicted on learning this, that nothing could alleviate her distress. Her noble husband endeavoured in vain to persuade her to consent to his departure. His aged father said to her,

"I also, when I was young, crossed the seas. I took the cross without the knowledge of my father, and my good mother was sorely distressed at it. Still both were rejoiced when I returned home, covered with honours. Surely, lady, your husband could not see his sovereign lead this expedition and remain behind. Is he not thirty years of age? the time for every man to distinguish himself. Why then should you wish him to remain on this estate to reap nothing but shame and dishonour?"

The good lady at length gave way, and agreed to the departure of her lord. He took with him his two brothers, Roger and Godfrey, and twenty-seven esquires followed in their suite.

When the terrible moment of separation arrived, the lady could not refrain from weeping bitterly, as Raoul, with emotion, swore to be true and constant to her. He took from her finger the nuptial ring, which she had received with such joy; and, breaking it in two, gave one part to his bride, keeping the other himself.

"This half of the ring which was blessed at our marriage," said he, "I will always keep as a true and loyal husband, and when I return from my pilgrimage I will give you back this pledge of my constancy."

He held his lady by the hand, and leading her to his aged father, besought him to love and cherish her as his own daughter. The old count promised to do so, and embraced the weeping lady. The knight then knelt before him, and said,

"Dear sir, and father, that my days may be

happy, bless me; and let your prayers and good wishes accompany me in my journey."

The old man, spreading his hands over his son's head, invoked the blessing of God upon him.

"Almighty Lord," said he, "bless my son in this war, which he undertakes in your holy name. And you, dearest Virgin, our Sovereign Lady, be his guardian; protect him from danger, and bring him back without blemish to his native land."

The good old man then blessed his other sons, and embraced them, as well as the esquires who accompanied them.

The lord of Crequy and his companions leaped on their chargers; at the sound of clarions and trumpets the noble troop set forth on their way, preceded by a herald who bore the standard of the cross. They made such haste, that they soon joined the main army, which was in advance by several days' march. "Never," say the ballads of the day, "was seen such a host of noble, gentle, and valiant youths." The record of their deeds would fill a large volume; we have here only to deal with those which relate to the lord of Crequy.

He had left a wife and father in deep sorrow; and in those days the pang of separation could not be alleviated by frequent correspondence. In due time the Countess of Crequy gave birth to a child —a sweet boy, in whom she found some consolation for the absence of her husband. The old count was quite overjoyed, and felt himself young again at the sight of his grandson. A special messenger was despatched to carry the joyful news to his son, who was found at the port of Satalia.

Raoul de Crequy made great rejoicings with his friends on this occasion. But his happiness was, alas! soon to be changed into sorrow.

An engagement shortly afterwards took place between the Crusaders and the Saracens. Raoul and his companions led the van of the army. Carried away by his ardour, he entered a narrow pass, followed only by two small troops, led by the lords of Breteuil and Varennes. These three companies formed but a hundred lances. The Saracens held possession of the heights overlooking this perilous pass. They let fall a rain of arrows upon the Christians, who fought manfully to gain a passage. Roger and Godfrey, the count's brothers, with twenty of the esquires, fell mortally wounded. But the Christians did not retire. Although they saw nothing but death before them, they earnestly pressed forward. In the encounter, besides the two brothers before mentioned, the lords of Breteuil, Varennes, Montjoy, Maumey, Brimen, Báuraing, Esseike, Mesgrigny, Sempey, and Suresnes perished; and many a beardless youth lay stretched in the dust.

The Lord of Crequy, as a man of high and undaunted valour, would not retire; but continued to fight, invoking our Lady's aid, till, exhausted by the number of his wounds, he at length fell to the earth.

When the seven knights, who alone remained, saw their leader slain, they fled precipitately to the camp, and announced their sad disaster. The enemies, remaining masters of the field, began to strip the dead, when they perceived that the Lord of Crequy still moved; and it was determined not to dispatch him, but to endeavour to heal his wounds and preserve his life, for the sake of the ransom which so noble a knight would fetch.

He was gently carried to the Saracen camp, where it was discovered that his wounds, though dangerous, were not mortal. They were skilfully dressed. But so weakened was he by the loss of blood, that Raoul remained for some time in an inanimate state. His youth, however, was in his favour, and he soon recovered his strength.

But how bitter were his first thoughts in finding himself a slave of the Saracens, and that he had fallen into the hands of one who was inclined to show him no favour? The Saracen gave him his hand to kiss. This the knight did so cheerfully, that he had courage to ask for a small relic—the half of a ring, of which he had been plundered. This, to his great joy, was restored to him.

As soon as he was convalescent, profiting of the offer of his master to accept two hundred pieces of gold for his ransom, Raoul sent a messenger to the Christian camp. This man chanced to arrive at the time that the Crusaders were attacking and massacring the Saracen army, and he was slain with the others. The Saracens, completely routed in this encounter, retired to the very spot where Raoul was confined, and who lay in hopes that his brethren in arms would soon break his chains, and receive him with joy again into their ranks. But his master waited not their arrival, but hastily fled, carrying his prisoner with him, and did not stop, so great was his terror, until he had reached the boundary of Syria.

In proportion as he was farther from the Christian camp, Raoul found his captivity more galling. He wrote many letters, none of which reached the king or France. All the army believed him dead; and the first couriers sent to France were commissioned to announce their loss to his father and wife. The latter, on hearing the fatal news, swooned. "Never from that instant," says the old ballad, " did his father enjoy an hour's health." He lingered and died. Lady de Crequy would have envied his lot, had not her son required her life; but she wept day and night. The youngest of the brothers, Baudoin, who had remained in France, seized upon the territories, and assumed the title of Lord of Crequy and other places, in injury to his brother's child. The lady's father was a powerful noble of Brittany; and being aged, and at a distance, was unable to assert and defend his grandson's rights. But, seeing his daughter a widow and unprotected, he advised her to marry the Lord of Renty, a nobleman, who, charmed with her amiable qualities, sought her in marriage. She, however, refused, notwithstanding her trials and defenceless state, to enter again into the bonds of wedlock, still lamenting her first spouse, and flattering herself with faint hopes of his returning to her.

Many years thus passed—long and bitter ones for the lady, hard and painful for the knight. His master made him wait on and serve him until he should be ransomed. His occupation consisted in watching the flocks, under the direction of the first shepherd, who had the management of the cattle. Hourly did he pray to God while engaged in the fields, and besought our Blessed Lady to obtain his deliverance from his durance; still he supported with resignation the state to which he fancied the neglect of his friends had reduced him.

Seven years had elapsed since his captivity, when his master died. He was then led to the market and sold with the other slaves. He fetched a good price on account of his great height and strength. The probability also of his being one day ransomed added to his value. He fell to the lot of a severe master, who hated the Christians; and he immediately commenced a series of persecutions on the person of the captive knight.

"You see," said his master to him one day, "that your country has abandoned you; deny your faith, invoke our prophet, and I will give you some land, money, and a wife."

But the Lord of Crequy would rather have suffered any outrage, or death itself, rather than renounce his faith and his plighted love to his dear spouse.

Hoping to reduce him to compliance with his wishes, his master confined him in an old tower, loaded him with chains, and inflicted many other hardships and tortures upon him.

This half-ruined tower had no roof. The sun darted its fiercest rays into the captive's cell. His hands and feet were linked together, and his body attached to the wall by a chain. He received every morning a handful of rice, a piece of black bread, and a jug of water.

His master often came to urge him to change his religion; and on his persevering in his faith, caused him to be whipped till the blood streamed down his body. These persecutions were continued at intervals during three years, without effecting in the least the knight's confidence in God.

After ten years' captivity, abandoning all hope of regaining his liberty, he ardently desired death. Not long after his master said to him, "Well, as it does not seem likely you will be ransomed, and you are obstinate in adhering to your faith, I shall have you strangled to-morrow."

A feeling of satisfaction came over him; but it was soon changed into one of regret, when he thought of his home, his aged father, and above all his dear spouse and young son, whom he was never to behold. However, he said, with firmness, his evening prayers, and recommended his soul into the hands of his Creator; begging of our dear Lady, that since he could no more see those beloved beings, to take them into her special care and protection. He recommended his child, soon to be an orphan, to the patronage of St. Nicholas, the tutelar saint of Christian children. And, placing himself for life or death into the hands of our Blessed Lady, he stretched himself on his hard couch, and soon fell into a deep sleep.

In his sleep he saw an unknown lady, whose features he thought he remembered in the chapel of Crequy. She bent over him, and seemed to free him from his chains and fetters. The delight this caused him awakened him. He then discovered that he was in very deed freed from his chains. Yet he still fancied he was under the influence of a dream, for he was out of prison and walked about in the air. The sun shone forth brightly, but did not oppress him by its heat.

He looked around him, and surprise following surprise, he found himself in a wood.

His first impulse was to fall on his knees and thank God and our Lady for his deliverance, and for the delightful sensations he now felt.

These feelings were so delicious, that he doubted whether or not he had been strangled in the night, and was now in paradise.

But the singing of the birds, the trees waving in the wind, the animals who grazed in the verdant meadows, everything around tended to convince him that he was still on this earth, though the air he breathed was milder than that to which he had been accustomed; and he was free. Yes, free! he had been delivered from his captivity by some unknown hand. Whose could it be but that of Mary? But was he quite safe from his master's pursuit? How far was he from his abode? How should he be able to return to Europe?

These questions, and other apprehensions, were beginning to excite some misgivings in his mind, when he saw, at the end of the pathway, a peasant cutting wood. He ran towards him. But no sooner did the poor man perceive him, than, taking him for a spectre, he threw down his hatchet, and ran for his life. The knight had not had time to reflect on his personal appearance.

Reduced almost to a state of emaciation, and darkened by the heats of the African sun, with no clothing but a piece of coarse sacking only partially covering the upper part of his body, with a long beard, a shaven head, and dark skin, he certainly presented a most extraordinary appearance. He, however, managed to reach the woodman; and seizing hold of him, asked him, in Syriac, the way out of the wood. The man, hearing him speak, a faculty which he thought was denied to spectres, changed his opinion concerning him, and now took him for one of those Saracen slaves who were sometimes brought by Crusaders into Europe. He answered him in French,

"I do not understand what you say."

At this moment Raoul de Crequy was experiencing the same sensations as did the three knights of Eppe on a like occasion, as before narrated.

"My good man," said he, in French, and breathing hard at each syllable, "tell me whether I am dreaming or under some delusion? Tell me, where am I? I am lost, and know no one in this country."

"This wood is called the forest of Crequy," replied the woodman: "it is on the borders of Flanders. But tell me who you are? Poor man, I suppose you are a Christian captive, who have escaped from some ship which has been wrecked on the neighbouring coasts?"

But the knight heard him not. After he had learnt that he was in his own country and native place, he had fallen on the ground; and, extending his hands in the form of a cross, he exclaimed,

"O Almighty God! O most holy Virgin! my sweet Protectress, my help, and my deliverer, by what miracle have you brought me hither?"

He then rose and asked the woodman, who was regarding him compassionately, whether the aged lord was still alive, and whether the young countess and her son were living, and in good health?

"What, you know them?" said the man: "it is many years since the old count died of grief, bewailing the loss of his three eldest sons. His youngest, Baudoin, has endeavoured to take possession of the title and estate, and has behaved ill to his brother's widow and child. But the lady's father, who still lives, is now with her. He came expressly from his distant home in Brittany to endeavour to persuade his daughter to marry again, in order to secure her son's inheritance. For the Lord of Renty has promised to protect his rights, and to cherish him as the son of his dear friend, our late Lord Raoul, to whose soul God grant rest! He is a rich and powerful lord, and our lady cannot do better than accept his hand. But she had hitherto continually refused to listen to any project of marriage until within the last few days, when she consented, for the sake of her dear son; and to-day she is to be led to the altar by the Lord of Renty at the hour of six. There will be a grand *fête* and rejoicing at the castle, and all will be welcome; and you, too, poor man, will, I trust, receive some alms on the occasion."

The knight replied not, but followed the woodman to the castle gate, which he recognised with joy. The attendants who surrounded it, seeing the miserable plight of the pilgrim, would not allow him to pass.

"What do you want?" asked they: "whence come you, to be in that wretched state? Are you some prisoner escaped from slavery?"

"I am a pilgrim from the Holy Land," answered the knight, "and wish to see the Lady of Crequy on business of great importance."

"A man in your condition cannot enter the castle; besides, no one can speak to our lady to-day; she is even now being vested in her nuptial garments. You can step on one side and see her pass."

The count waited in silence; and shortly the Lady of Crequy, richly dressed, and seated on a highly-decorated mare, led by the Count of Renty, and followed by her father, son, and relatives, who had been invited to attend the ceremony, came forth from the castle on her way to the neighbouring abbey, in the church of which she was to be married. She bore the marks of sadness and of tears upon her pale face; and the frequent looks of love she gave her son showed that she was seeking his interest and welfare, and not her own.

Raoul, mastering his emotions, stopped the countess, and said:

"I come, noble lady, from the East. I bring news of the Lord of Crequy, who has endured a captivity of ten years."

The lady, at these words, dismounted, so great was her emotion. But on recovering the first shock, she looked earnestly at the pilgrim, and said:

"Your report, alas! is I fear incorrect. My lord fell with his brothers and their squires leading on their banner with honour. All who accompanied him perished, with the exception of seven who escaped by flight."

"Raoul de Crequy did not perish, noble lady; behold him! he stands before you."

A general murmur and excitement was expressed by the attendants at these words.

"Look at me," continued the count. "Despite so much misery and the many hardships I have suffered, can you not recognise your faithful husband, once so dear to you?"

"I can scarce believe you," exclaimed the lady, interrupting her sobs, "unless you give me some proof. If you are my husband, tell me what you did on the day of your departure for the Holy Land?"

"I broke in two your wedding-ring: I left you one half, and took the other with me, and I have kept it in pledge of my love. Here it is."

The knight removed, from round his neck, a little reliquary, from which he took the half ring, and presented it to the lady. On seeing it, she fell on his neck embracing him, and exclaimed:

"You are, indeed, my beloved husband! You are my dear lord!"

She then gave full vent to her raptures on recovering him, which excited the greatest sympathy in the bystanders.

The Lord of Renty, relative and friend of the Count of Crequy, was still incredulous of a fact which deprived him of a charming wife. A struggle arose in his heart between friendship and love.

"He certainly possesses the form and size of Raoul," thought he, "but I cannot recognise his features."

The countess's father, however, said:

"I now see the features of my lost son-in-law, although suffering has somewhat altered them. When we see him dressed, I think you will all recognise in him your long-lost lord."

The child, who was now ten years old, had also timidly approached. He felt new sensations come over him on hearing that his father lived; and when his mother took his hand and said, "Behold, my dear son, your father! show him how you love him," the child threw his arms round his father's neck, rejoicing at his recovery. The count covered the boy's face with tears of joy, and pressed him to his heart. The boy seemed not to have any childish fears at the uncouth appearance of his father, but said:

"It was for you that my dear mamma wept so often, continually repeating, 'We have lost everything, my son, in losing your father, my beloved husband.'"

The ladies and knights who had been invited to the wedding pressed round to see and speak to the count. The abbot of the monastery was apprised that the wedding would not take place, and was summoned to attend at the castle. The count having been shaved, and dressed according to his rank, and wearing a wig, which quite changed his former wild and eastern appearance, led his lady to the banquet which had been prepared for the marriage feast. The whole of the company were also invited to seat themselves; and having recounted to them his sufferings, and miraculous deliverance, and sudden transportation to the forest, the hall resounded with toasts to the health and long *vivas* to Raoul, Lord of Crequy.

He even invited his brother Baudoin; and having pardoned him his treachery towards his wife and child, made him sit by his side. The *fêtes* were continued for some days; and the people, who came from far and near to see the long-lost Count de Crequy, were well received and entertained.

The chains with which he had been loaded in his dungeon were found in the forest near the spot where he awoke; and the count, in thanksgiving, built a monastery in the wood, and richly endowed it. He also made presents to all the neighbouring chapels of our Blessed Lady.*

* This legend has some affinity with that of the Three Knights of St. John, before narrated. A still more extraordinary legend is familiar to the people of Brittany. The Lord of Garo was taken prisoner, with his esquire, in Palestine, by the Saracens, near Bethlehem. They were placed in a large strong box, and told by the infidels to ask their God to get them out of it if He could. They then closed it, and were about to bury it in the earth. The esquire began to lament, but the Count Garo commended himself to God, and most particularly our dear Lady of Bethlehem—vowing to erect a chapel in her honour, if he should escape his dreadful entombment alive. They then felt that they were moving; and the esquire, after some time, said, "Why, surely it is the cock of Garo I hear crow!" The count at these words blessed heaven and our Lady, who he felt confident had saved them and trans-

LEGEND OF THE LORD OF CREQUY. 241

ported them to their native land. Shortly some peasants passed, and seeing this large trunk on the wayside, opened it, and set free the Lord of Garo and his esquire, whom they recognised with astonishment. He instantly fulfilled his vow, and erected a charming Gothic chapel in honour of our Lady of Bethlehem, which is to be seen at the present day, with its old stained glass recording pictorially the wonderful deliverance of Count Garo out of the hands of the Saracens, and his miraculous transmission to his own estate in Brittany.

The Battle of Lepanto.

"Auxilium Christianorum."   "Help of Christians."

WHILE the terrible evils which followed the pretended reformation in the sixteenth century were raging, the Turks eagerly took advantage of our internal commotions, and hurried to the conquest of Southern Europe. They took and sacked the island of Cyprus, and were now menacing Venice; and, flushed with success, swore they would not cease their career until the whole of Christendom had succumbed to the Crescent. Confident in the resources of an immense empire, they possessed a formidable army, an extensive navy, abundant ammunition and arms, and, greater than all these, that boldness which the habit of conquest imparts. The European monarchs, in an inconceivable delusion, quietly allowed these encroachments on Christianity to take place.

Like those Greeks of the Lower Empire, who attended the lectures of rhetoricians while Mahomet II. besieged Constantinople, the Christians of Europe were taken up with the arguments of the pretended reformers, while their country and faith were menaced by the infidels. Happily, a man was found of sufficient intelligence to understand the danger, courageous enough to oppose the enemy, and whose humility told him that God alone could save Europe. This man was Pope Pius V.

This worthy Pontiff (whom the Church now honours among her saints, and the world then looked upon as one of the greatest of the popes) called upon Christendom, in 1570, to form a league against the common enemy. Selim II. was about to invade Venice, whence to attack the West. The peril was imminent. The Venetians, and Philip II., king of Spain, alone responded to the Pope's appeal. The other nations, overwhelmed with internal disturbances, let him know that they could no nothing.

Pius V. did not lose courage at this announcement. He pursued his noble object, and, notwithstanding his weakness, gave instructions not to wait for Selim's fleet, but to go and meet it.

The league was signed in the month of May, 1571, and the Pope, who had originated it, was declared its head. He nominated the Archduke John of Austria, natural brother of Philip II., general-in-chief of the Christian forces. These were supplied by the states of the Church, the republic of Venice, the Spanish provinces, the province of Avignon (which had been kept in tranquillity by Pius V., in the midst of the troubles which desolated the south of France), that portion of the Low Countries which had remained faithful, and by some devoted Frenchmen. This army was not very numerous to attack the most redoubtable forces. However, the holy Pontiff enjoined John of Austria to dismiss all the men of irregular life, robbers, and other bad characters, hoping that true Christian troops would meet with greater success. Before embarking, the general-in-chief received the standard under which he was to fight, and the blessing of the Sovereign Pontiff.

The army of the Pope's league were drawn up in the isle of Corfu, which is near the mouth of the Gulf of Venice. Thence they set sail in search of the hostile fleet.

They soon found it at anchor in the Gulf of Lepanto, forty leagues from Athens. The next morning, 7th of October, 1571, the Turks, rejoicing in the thought of the conquest they felt so sure of gaining that day, arranged their fleet in the form of a crescent, according to their custom. Their line was of much greater extent than that of the Christians, had it been disposed in the same order. But they, on the contrary, drew up their fleet in the shape of a cross. The van was composed of Venetian galeasses, the rear was commanded by the marquis of St. Croix, the right wing was under the command of Andrew Doria, and the left obeyed Augustine Barbarigo. The Archduke John was in the centre, assisted by Colonna and Véniéri.

Each ship had some Franciscan monks on board. Their exhortations had prepared every man to fight generously for the holy cause, and, if necessary, to die fearlessly; for all had been reconciled to God. The moment before the engagement took place, each officer harangued his troop in a few short but impressive words. The soldiers then fell on their knees before the crucifix, threw their beads round their necks, and rose only as the fleets met. Immediately Duke John of Austria, from the admiral's ship, raised the banner he had received from the Pope. It bore a representation of the Blessed Virgin presenting to us her Divine Son, whose invincible cross surmounted it. A general shout from the whole Christian force saluted the blessed standard, which at the same moment received the first charge of the Turkish artillery. But no shot, either then, or during the whole day, touched the sacred banner.

The Mussulmans, not doubting of the victory, and well knowing that the defeat of this fleet would open Europe to them, charged with all that impetuous fury which distinguishes them. Every advantage was on their side,—strength, numbers, and the wind. But the Christian warriors, who had sung the EXURGAT DEUS, the psalm of holy battles, forgot not that success was in the hands of God, and all braving death, which they feared not, fought like heroes.

During this terrible conflict, Pius V., who could not have imagined that the battle had so soon begun, was engaged with the cardinals. He suddenly rose, opened a window, and looked for an instant upon the sky. What saw he there? for instantly he exclaimed, "Away with business! Let our only thought now be to return thanks to the Almighty for the victory which he has granted to the Christian forces."

The astonished cardinals followed the Pope, who repaired to the Basilica of St. Peter. They asked one another what this revelation accorded to the holy father could mean? They soon learnt, and spread the news among the people, who attributed this prodigy to the Blessed Virgin, the protector of the fleet. Her litany was immediately sung everywhere throughout the city of Rome, and on that occasion Pius V. introduced a new invocation,—that of "Auxilium Christianorum,—*Help of Christians.*"

He also instituted a new festival for the 7th of October, dedicated to the rosary of the Blessed Virgin, to whom he gave the title of *Our Lady of Victory*. This feast is still kept by the whole Church.

Thus was celebrated at Rome by public rejoicings a victory which was simultaneously gained at a distance of three hundred leagues, or nine hundred miles. Nor was this joy premature. The Christians had won that day. The wind suddenly had changed in their favour. The Archduke John slew Hali, who commanded the Turkish fleet, and at six o'clock in the evening, after twelve hours' fighting, the Mussulman had lost thirty thousand men, two hundred ships were sunk or taken, and ninety others were fired. The conquerors brought back with them three hundred and seventy-two pieces of cannon, and, what was of infinitely more value, twenty-five thousand Christian slaves restored to liberty.

The Turks sustained a defeat at Lepanto from which they never recovered. Henceforward, that terror which they had exercised over the Christians changed sides.

The holy Pontiff decreed a triumph in the ancient style to the Archduke John of Austria, the happy instrument of this great victory, and he magnificently rewarded his brave little army, who well knew, however, to *whom* really the laurels and crowns were due.

Our Lady ad Nives.

(NOTRE DAME DES NEIGES.)

"Regina Angelorum." "Queen of Angels."

HE patrician John, and his noble spouse, were held in great estimation at Rome in the fourth century, on account of their riches, but especially for the excellent manner in which they spent their wealth. The flame of charity burnt brightly in their souls, and not a day passed which did not bring forth many good works.

They who give to God never become poor. In their old age, John and his wife were still rich, although their charities were constant; and having no children, they resolved to choose their heirs before they died.

As our wants are twofold; namely, those of the body and those of the soul, so has charity a double character. One part, therefore, of John's riches he portioned out for the relief of the wants of the body; the other he gave for the providing for the spiritual comfort of souls. This second portion the good couple thought they could not place in better hands than those of the Blessed Virgin, whom they had ever faithfully honoured and tenderly loved. "We will raise a temple to her honour," said they, "and beseech her to succour and comfort those who shall ask anything of her within its sacred precincts."

Wishing to accomplish this object before their death, they immediately commenced to put it into execution; and tradition informs us that our Lady herself appeared to them during the night. She told them that she accepted their pious intention. She traced out the plan of the new sanctuary, and told them to erect it on Mount Esquiline, one of the seven hills of Rome, on the spot which in the morning they should find covered with snow.

That day was the 5th of August, 365 or 367, and the heat was excessive.

The patrician went to the Esquiline mount, accompanied by his wife. At the foot of the hill they met Pope Liberius, who, having had the same vision, had come to witness the miracle. They found in the centre of ground burnt up by the piercing rays of the sun, a thick mass of snow, covering space enough whereon to build a church. The saintly personages fell on their knees and thanked the Almighty for this manifestation of his divine will, and on that very day was laid the first stone of Our Lady's Church.

The church thus founded is known to all the Christian world under the name of *St. Mary Major* (or the Greater), because it is the largest, most important, and one of the first churches built in Rome under the dedication of our Blessed Lady. It is, however, still more generally known to the people by its primeval name of *Our Lady ad Nives* (of the snow), on account of the extraordinary circumstance just mentioned. It is also designated, by the old historians, the Liberian Basilic, in memory of the Pope in whose reign and by whom its erection was commenced. It is also called our Lady's of the Cradle, on account of its possessing the crib of the Infant Jesus,* which was presented to the church in the seventh century, under the pontificate of Theodore the First.

Liberius lived only to see the work begun, for he died in September, 367. It was finished and dedicated under Sixtus III., in 432.

Another valuable relic is kept in this church. It is a picture of the Blessed Virgin, said to have been painted by St. Luke. It was presented to the church by St. Helena, on her return from Jerusalem. It cannot be doubted that St. Luke was a painter. Indeed such is positively asserted by many early writers:—among others, Nicephorus and Theodore. The number of sanctuaries which claim possession of a portrait of our Lady, by St. Luke, would lead us to believe that an opinion so generally received cannot be without foundation.†

The picture at St. Mary Major's is painted on wood. It is three feet high and two and a half

---

* It is the wooden portion of our Lord's resting-place at his birth. It is inclosed in a silver shrine, and preserved in the Sixtine chapel, being only exposed [to the veneration of the faithful during the Octave of Christmas. Upon its summit is a figure of the infant Jesus reclining on some straw, in gold. St. Jerome had a particular devotion to the stable of Bethlehem. He spent some years there, and now his body lies in St. Mary Major's, near this portion of his Lord's crib.

† These doubtless are very early paintings, and probably copies of portraits, by St. Luke. Theodore, who flourished at Constantinople in 518, says, that a picture, by St. Luke, was sent to the Empress Pulcheria, in the fifth century. Some statues are also attributed to St. Luke. We have no authority, however, for supposing him to have been a sculptor. As these images are generally painted in polychrome, they may have been painted by him; but we know nothing certain on this subject.

broad. The two pieces, of which the panel is composed, have become slightly disjointed by time. The Blessed Virgin has a sweet countenance, and her head is covered with a blue veil. The infant is most beautiful, and is seated on his mother's knee. He holds a book in the left, and the right hand is held up in the act of blessing. Every Saturday it is exposed to the veneration of the faithful, who crowd to pray before it, and whose confidence in asking for favours is proportioned to the numberless graces which have been obtained by others on the same spot.

We give an account of the most celebrated miracle connected with St. Luke's portrait of our Blessed Lady.

In the year 590, Rome was visited by the plague. It spread desolation over the city, nothing was heard but weeping and lamentation, and on every side were seen the dead carried to the grave by the dying.* As Easter drew near, the disease was raging at its greatest fury, when St. Gregory the Great, who then worthily sat in the chair of Peter, assembled such of the faithful as were able to leave their houses, in the church of St. Mary Major. One-half the inhabitants had died. Gregory ordered a penitential procession for Easter Sunday, well knowing that disease is sent us in punishment of our sins, and trusting to the divine mercy to remove the scourge on that glorious day of our Blessed Lord's triumph over death and hell.

He omitted nothing which could move the

* It is said that this disorder particularly affected the fibres of the brain, and produced sneezing. Hence, some say, arose the custom of saying "*God bless you*" to those who sneeze.

goodness of God: the venerated picture was taken down, and the suppliant crowd, grouped around the holy image, went in procession through the city amid a concert of sobs and lamentations, bareheaded, and with naked feet. The impure air was dissipated, and the pestilence fled at the approach of the sacred picture. The sick grew better. They and the holy Pope heard in the air choirs of angels saluting their queen in these words :*

> " Joy to thee, O Queen of Heaven, Alleluia.
> He whom thou wast meet to bear, Alleluia,
> As He promised, hath arisen, Alleluia."

The legend adds, that the holy Pontiff, animated by this wonderful event, joined his voice to those of the angelic choir, in humbly adding to their canticle the following line of supplication, in a voice trembling with emotion : †

> " Pour for us to him your prayer, Alleluia."

This angelic hymn was henceforth adopted by the Church, and is sung during the Paschal time.

The prayer of the saintly Pope was instantly granted; the plague ceased its ravages. Another wonderful event also signalized this period. When the procession was passing Adrian's tomb, an immense building, now a citadel, an angel was seen on its summit to place his bloody sword, with which he had menaced the city, in its scabbard. Hence the tomb is now called the Castle of St. Angelo, and a large bronze angel has been erected on its summit, in the act of sheathing a sword, in commemoration of this event.

---

* Regina cœli lætare, Alleluia.
 Quia quem meruisti portare, Alleluia,
 Resurrexit sicut dixit, Alleluia.
† Ora pro nobis, Deum, Alleluia.

Our Lady of the Angels.*

"Regina Angelorum."   "Queen of Angels."

DURING the last century, which set little value on humility and self-denial, many attempts were made to disparage the character of St. Francis of Assisi. Luxury and indulgence have no sympathy with the life and works of this great saint. Still was he a great saint and a man of genius. Goerres has well demonstrated this fact. We will content ourselves with a few lines to consider the founder of the Friar Minors under this twofold aspect.

It was not through his genius that St. Francis of Assisi acquired the extraordinary graces by which he was so elevated above the rest of mankind. It was the pure and humble dispositions of his heart which caused the Almighty to shower upon him his choicest favours. When he had to choose, in his twenty-fifth year, between God and the world, he unhesitatingly chose the former.

Ardently devoted to the Blessed Virgin and the celestial spirits, he went to seek repose in the little chapel of *our Lady of the Angels*. Whence do you imagine this sanctuary obtained so charming an appellation? A general tradition tells us that the heavenly choirs delighted in singing the

* Notre Dame des Anges.

praises of their Queen in this chapel. On several occasions has their divine melody been heard by the neighbouring peasants; and they also assert that, attracted by the sounds, they have respectfully approached the chapel, and seen amidst a mysterious light, which filled the sanctuary, groups of angels surrounding the sweet image of their Queen.

According to the local traditions, this image of the Blessed Virgin was brought into the country about the year 352, by four pious hermits from the Holy Land. They had obtained permission from Pope Liberius to inhabit the valley of Spoletto, and had constructed a small chapel, wherein they placed a relic from the tomb of the Blessed Virgin; whence it was at first called Our Lady of Josaphat. The monks of St. Benedict enlarged it in the sixth century, and at the same time, on account of the wondrous visits of the angels above related, it took the name of Our Lady of the Angels. It was also called *Portiuncula*, because the field in which it stood was a small portion of the property of the Benedictines of Mount Subiaco, near Assisi. Francis, while at prayer in this chapel, was favoured with such visions and other singular gifts, that he exclaimed, " Truly this is the abode of angels, and one of the most favourite of our dear Lady's shrines."

He was joined in his retirement by several companions. They numbered twelve, while as yet their only habitation was a common cottage. The saint was, therefore, overjoyed when the Benedictines gave him the chapel and the small house attached to it. The good priest who had hitherto resided there gave it up to St. Francis, embraced him, and said, "Bring hither your brethren and their furniture." This was soon and easily effected, for of furniture they had none.

Thus arose the order of St. Francis, which has rendered such services to the world, and has been repaid with such ingratitude.

When the order grew into great repute, it still (as was agreed in the deed of gift) kept the *Portiuncula* for its chief house, and it was to its dear church that St. Francis was most attached, and in which he received his greatest gifts from heaven. We are not able here to recount all these favours, but we cannot pass over one important fact.

One day, in the year 1221, that St. Francis was praying there with great fervour, imploring Heaven's favour for his brethren, and for all those who, with pious intentions, visited the church of the *Portiuncula*, he had a vision, in which Jesus and Mary appeared to him surrounded by the angelic host. Our Saviour told him that his prayer was granted, and that the Sovereign Pontiff (to whom he enjoined him to apply) would grant a plenary indulgence for all true penitents who should visit the church. Francis went and threw himself at the foot of St. Peter's successor, Honorius III., who issued the celebrated indulgence called that of *Portiuncula*. Two years afterwards, by another favour, seven bishops were especially designed to go and publish with solemnity this indulgence in the privileged church.

This indulgence was at first attached to the feast of our Lady of the Angels, and only to the chapel of the *Portiuncula*, which is at present in the centre of the great church, and to which it gives its name; but it was afterwards extended by Pope Innocent XII. to every day in the year for this church, and by Alexander IV. and Urban VIII. to all the churches and chapels of the Franciscan order for the 2nd of August.

If our *Lady of the Angels* does not permit us to enjoy the same divine communications as she did her servant Francis, it is, doubtless, because we are too much fascinated with the deceitful pomps and pleasures of earth.

The Scapular.

"Regina Patriarcharum."   "Queen of Patriarchs."

THE hermits of Mount Carmel are the most ancient order of religious in the world. They claim descendance from the patriarchs, and regard Elias as their founder. In the days of St. John the Baptist, according to some, there were solitaries living on Mount Carmel, who walked in the paths of strict virtue, and believed in Christ the moment they heard of him. His Blessed Mother was venerated here at a very early period, and we are informed that, during her life, she honoured the hermits of Carmel with several communications; so has she ever been an especial object of veneration to the good religious.

St. Simon Stock,* who flourished in the middle of the thirteenth century, and who was raised by his eminent virtues to the dignity of general of the Children of Elias (better known by the name of Carmelites), cherished a particular devotion

---

* *Stock*, in many of the northern languages, means the trunk of a tree. This surname was given to the saint because, at the age of twelve years, having retired into solitude, to live more intimately with God, he spent twenty years therein, having no other abode but the hollow trunk of a tree.—*Trans.*

towards the Blessed Virgin. Wishing to revive in Europe an order which had ever shown itself so devoted to Mary, he daily addressed her in these sweet words, which the Church still sings :*

> Flower of Carmel!
> Flowering vine!
> Shed thy gifts
> On us who are thine.
> Virginal Mother!
> Star of the Sea!
> Glory of Heaven!
> We cry to Thee.

It is said that, on the 16th day of July, 1251, the Blessed Virgin graciously deigned to appear to St. Simon Stock, holding in her hand a scapular,† which she presented to him with these words :‡

" Receive for yourself and your order, my dear son, this privileged emblem which you so much desired; it shall be the distinguishing mark of my confraternity, it shall be a pledge of peace and eternal alliance, the symbol of salvation, and the safeguard in dangers; and they who die after having faithfully borne the scapular shall not perish everlastingly."

---

* Flos Carmeli, vitis florigera,
Splendor cœli, Virgo puerpera,
Mater mitis, sed viri nescia,
Carmelitis da privilegia,
Stella maris!

† The scapular is composed of two pieces of linen, bearing representations of the Blessed Virgin, and other emblems. It derives its name from being worn hanging over the shoulders.

‡ Accipe, dilectissime fili, tui ordinis scapulare, tibi et cunctis Carmelitis privilegium, signum confraternitatis meæ, fœdus pacis et pacti sempiterni; ecce signum salutis, salus in periculis; in hoc moriens æternum non patietur incendium.

Hostile critics have taken up these expressions, as if they meant that it was only necessary to wear a scapular to be saved! But he who wears the scapular worthily must fulfil the conditions it imposes; and to do this, is to lead a perfect Christian life.

Many pontiffs have granted privileges to the confraternity of the Scapular; and since the time of St. Simon Stock, who healed many sick persons by giving them this holy sign, innumerable graces have been granted to those who wear it. It is embarrassing to choose out of so many historically-attested facts, and others which rest upon less weighty authority.

Louis XIII. received the scapular on the following occasion. At the siege of Montpellier, where he commanded in person, M. de Beauregard, who was near him, received two musket-shots. He staggered, but did not fall, like a man who had merely received a slight blow. He was instantly undressed, when it was perceived that the two balls had struck the scapular he wore, while his body remained unhurt.

M. de Montigny, governor of Dieppe, going by sea to Toulon, was surprised by a tempest, which threatened to destroy his vessel. He was washed overboard, and saving himself contrary to every probability, attributed his safety to the scapular which he wore.

On Christmas-day, 1648, the château of Raguin, in Anjou, took fire. The Baron de Souche threw his scapular into the flames, which immediately ceased. The same effect was caused by the same means in many other places, and particularly at Paris, in 1664. The flames were in like manner arrested by a scapular, on the 9th July, 1719, in the village of Arnaville. The Bishop of Metz caused this miracle to be examined into, and published it in a pastoral letter, dated the 12th of January, 1720.

Of the miracles recorded of St. Simon Stock, we will give the following. A gentleman, who had led a bad life, was dying in despair, gnashing his teeth, swearing, blaspheming, and foaming with rage. This was reported to the saint, who hastened to the bedside of the unhappy man, invested him with his scapular, and as if the bad spirits who agitated the dying man had suddenly vanished, he became calm, alive to a sense of his awful position, and bewailing and confessing his sins, died a penitent.

A student of Padua, whose disorders had led him to a state of despair, in the hope of ending his life, stabbed himself thrice; but the dagger struck the scapular, which he had taken in his early youth, and did him no harm. This miracle effected his conversion; for he repented of his sins, and repaired for the excesses of his youth by a life of penance.

A Flemish soldier having seriously disobeyed his officer, was condemned to be shot, and led to the place of execution. His comrades fired three discharges without any effect. All the bullets fell at his feet. The officers were so struck by this incident, that they had him stripped and examined, to see whether he had not a coat of mail concealed beneath his clothes, but finding only the scapular there, he was pardoned in honour of the Blessed Virgin.

In the year 1336, a young man of Lorraine, named Coquart, was shot by a pistol held close to him. Seeing it had no effect, the assassin fired again, aiming at his heart. The balls pierced his clothes without injuring him. The astonished man stripped his intended victim, and finding the scapular on him, gave him his life.

The same author relates that, in Lorraine, three men having been surprised by a band of robbers, two were shot, but the third escaped, having been protected by our Lady's livery.

After the siege of Ypres, the Archduke Leopold was presented with a musket-ball, quite flattened, which had been fired at a soldier whom it had struck without injuring him. The image of the Blessed Virgin, like to that on the scapular which it had struck, was found impressed upon it.

The number of these incidents are innumerable, and all resting upon respectable testimony; they show how powerful is the Blessed Virgin, and how she protects those who wear her scapular, and faithfully observe the duties it imposes.

Our Lady of the Pillar.*

"Regina Apostolorum."   "Queen of Apostles."

AN incontestable tradition, resting upon the testimony of St. Jerome, St. Isidore, the ancient liturgies of Spain, and supported by a host of authorities and monuments, which treat it as a matter of history, tells us that St. James the Greater carried the Gospel to Spain. According to the best authorities, he undertook this mission soon after the martyrdom of St. Stephen. Thus, in the year following the ascension of our Lord, Spain had the Gospel preached to her.

But a more extraordinary legend is attached to this apostolic visit, which attributes to St. James himself the foundation of the church of our Lady del Pilar, venerated from time immemorial at Saragossa. Let us examine the foundation of this legend.

So many contradictions had arisen concerning the miraculous origin of the church, that Spain addressed herself to the Holy See, the guide of faith, to settle the controversy. Innocent XIII. then sat in St. Peter's chair. After a minute, exact, and careful investigation, the twelve cardinals, in whose hands the affair rested, adopted the following account, which was approved by the

* Notre Dame del Pilar.

Sacred Congregation of Rites on the 7th of August, 1723, and since inserted in the lessons of the office of the feast of our Lady del Pilar, celebrated on the 12th of October.

"Of all places which Spain offers to the veneration of the devout, the most illustrious is doubtless the sanctuary consecrated to God under the invocation of the Blessed Virgin, under the title of our Lady del Pilar, at Saragossa.

"According to ancient and pious tradition, St. James the Greater, led by Providence into Spain, spent some time at Saragossa.* He there received a signal favour from the Blessed Virgin. As he was praying with his disciples one night, upon the banks of the Ebro, as the same tradition informs us, the Mother of God, who still lived, appeared to him, and commanded him to erect an oratory in that place.

"The apostle delayed not to obey this injunction, and with the assistance of his disciples soon constructed a small chapel. In the course of time a larger church was built and dedicated, which, with the dedication of St. Saviour's, is kept as a festival in the city and diocese of Saragossa on the 4th of October."

Before the publication of this statement, Pope Calixtus III., in a bull dated 1456, had encouraged pilgrimages to our Lady del Pilar, acknowledged the miracles performed at her shrine, and the prodigy of its foundation. The popular legends, however, are much fuller than the one we have just given. They add that St. James, having visited Oviedo and other places, stopped for some time at Saragossa, where he increased the number of his disciples to such an extent that he assembled

* Then called *Cæsar-Augusta.*

them every evening in a quiet spot on the banks of the Ebro, where he instructed them in the faith, and told them of the mysteries of the kingdom of God. When one evening, near midnight, the faithful who surrounded the holy apostle heard choirs of angels chanting *Ave Maria gratia plena*; and at the same time they beheld, in the midst of the heavenly troop, the figure of a lady, of exquisite beauty, seated on a marble pillar. St. James, recognising the Mother of God, fell on his knees before her.

She told him to erect a church on the spot where she appeared; and the marble pillar was allowed to remain as a testimony of the truth of the apparition. The apostle obeyed. A chapel was erected, and an image of the Blessed Virgin placed on the miraculous pillar, which still attracts the notice of pious pilgrims. Such is the tradition. The Blessed Virgin is represented erect with her Divine Son in her arms, who holds a dove in his hand.

The piety of the Spaniards afterwards erected a handsome church on this spot; the ancient chapel now forms a crypt under the chancel. It is 36 feet long by 25 feet broad. Many believe it to be the original chapel; but this is scarcely probable. It is splendidly decorated; and though the wars in the early part of this century have despoiled it of a great portion of its wealth, it still remains a splendid sanctuary.*

* St. James returned from Spain to Jerusalem, where he was the first of the apostles to suffer martyrdom. It is said that he took with him some disciples from Spain who returned with his body to their native country. St. James is reverenced as the apostle of Spain, and has on many occasions specially protected that great Catholic

Among the many miracles which have been obtained by the intercession of the Blessed Virgin in her chapel at Saragossa, the following is perhaps the most remarkable and the most astonishing. We also are guided in our selection by the many proofs and testimonies which are attached to it, and to its being given by the *Bollandists*, whose learning and critical acumen we suppose no one will deny.

"The miracle we are about to record happened in our own time. It occurred to a young man who recovered the use of a leg through the intercession of our Lady of the Pillar.

"His name was Michael Pellicer. His parents were poor people of Calanda, in Arragon; but he worked with one of his uncles in Valencia. At the age of nineteen, he fell from a cart, heavily laden with corn; and the wheel passed over his right leg, which was broken. This happened in the year 1638.

"The uncle and nephew being both poor, the wounded man was taken to the hospital at Valencia. Several remedies were applied to the broken limb without success. As he grew worse, they yielded to his entreaties to be taken to the great hospital at Saragossa, where his devotion to our Lady of the Pillar led him to hope for succour.

"Before entering the ward, he begged to be laid in the subterranean chapel before our Lady's venerated image. Suffering as he was, he made

---

country. The place where his relics are kept has long been a famous resort of pilgrims; and there is no one who has not heard of Compostelo. The name of this city itself is a corruption of St. James the apostle. It was first called in Spanish *Giacomo Apostolo*, then *Como Postolo*, and finally *Compostelo*.

his confession, heard mass, and received the holy communion. He then, with perfect resignation, was conveyed to the hospital, and placed under the care of Dr. John D'Estranga, a surgeon of great eminence at that time.

"This surgeon was alarmed at the sight of his patient's leg, and instantly declared there was no hope, save in amputation. The leg was accordingly cut off a little below the knee, and the dead limb buried.

"Michael Pellicer thought that it had not pleased our Lady to heal him, and that he merited his sufferings, which he endured with the greatest patience and submission to the will of God. During the painful operation, the only exclamations heard to escape his lips were fervent aspirations to his dear Patroness—our Blessed Lady, whom he most tenderly loved. When the amputation was over, and the part bound up, he went on crutches to our Lady's shrine, and returned thanks for the strength given him to undergo the operation. While engaged in prayer, feeling his wound sore, he thought of rubbing it with some of the oil of the lamp which hung before the image, but was told it would do him harm, unless a miracle changed its nature. He, however, still persisted in applying the oil to his leg. The wound healed, and he lived for two years in Saragossa, well known for his devotion to our Blessed Lady, at the entrance to whose chapel he received the alms of the people.

"In the beginning of the year 1640, a good canon, hearing that the poor cripple greatly desired to visit his parents, gave him a little mule. Michael Pellicer mounted it, and returned to Calanda. As he passed through the neighbouring villages, he received alms from the people, and visited the different churches.

"One evening after his return (it was the 29th of March), feeling very fatigued, he placed his crutches by the fireside, where his parents sat, and went to bed. At eleven o'clock, before retiring to her room, the mother went to see whether her son was asleep, or whether his fatigues had made him unwell. She rubbed her eyes with astonishment at the sight of two feet at the end of the bed, having left her son three hours ago with but one leg. She thought that it might be one of the soldiers, then quartered in the town, who had taken possession of her son's bed, and ran to call her husband.

"He uncovered the face, and instantly recognised his son in the sleeping man. The noise of their movements awoke Michael, who exclaimed:

"'Oh, why did you awaken me from so sweet a dream, and so beautiful a sight? I was in the holy chapel of our Lady of the Pillar, and there, in the presence of my dear Protectress, two angels restored to me my lost leg in recompense for my persevering confidence in the Mother of my Lord.'

"'Give thanks to God and our Lady, my dear son,' cried both parents; 'you have not had a vain dream, for your leg is indeed restored to you.'

"Michael Pellicer was yet ignorant of the miracle which had been wrought upon him; but he sprang out of bed, and the neighbours, hearing the cries of joy, ran in, and joining the good parents in their wish to render thanks for the miracle, conducted the young man in triumph to the church.

"A singular circumstance was attached to this

miraculous cure, and which it would seem to baffle the reasoning of the incredulous—the restored leg was reversed. Was it to afford another trial of the young man's faith? Was it a sign that certain extraordinary favours are only completed in the sanctuary? Was it to make the miracle more manifest? However we may judge, so it was. As soon as Michael Pellicer had prostrated himself at the foot of our Lady's altar, and poured forth, in company with the rector, a fervent prayer, and while the people sung the *Salve Regina*, the leg turned to its proper position; and he rose and stood firm on both legs, who the day before could not move six steps without the aid of his crutches.

"Many of his friends accompanied him to Saragossa, where he went to return thanks in the chapel of our Lady of the Pillar. The miracle was juridically examined, and all the facts connected with it were attested by many witnesses, and authenticated by notaries, professors, and surgeons. A bright red line appeared round the leg, and remained there during the life of Pellicer. The miracle was authentically published on the 27th of April, 1641, by the Archbishop of Saragossa."

A Legend of the Rosary.

"Regina Martyrum."   "Queen of Martyrs."

ODERN heresies, and in their track many modern writers, have attacked and shamefully calumniated the memory of an eminent man, who is only known to many through these defiled mediums. His great meekness has been wickedly turned into rigour, his tender zeal into harshness, his charity into fanaticism, his humility into pride. He even has been made a grand inquisitor of, though that office had no existence until twelve years after his death. He spent his life in restoring to the cruel and ferocious men of his time, pardon, indulgence, and the quiet virtues of peace; but as he was a great defender of the Church, his enemies have maligned him. History has grievously sinned in his regard. But, let us add, it is that shameless history, written by those whose bile is excited by the very name of the Roman Church—pretended historians, who, unfortunately, for three centuries have had too much sway over our annals. Many will have guessed that the person we speak of is St. Dominic.*

* St. Dominic died in 1221, and it was in 1233 that Pope Gregory IX. attached the Dominicans to the Inquisition, and named Father Peter the first Inquisitor-General. He was assassinated by the Albigenses.

It is related of this saint, that he had a most tender devotion to the Blessed Virgin from his childhood, and that she appeared to him and revealed the sweet devotion of the Rosary. Without stopping to examine the details of this incident, we will assert an incontrovertible fact, that if St. Dominic was not the founder of the Rosary, he was the restorer of this devotion, so dear to all Catholic hearts, now so universally used; and this is enough for those who follow the standard of the prince of this world to make them hate this great servant of Mary.

Dominic lived at a period of great ignorance, when few Christians knew how to read. He knew and had experienced the admirable power of prayer; and it was a worthy inspiration of the tender Mother of the Faithful, to institute in their favour a method of supplying the one hundred and fifty psalms of the Psalter, by one hundred and fifty Hail Marys. Thus, many popes have called the Rosary, the Psalter of the Blessed Virgin.

He divided this garland of flowers, which he offered to the mystical rose (and which he called by the sweet name of the Rosary) into fifteen decades, each commencing with the Our Father. It is thus composed of the most holy prayers— the Our Father, taught us by our Lord himself; and the Angelic Salutation, composed of the words of the angel Gabriel, when he announced the redemption of men; those of St. Elizabeth, the first to recognise Mary as the Mother of God; and finally, the invocation added by the holy Council of Ephesus.

He made each decade terminate with the Doxology, &c., in honour of the Blessed Trinity, and commence with the Creed, followed by three Hail Marys, in honour of the three theological virtues.

The fifteen decades relate to the principal mysteries of the Incarnation of our Blessed Redeemer.

The first five, called the Joyful Mysteries, are the Annunciation, the Visitation, Our Lord's Nativity, His Presentation, and Finding in the Temple.

The second five, called the Dolorous Mysteries, are the Agony in the Garden of Olives, the Scourging at the Pillar, the Crowning with Thorns, the Carrying of the Cross, and the Crucifixion.

The third five, called the Glorious Mysteries, are the Resurrection, the Ascension, the Descent of the Holy Ghost, the Assumption and Coronation of the Blessed Virgin in Heaven, where she sits, enthroned by her Divine Son, Queen of Heaven and Earth.

Thus is this beautiful devotion easy to the most simple and unlettered. It has been most successful, and has much contributed to destroy the perfidious heresy it was destined to combat; and it will continue to be a powerful ally of the Church in the assaults of the old enemy.*

In the year 1221, in the general chapter of the rising order of the Preaching Friars, assembled at

* The laity being rarely able to recite the whole of the Rosary at once, it is divided into three portions, of five mysteries each, which is called a *chapelet* (the beads), from the ancient custom of adorning the hair with beads, thus forming, as it were, a little chapel. We see in Froissart (1349), Edward III. of England detach his pearl beads from his girdle, and give them to Sir Eustace of Ribaumont. In Italy the beads are called a *crown*.

Bologna, St. Dominic, a few days before his death, blessed the large body of religious, who recognised him as their father, and who were henceforth to disperse themselves throughout the world.

The people who spoke dialects derived from the language of the Church very generally followed the standard of Catholicism. But in the countries where the Slavonic, Teutonic, and other rude German idioms prevailed, the most gross superstition still reigned. It was to these barbarous regions that the patriarch of the Preaching Friars, or Dominicans, wished his followers to betake themselves. He gave these young soldiers of the Church (who undertook a no less perilous task than their brethren, who took arms for the recovery of the holy sepulchre) the protection of Mary for their riches and her Rosary for their armour.

In their journeys, they recited it daily, and gained strength and perseverance from the habit. Thrown like lambs among wolves, they well knew that, in persevering to the end, they should gain the victory, and that their words, blessed from above, would tend to spread the kingdom of Christ, if they but watered the seed they set by their blood in martyrdom.

In the number of those who thus set out in the track of the apostles, in 1221, there was a young man, full of faith and zeal, called Sadoc. We know no more of his country than that it was in the north. He traversed for many years, amidst pains and troubles, Hungary and its neighbouring states. He led the laborious life of a missionary with indefatigable patience and unbounded devotion, daily sowing the seed of good tidings in savage breasts, and rarely receiving any other pay than injuries and insults. Still he was consoled by the immense happiness of treading in the footsteps of his Saviour, gaining a few souls, receiving innumerable graces and superhuman joys from above, and the constant and sweet protection of his dear Mary, whose praises he never tired of singing.

He continued his course in spotless purity, though reproaching himself for those slight faults into which even the just man falls, and ardently desired the happiness of receiving martyrdom. But he was doomed to wait long for his crown, for in 1259, thirty-eight years after he had left Bologne, he was still wandering among the Poles at Sandomir, preaching to and civilizing that people.

Forty young religious laboured under his direction, and all led the most perfect lives. Every evening they recited the Rosary in common, concluding with the *Salve Regina*. Not one of them would suffer anything to interfere with this holy exercise, and Sadoc had never once been absent from it. Their constant prayer to our Lady was for the gift of perseverance, without which nothing can avail, and the grace to be able to prepare themselves well for death; for at this time the Tartars made frequent and sudden irruptions into the Polish territories, and they daily expected to fall a prey to these enemies of Christianity.

Under these circumstances, all the brethren being seated at supper on the 1st of June, 1259, the lector, who, according to custom, was reading the martyrology of the next day, saw the following words (which he read aloud) written in the book:

"At Sandomir, the martyrdom of forty-one Christians. . . . . "

These words were applied to the 2nd of June. After having read them, the brother paused. The astonished religious knew not what these words could signify; for Christian blood had never yet flowed in the place where they were. How came the words inserted in the book, for no one had ever seen them there before? Sadoc began to believe that our Lady had granted them their fervent prayer, and that they were thus warned, in order to prepare for death. But what death would it be? They neither knew nor cared, but, bent in submission to the will of God, they passed the night in silent meditation and prayer. At daybreak, the pious superior having confessed the brothers, solemnly celebrated the sacred mysteries, and distributed to all the holy communion, which they received as the viaticum. After mass, they all commenced singing the *Salve Regina*, when they were startled by a loud noise, succeeded by terrific screams. The Tartars had surprised Sandomir, broken into the town and massacred the inhabitants, and in a few moments entered the humble abode of the Dominicans, brandishing swords and axes, which they used for the murder of the brothers, who still continued their holy chant. Sadoc was the last to fall by a blow from an axe, just as he had finished alone the last words of the hymn: "*O clemens, O pia! O dulcis Virgo Maria!*"*

* These martyrs have been honoured at Sandomir since the thirteenth century.

The Iconoclasts.

"Regina Confessorum."   "Queen of Confessors."

THE history of St. Mary of Egypt shows us, that about the year 380 the public veneration of images was established and generally practised in Jerusalem. We may also see from the lives and works of St. Paulinus of Nola, St. Prudentius, St. Gregory of Nyssa, St. Ephrem, and of many Fathers of the first four centuries, that images were publicly and universally venerated wherever the Church enjoyed any liberty. Eusebius, who wrote in the early part of the fourth century, speaks of the miracles wrought at Paneas, in Palestine, before the carved image of the woman cured by our Divine Redeemer of a bloody flux. About the same time, St. Epiphanius, archbishop of Salamis, suppressed a painted image of a saint honoured by the people, to replace it by one more worthy.

The veneration of relics and holy images can be traced to the time of the apostles, by incontestable traditions, and was therefore everywhere established, when Leo the Isaurian, an ignorant and brutal soldier, having raised himself to the imperial dignity, issued, in the year 726, an edict against images, and planted in blood the first standard of the Iconoclasts. Although he had sworn at his elevation to maintain and protect the Catholic Church, he leagued himself with the Jews and Saracens, under the pretence of reforming the Church! Immediately after the publication of his edict, he caused his soldiers to destroy every image in the churches and elsewhere, beginning with the figures of our Lord. This took place at Constantinople. The indignant people rose in rebellion; they were massacred by the soldiers, who, on pretence of seeking the prohibited images, entered their dwellings and laid them waste. The patriarch Germain, a venerable man, nearly a century old, raised his voice in defence of the Christian worship, but in vain; he was deposed and banished. The men of genius, also, protested against an edict, which struck as much at art as at religion. But Leo, alike hostile to religion and education, issued another edict, suppressing the public schools. To complete his purpose, he shut the teachers up in the great library of Constantinople, and then, worthy ally of the children of Omar, ordered the building to be destroyed by fire.

The horrible heresy of the Iconoclasts could not, however, make any way in Italy or Gaul. The emperor tried in vain to introduce it into these countries. He sent his edict to Rome, where Gregory II. indignantly rejected it, and the people tore it in pieces. Leo, in his fury, sent assassins to Rome for the purpose of killing Gregory; but the Roman people pursued the bandits, put them to death, and were only prevented from rushing into rebellion by the prayers and entreaties of the holy pontiff.

But while the West remained firm in the faith, religious images were being destroyed throughout the East. Every opposing voice was silenced by exile or death. God, however, abandoned not his holy cause. He raised up a man for the support of the Church, who though living near the tyrant, was beyond his control. It was John, governor of Damascus, whose name is illustrious in the ecclesiastical annals as St. John Damascen.

Damascus having been taken from the Christians, was in the hands of the Mussulman, and the caliphs, successors of Ali, resided there. These princes treated the Christians with mildness. Gezyd I., at the close of the seventh century, had even among his ministers a Christian, for whom he entertained a strong affection. He was a man of great wisdom and ardent charity, who devoted the bulk of his property to the ransom of Christian slaves. Heaven, for his reward, sent him one day, among the slaves, a Greek religious, named Cosmas, deeply versed in both secular and sacred learning. The caliph's minister retained him in his house, and intrusted him with the education of his son John, whom he earnestly desired to have well brought up.

The happy disposition of John heartily responded to the desires of his father and the exertions of his preceptor. As he advanced in years, he became so beloved by all the Saracens, that Gezyd II. appointed him governor of Damascus, which office he was most worthily filling when the edict of Leo was promulgated.

John Damascen was deprived of the presence of his preceptor Cosmas, who had retired among the solitaries of St. Sabas, near Jerusalem; but he had preserved his spirit, and his counsels were ever in his mind. He felt that he owed the faithful the assistance of his knowledge and position, and that a Catholic who is silent when the Church is assailed is an unworthy child of his mother. He wrote several letters on the subject of sacred images, setting forth the principle, that the Church cannot err, and consequently can never fall into idolatry. He clearly showed that the veneration given to relics and images is very distinct from the worship due to the Almighty. He next remarked, that the prohibition of images in the Old Testament was confined to idols. He also proved that the Iconoclasts were inconsistent, since they themselves honoured Calvaries, Crosses, the books of the Gospels, the stone of the holy sepulchre, and the sacred vessels. He then proceeded to establish the veneration of relics from apostolic times, its uninterrupted continuation to the days in which he wrote, and the constant tradition and authority of the Fathers. From these reasons he contended that the emperor's edict ought not to be observed. " The government of the state," said he, " belongs to princes; but the doctrine of the Church is independent of their authority."

John wrote several copies of these letters with his own hand, and sent them to the principal churches in Asia to support the faithful. They produced such a sensation that it soon reached the ears of Leo the Isaurian, and greatly irritated him. Not being able to chastise, stifle, or burn the author, who was the caliph's subject, he conceived a most diabolical idea. He procured one of the letters in John's own handwriting, which he set before his secretaries, threatening them with death if they did not quickly succeed in imitating it. He then caused them to write, as coming from John, a letter to himself, engaging him to surprise and take the city of the caliphs, offering to afford him every assistance in his power.

Leo then sent this forgery to the caliph, with a letter from himself, in which he assumed the part of a friend, in thus exposing a traitor to his lawful prince.

Notwithstanding their habitual fair treatment of the Christians, the caliphs had lost none of their Asiatic character. Their resolutions were hasty, and their execution rapid. Leo had reckoned upon this. As soon as Gezyd II. opened the supposititions letter, he recognised John's writing; and in the surprise he experienced, let it fall from his hands. He snatched it up, read it again and again, and decided that it must be the governor's writing. A struggle arose in his mind between the affection he bore to John and the horror with which such deep ingratitude had struck him. He was in the audience-chamber dispensing justice, and surrounded by his soldiers, who were the prompt executors of the sentences he passed, according to the oriental custom. He said, coldly, "Let Mansour appear;" such was the name by which John was called by the Saracens.

The caliph considered the letter so extraordinary a production, that he hesitated to believe John's guilt until he should see him, and the effect it should produce upon him when he saw it. Shortly after the messenger had departed, Gezyd said to one of his officers:

"When Mansour leaves, if I dismiss him with the word 'go,' you will follow him, and instantly have his right hand cut off; you will then expose him in the public place, and show his hand to the people as that of a traitor."

The officer bowed assent, and John entered.

He advanced to the caliph's feet, who, without saying a word, gave him the letter, and fixed his eyes upon him while he read it.

John, suspecting nothing, and not having heard of any plot, was astounded at the sight of a letter, in what evidently was his own handwriting; and as he read, was so thunderstruck at the perfidy it contained, that he lost his voice, and became so agitated by contending emotions, that the caliph, fancying his confusion to arise from a sense of guilt, said to him,

"You will explain this to me when you become more calm—go!"

The officer immediately followed John; and when they had left the apartment, explained to him his sad commission. He then ordered one of the soldiers to cut off the right hand of John, who remained still more astounded, but offered no resistance to the barbarous sentence. When it was accomplished, the officer led him to the public place; and holding up the hand, exclaimed, "Behold the hand of a traitor."

The day was well-nigh spent. John returned to his house, offering his suffering and opprobrium to the Almighty, as an atonement for his sins; while the people, by whom he was beloved, and who could not believe him guilty, surrounded the messenger who brought the king's despatches, and with threats learned from him that he had brought the letter from Leo, who, they hesitated not to declare, had caused it to be forged.

The tumult spreading, one of the governor's friends went to the caliph, protested that John was innocent, but that his defence of religious images had drawn down upon him the rage of the emperor—the chief of the Iconoclasts. He therefore begged that at least John's hand should be restored to him, and thus somewhat lessen the indignity he had already suffered. Gezyd consented readily to this, and expressed his regret at having acted so hastily with one whom he had every reason to believe was sincerely attached to him. The hand was accordingly restored to John Damascen.

The foregoing relation is incontestable, but the truth of what follows has been severely contested. The life of St. John Damascen, which has come down to us, and which was written in Greek and Latin by the Bollandists, was not published, it is said, until two centuries after his death. On this account many critics have looked upon the following narration as a popular legend—beautiful and elegant it is true, but with little foundation. Still, as it is well known that his life was written by John IV., patriarch of Jerusalem, it seems worthy of some credit. Baillet himself, whose criticisms are most rigid, does not actually reject the fact, but denies that it can be clearly proved; and adds, that if it be rejected, the whole of what precedes must also be denied, and thus the whole event be erased from the book of history.

When his hand was brought to John, he was found in tears in his oratory, kneeling before a figure of the Blessed Virgin, offering the Almighty, through her intercession, his deep-felt sorrow. He regained his strength in prayer, and rejoiced in having suffered for the faith, with entire submission to the mysterious designs of Divine Providence. He might, perhaps, have regretted the loss of a hand, which he had ever devoted with zeal to the service of the Almighty and the defence of the Church. So that when the dead member was given him, he laid it down before the image; and placing his mutilated arm near it, said:

"You know, O Holy Virgin! why this hand has been severed from my arm. It was consecrated to you, and with your aid would have still better served you. O Heavenly Queen! if it be agreeable to the will of God, let thy power restore this hand to me, of which thy enemies have deprived me? It shall be more than ever devoted to thy service."

While praying thus, he felt his pain leave him; and he shortly after fell into a gentle slumber. In his sleep a beautiful vision appeared to him. It was no other than the Blessed Virgin herself, who, sweetly smiling on him, said:

"Keep your promise, my son; write no more for the vain objects of this world, but for God and His holy Church alone, for your prayer is heard, and your cure granted!"*

The saint awoke, says the legend, and was delightfully surprised to find his hand reunited to his arm, without any appearance of its ever having

---

* Some say that the image before which St. John Damascen prayed is the same that is celebrated in legends under the name of our Lady of Damascus. "The Syrians and Arabs, the Saracens and Jews, as well as the Christians, render it a homage, founded upon the extraordinary graces obtained at its shrine; she was their resource for the cure of their ills. It was of carved wood; and at times the perspiration ran down its forehead, which was most preciously collected and religiously preserved. A phial of it was kept at Cluny. This image, it is said, was not made by the hands of man; and even during the last century it attracted crowds of the sick in body and mind, and it is doubtless still honoured at the present day in a Greek monastery, called Seidnaia, about six leagues from Damascus."—*Baillet.*

been separated, except a thin red line, running like a bracelet round his wrist, as a perpetual memorial of the miracle.

The caliph, on hearing the next morning of this wondrous cure, and being convinced of the entire innocence of the governor, was anxious to make some atonement for the wrong he had inflicted, by heaping new honours upon him. But John, who had hitherto only lived in the world with regret, and worn its honours with fear, threw himself at his prince's feet, and besought him to grant him the liberty of devoting himself to the service of his God.

"I ought to serve no other in future than God, who has healed me, and the Blessed Virgin, to whom I have vowed this hand, and whom I have promised never to write in any other cause than that of the Church."

Gezyd II., though loath to part with John Damascen, yet granted his request. The happy saint took refuge with Cosmas, his good master, among the religious of St. Sabas, where he led a most austere life. Still, in accordance with his promise, confirmed by the commands of his superiors, he wrote, with indefatigable industry, so many treatises, that he earned the glorious title of a Father of the Church. He completed his former work on holy images. It forms three important treatises in his works. He also wrote several very fine panegyrics on the Blessed Virgin. He was raised to the priesthood by the Patriarch of Jerusalem; and on receiving the sacred unction, he did not content himself with writing, but travelled through Palestine to confirm the faith of the Christians by his impassioned discourses. He also went to Constantinople for the same purpose, in spite of the fury of Constantine Copronymus, worthy successor to the crown and vices of Leo the Isaurian. On his return to his solitude, he continued to write in defence of the faith, under the domination of the Saracens. He died in his humble cell about the year 780.

The Cure.

"Regina Virginum." "Queen of Virgins."

N the 20th of September, 1825, a young Roman lady, named Constantia Tondini, after having prayed in St. Augustine's church before the image of the Blessed Virgin (so admired by artists as one of the *chefs d'œuvre* of Sansovino, and so honoured by Christians for the innumerable graces conferred by Mary on those who ask for them before it), resolved to embrace, under our Lady's protection, the perfect life of a virgin, and immediately set out for Terni, where she intended to take the veil in the convent of Clares, known by the name of the Annunciation.

This young person was eighteen years of age, and possessed a good constitution and great courage. She had, however, a disagreeable journey, and reached her destination very ill, being seized with severe pains in the stomach. Her symptoms grew worse, and for six months she was confined to the convent infirmary.

God sometimes sends his children trials, which to us remain impenetrable mysteries. The physicians ordered Constantia to return to Rome, in the hopes that her native air would restore that health which they acknowledged their own art unable to accomplish.

The poor girl was therefore taken back to her parents. It was then the month of March, 1826. But neither the good effect of her native air, nor the mild influence of spring, nor the resources of medical art, could cure her disease, which, on the contrary, continued daily to grow worse. It consisted of spasms, contraction of the nerves, convulsions, partial paralysis, and a greater complication of pains than can be defined.

The sick girl earnestly besought the Almighty to grant that cure she sought from others in vain, or that if it was His will that she should quit this world, she implored the Blessed Virgin to assist her to make a good end.

She bitterly bewailed her inability to throw herself at the foot of her dear image at St. Augustine's, for it was constantly before her mind. She, however, obtained a copy of it, which was placed in her room near her bed. At this time she had been eleven months in Rome; and so great was her weakness, and so frequent her fainting fits, that her death was expected before many days had elapsed.

The blessed viaticum was administered to her on the 3rd of February, 1827, after which she lost her speech, and could only pray from her heart. Her faith, so long tried, failed not. She did not for an instant lose sight of her dear little image of our Lady; and even when the violence of her spasms caused her to close her eyes, one could still see her face turned towards the place it occupied. On the 6th of February, the physicians having declared that her death was at hand, her sisters begged her confessor to administer extreme unction. The holy man was rector of St. Mary's on the Minerva. While assisting him, the sisters, seeing the sick girl losing her senses, fell on their knees before the little image of the Madonna of St. Augustine's, recited the litany of the Blessed Virgin, and recommended the soul of their dying sister to her protection. At this moment, one of Constantia's friends arrived with some of the oil from the lamp which burned in St. Augustine's church before the figure carved by Sansovino. They anointed the limbs of the dying girl with this oil. At about sunset, Constantia awoke, and felt as if she had been aroused from a dream. She had regained her speech, but felt doubtful of her being awake, for her pains had left her. Her contracted limbs regained all their former suppleness, her tumours had disappeared, as had also her paralysis. She rose from her bed, asked for her clothes, which she put on, to the delight and astonishment of her family, and walking into the centre of the room, begged to be allowed to eat something; and when her confessor returned to give her the last blessing, he found her on her knees before the little image of the Blessed Virgin.

"Our Lady of St. Augustine's has cured me," said she; "I am now, thanks to her, quite recovered." She then related how, when she had lost her senses, she saw the Blessed Virgin, under the familiar form of the image she so loved, come and anoint her with cotton soaked in oil, and then disappear. She awoke perfectly recovered.

She supped with the family, eating heartily of what her sisters did.

The next morning, the physician, on seeing her up and well, was struck with the greatest astonishment. He accompanied her to St. Augustine's church, where she returned most grateful thanks to our Lady for her cure. This miracle having been juridically examined by order of Leo XII., was confirmed in a decree, dated 14th of September, 1827, which declares, " that the instantaneous and complete cure of Constantia Tondini, afflicted by a multiplicity of mortal maladies, is a great miracle obtained from the Almighty, by the intercession of the Blessed Virgin Mary."

The Abbey of Afflighem.

"Regina sanctorum omnium."   "Queen of all Saints."

THE bull of Pope Eugenius III., which proclaimed the second crusade, charged St. Bernard to preach it. His fervent eloquence, strengthened by the sanctity of his life, produced such a general sensation, that a distaff and spindle were sent to every knight who refused to take arms.

The better to fulfil his great mission, St. Bernard traversed France, the Low Countries, and the Rhenish provinces. Many a town still retains some tradition of his visit on this occasion. He is not forgotten at Mechlin, nor at Brussels; both these cities are proud of having held within their antique walls the last Father of the Church. Then, as in 1131, when he visited these countries in company with Pope Innocent II., Bernard delighted in escaping from the crowd and going to refresh his soul in a solitude, which had been founded about sixty years, by the munificence of the dukes of Brabant, and shed throughout the land the good odour of its virtues. This holy asylum was the abbey of Afflighem, which flourished in all its purity under the rule of St. Benet.

Bernard was so charmed with the sanctity of these religious, that he said, " I here find angels, whilst elsewhere I scarcely meet men."

Ardently devoted to the worship of the Blessed Virgin, Bernard let no opportunity of extending it pass, and in one of his retreats at Afflighem, he delivered a panegyric of Mary, which contains this passage:—

" Mary is the great and brilliant star, which God, in his goodness, has caused to shine over the immense ocean of this life. If she dazzles us by her privileges, she illumines us by her example. O Christians, whoever you be, know that your life here below is not a quiet promenade, but a perilous voyage, through rocks and tempests. Turn not, then, your eyes from the star which lights and guides you, if you would not be swallowed up in the gulf. If the winds of temptation assault you, if tribulations encompass you, turn your eyes towards the star, invoke Mary.* If the waves of pride burst over you, if you fear being carried away by the tide of ambition, injustice, or envy, look on the star, invoke Mary. If anger, malice, avarice, sensuality, beat against the frail bark of your soul, turn your eyes towards Mary. If you are troubled by remorse for your crimes, tormented by a conscience overwhelmed with horrible remembrances, terrified at the thought of judgment; if you feel the gulf of sadness before you, and the abyss of despair ready to swallow you, think of Mary. In perils, in troubles, in doubts, think of Mary, invoke Mary. Let her name be ever on your lips, the thought of her ever in your mind, the love of her ever in your heart; and to

---

* Respice stellam, voca Mariam.

obtain a favourable hearing with her, neglect not to follow the example she has given you."

On another occasion he exclaimed:

"Holy Virgin! let him cease to praise your goodness, who has never experienced its fruits, when he invoked you in his distress."

The good monks, one evening that Bernard had delighted them with his discourse, besought him to intone, in his own dear voice, the *Salve Regina*, —that moving invocation by which the Church every year salutes Mary, and which the monks of Afflighem were accustomed to sing every evening before her loved image. The saint could not refuse their desire; and when all the lamps were extinguished, with the exception of one, which, emblem of the mystical star burnt before Mary's venerated image, Bernard, in his sweet and touching voice, intoned the *Salve Regina*, and sang it through with the monks, who seemed to fancy that they saw a gracious smile on our Lady's face.

When they had sung, *Et Jesum benedictum fructum ventris tui, nobis post hoc exilium ostende*, all the voices ceased, for at that time the hymn concluded with these words.* But the inspired voice of Bernard continued, and he sent forth from

---

* We here give a translation of this beautiful hymn sung in the church office after Complin, from the feast of the most Holy Trinity to the Saturday before Advent:—

Hail! Heavenly Queen! Mother of pity, hail!
Hail! Thou our life, our hope, our solace, hail!
　Children of Eve,
To thee we cry from our sad banishment;
　To thee we send our sighs,
Weeping and mourning in this tearful vale,
　Come, then, our Advocate.

his heart those three sweet invocations which have ever since been added to the hymn—*O clemens! O pia! O dulcis Virgo Maria.**

The legend adds, that after a silence of some seconds, the saint again chanted the words *Salve Maria!* and that the glorious image of Afflighem immediately inclined its head, and distinctly uttered the words *Salve Bernarde!*

The truth of this legend was attested by the fact that the head of the image remained bent forward ever afterwards.

> Oh! turn on us those pitying eyes of thine,
>   And our long exile past
>   Show us at last,
> Jesus, of thy pure womb, the fruit divine.
>
>   O Virgin Mary, Mother blest!
>   O sweetest, gentlest, holiest!

* According to another account, the saint pronounced these invocations while in a state of ecstasy, at Spire, where, in commemoration of the fact, the hymn is sung daily with great solemnity.

A Legend of Duns Scot.

"Regina sine labe originali concepta."   "Queen conceived without original sin."

THE singular fact we are about to record has great affinity with that which precedes it. Another devout servant of Mary is the hero John Duns Scot. This celebrated theologian taught with great success in Paris towards the close of the thirteenth century. He was called the *subtle doctor*, on account of his writing and speaking with such wonderful clearness and precision, as may be seen in his works. He was one of the most earnest advocates of the doctrine of the Immaculate Conception of the Blessed Virgin; which means, that Mary, by a unique privilege, was born free from original sin, and pure as Eve before her fall.

For some time this belief had become dear to the school of Paris, and the Church of Paris then celebrated the Feast of the Immaculate Conception.* But as the Church had not decided

---

* There existed in the church of St. Severin, in Paris, a confraternity of the Immaculate Conception of the Blessed Virgin in the fourteenth century. It was a branch of an association which had been established in London in the previous century. It still exists in the same church (St. Severin) under the title of the Confraternity of our Lady of Holy Hope.—*Trans.*

this point, it was open to controversy, and found some adversaries even in the ranks of the pious.

Though this belief had been advanced before his time, Duns Scot is generally called the first defender of the doctrine, on account of the triumphant manner in which he silenced its impugners.

In this controversy he rested not on his intellect and learning alone, but sought inspiration in prayer, knowing well that prayer, if it penetrates to the throne of Divine power, draws down victorious graces, the powerful seed of a glorious harvest.

There existed at this time by the doorway of the crypt of the *Sainte-Chapelle*,* that beautiful jewel with which St. Louis endowed the city of Paris, which the Convention transformed into a record office, and which, by the return of religion and good taste, is now being restored to its pristine beauty. Well, at the door of the crypt of this *Holy Chapel* stood a graceful figure of the Blessed Virgin. At the feet of this statue, the doctors and literati of the day loved to prostrate themselves and their works. There, it is said, the prayers of masters and students were poured forth; science and eloquence there sought their inspiration. The preacher ascended the pulpit with greater confidence, the professor spoke with greater force, when he had recommended his cause to our Lady before her image at the Sainte-Chapelle. And there was Duns Scot ever to be found before undertaking any great cause.

One day that he was to maintain his favourite thesis against some foreign doctors, who denied

* This lovely chapel was erected by St. Louis, on his return from the Holy Land, to receive the relics of our Lord's passion which he brought over with him.—*Trans.*

to our Lady her great privilege, he was kneeling before her loved image, praying more fervently and for a longer time than usual, to obtain grace to overcome his antagonists. Ancient traditions assert, that on this occasion, to show that she had granted especial favours and graces to her favourite champion, the image, at his request, bent forward its head. From this moment the head of the image remained inclined, and doubtless, before the restoration of the Sainte-Chapelle is completed, the faithful will again behold the long-venerated image of our Lady in its ancient niche.

Duns Scot triumphed. The cause of the Immaculate Conception is no longer opposed. In our days, Cardinal Lambruschini has published a polemical dissertation on the subject, in which he establishes that Mary was preserved from her happy conception from the least taint of even original sin. This has now become the general opinion of the whole Church, as it was of the holy fathers and doctors of ancient and modern times, and will soon receive the authoritative sanction of the Holy See, and become an article of Catholic faith.

Legend of the Lord of Champfleury.

IN the twelfth century there lived at Champfleury, in Champagne, a knight, of a more liberal disposition than prudence dictated, or his fortune allowed. Abandoning himself to pleasure, he squandered his wealth in feasting, and became a prey to the deepest distress. His friends, devoted to him while partakers of his cheer, deserted him in his poverty. He had married a young lady, whose amiability, modesty, candour, and grace were sufficient to have made him the happiest of husbands. Her dowry had disappeared with the rest, and nothing remained, save an old dilapidated manor-house wherein they resided. But not a murmur passed her lips, nor were questions asked or reproaches given.

While bewailing his fallen state, a messenger announced to the Lord of Champfleury that the Count of Champagne, his *suzerain*, or superior lord, would shortly pass by his domains, and intended to honour him with a visit. The knight, who was much addicted to vanity and magnificence, fell into a state of despair; and leaving his house, wandered to a retired spot, where he might weep unseen. After an hour's walk, he stopped in the midst of a vast plain, and threw himself on the ground, under the shade of seven stunted walnut-trees. Here he gave full vent to his grief, and endeavoured, in vain, to discover some means of entertaining his future guest in a worthy manner. The day was fast declining (it was in the month of May), when he heard the rapid steps of a knight approaching the spot where he reposed. He hastily dried his eyes; and rising, found in his presence a man of high stature, and of a commanding, but gloomy figure, mounted on an Arab steed as black as ebony. He regarded him attentively, but without being able to recollect having seen him before. The stranger dismounted, and addressing him, said:

"You are suffering from deep grief, Lord of Champfleury. Be not offended at my seeking the cause; but it is, perhaps, not unknown to me. If you will consent to serve me, I will undertake to bring you through your trouble with splendour. I am able to bestow on you much more wealth than you have lost."

Before replying, the knight paused to examine the stranger. His offer was not very extravagant or astonishing in an age when feudal lords delighted in knight errantry and stirring adventure. But, plainly clad in a suit of black mail, the stranger bore no arms, either on his cloak or his horse's caparisons, which would proclaim the powerful and wealthy lord. Besides, he was alone, having neither page nor servant. At length, the Lord of Champfleury answered:

"I am a vassal of the Count of Champagne. I willingly promise anything which will not cause me to break the pledge of loyalty and homage which I swore to him—that is, after I am convinced of the seriousness of your promise. But first I must know your name."

"If we come to terms, you shall know who I am," replied the stranger. "The homage I shall exact will not interfere with that which you owe to your *suzerain*, the Count of Champagne, who in two days will present himself with a brilliant suite at your gates."

These last words cruelly revived the agony which the knight had been suffering on this account.

"Whoever you be," said he, after a moment's silence, "and should I lose all but my honour, I am ready to do what you desire, for I was but now dying with despair. But," added he, with earnestness, "I must first learn *who you are*."

"Well," said the black knight, slowly, "be not dismayed; the terms will doubtless sound strangely in your Christian ears. Your suspicions are being realized. I am he who from an imprudent rebel became a reprobate chief. You understand; you see in me the object of your brethren's fears,—the fallen angel who dared to revolt against heaven."

"Satan!" cried the Lord of Champfleury, starting back; and he was about to raise his hand to make the sign of the cross in his defence, when the stranger seized his arm.

"Stay," said he, with a trembling voice; "you are about to insult me, and I am here to save you. Know I am not your greatest enemy. You are self-abandoned. Without my assistance you are lost. I come to restore you to wealth and honour."

"I doubt you not," said the knight, bitterly; "but I want not your gifts."

"As you will . . . and when the Count of Champagne arrives in two days . . . Well, good bye!"

The knight trembled. Then, fascinated by a look from the stranger, he continued, with apparent calmness,—

"What is the nature of the homage you require of me?"

"Oh! it is nothing very difficult," replied the demon, in as pleasing and friendly a tone as he could assume.

He appeared to retire a few paces, then he continued,—

"I shall exact three things: the first may appear strange to you; but I must have some pledge. The rest will be much easier. You must sell me the eternal salvation of your wife. You must bring her to this spot on this day twelvemonth."

The knight, although prepared for revolting propositions, was indignant at this. His heart rose in anger. But he was under an influence, the effects of which he soon felt; his indignation subsided; his anger cooled; he thought the fallen angel might have exacted something still worse; that a year still remained to take measures for thwarting his adversary; at length he muttered that it was not in his power to do what was required.

"I merely desire you to bring your wife to this place in a year from this day, alone, and without giving her any intimation of our agreement. The rest is my affair."

The Lord of Champfleury accepted this first condition, and signed with his blood, on a triangular piece of vellum, his promise to fulfil it.

The eyes of his infernal visitor shone with renewed brilliancy. He then told him that the second condition was to renounce God. The knight's hair stood on end, and he trembled with exceeding fear at this blasphemous proposal. He vehemently exclaimed against it, while the stranger the first impulses of passion have their sway in such an exigency. And when the knight had recovered from his first emotion, he resigned himself to his tempter, thinking he should have ample time to repent in the course of a year. Without daring to raise his eyes to the heavens he renounced, he repeated, trembling the while at his cowardice, the blasphemies which the demon dictated to him, and found sufficient strength to enable him to pronounce the odious words which cut him off from hopes of eternal felicity.

Thus he placed himself under the power of Satan. With trembling voice—the perspiration pouring down his face—he asked, in despair, what was the third condition of the compact? The demon replied, that this was the last he should require—it was simply that he should renounce the Blessed Virgin. The Lord of Champfleury started back at these words, and felt his courage return. Although well knowing that he had committed the greatest crime man could do, by renouncing his God, the third proposal was to him as the drop of water which causes the glass to overflow.

"Renounce the Blessed Virgin!" said he, "after two acts which are sufficient to damn my soul, to renounce the Mother of God! to forsake the patronage and protection of Mary!"

The demon trembled at this name.

"If I forsake her," thought the knight, "what support, what refuge, remains for me to effect my reconciliation with God?. No," he replied, aloud, "I will not subscribe to this proposition; you have already led me too far; you have ruined me. Release me and let me go."

He said this with such resolution, that the

contented himself with what he had already obtained. He greatly insisted on this forbearance, and finally told the knight in what part of his house he would discover immense sums of money and heaps of jewels. After which he mounted his horse, and soon disappeared. The knight sought his mansion in great distress. The treasures were found in the place indicated; he took them, without mentioning to any one the means by which they were discovered, and made great preparations for the expected visitors.

He received the Count of Champagne with such magnificence, that they who knew how he had squandered his wealth were amazed. He completely bewildered them; and one of the barons in the count's suite, reminding him that St. Bernard was preaching the second crusade, asked if he would not follow his lord's banner under King Louis the Young. To this the knight replied, that not being able to leave his estate he would willingly present two hundred golden crowns to his lordship the Count of Champagne, to assist in the equipment of the troops he proposed to lead to the Holy Land. The count took this large sum with great thanks, and all his court complimented the Lord of Champfleury, who soon increased his domains, embellished his castle, and was more renowned than ever for the sumptuousness of his feasts.

One circumstance, however, could not fail to be remarked. He had lost all his former gaiety. His countenance was ever shaded with grief. The joy of again possessing riches, the festivities which succeeded one another in his new career, the numerous occupations with which he sought to distract his mind, did not suffice to stifle the despair he felt at the promise he had made and signed with his blood; his heart was troubled, his slumbers were uneasy, and his pleasures a shadow without any reality. Nor could he bring himself to have recourse to prayer. The moment he entered a church, he felt a trembling come over him, and experienced such anguish of mind, that he was obliged to quit the sacred edifice without assisting at the divine offices. He had determined during the year to reconcile himself with the Almighty; but a wall of iron seemed to separate him from repentance. His gentle spouse had given birth to a son, and but four months had elapsed since this event, when the fatal day arrived.

The knight, whose pride shrunk from revealing to any one the source whence he had derived his riches, had never mentioned the compact he had made with the demon. As the terrible moment agreed on for its fulfilment approached, he regretted his folly in not having revealed the terrible secret to some holy religious; but now it was too late. One only hope remained. "Surely," thought he, "Heaven will never abandon one so holy and so pure as my sweet spouse!"

He called her, and saying that he wished her to ride out with him, bade her prepare, while he ordered the horses. The good lady gave her infant to the care of its nurse, said an *Ave*, and followed her husband.

"Shall we be long absent?" she asked.

"Oh, no! we are not going far," replied the embarrassed husband. They mounted and were soon out of sight.

On their way they passed a chapel, dedicated to the Blessed Virgin. The Lady of Champfleury, whose tender devotion to her sweet patroness was well known to her lord, asked permission to enter the chapel, for she never passed an oratory wherein our Lady was especially venerated, without pausing to invoke her protection. The knight assisted his lady to alight, and remained at the door with the two palfreys. After a short prayer the lady reappeared, and the Lord of Champfleury aiding her to remount, continued his way, his fear and trepidation increasing the nearer they approached the place of their destination.

Never had his young wife, of whom he felt that he was no longer worthy, at the moment when he was about to be separated from her,—never had his sweet Mary (for such was her name) seemed so dear to him. Her modest beauty, the calmness of her fair countenance, her sweet smile, now sweeter than ever, inspired him with a feeling of respect, blended with tenderness. But he dared only to give expression to his feelings in deep sighs. He was the slave of Satan, and he feared him, with whom he was allied, too much to think of breaking his oath; yet he felt that to snatch his dear young spouse from his bosom would be his death. Tears came to his relief, and his breast heaved with emotion when he saw the seven withered walnut-trees, where his interview with the demon had taken place. He drew his horse close to the side of his wife—he tried to take her hand, but dared not.

"Dearest Mary!" said he; but his tears stopped further utterance.

"You weep!" she replied. "You tremble! you are suffering." And she reined in her steed.

"O let us go on," said he; "I dare not delay."

A feeling had come over him, for which he could

not account, but which inspired him with a veneration for his wife, akin to that which is given to the saints in heaven. He dared not turn his eyes towards her; but spurring his horse, hurried on.

The moment he reached the fatal spot, he saw the dark knight to whom he had sold his spouse approach, followed this time by several esquires, clad, like him, in black. But no sooner had the stranger perceived the lady, than he became pale, trembled, cast his eyes on the ground, and seemed to be paralyzed with fear.

" Perjured man!" cried he, addressing the knight, "is this the manner in which you have fulfilled your oath?"

"What would you?" replied the Lord of Champfleury: "Am I not here at the stated time? Do I not bring you her who is dearer to me than life? But what means this strange conduct?"

" The compact is signed with your blood, base man," interrupted the demon. " You have reaped the fruits of it. Did you not promise to bring your wife to this spot; and instead of her you here present to me my most bitter enemy!"

The knight was amazed at these words, and boldly proclaimed his honour to be unsullied. He turned towards his companion. A ray of light encircled the countenance of the lady, and as it increased in brilliancy, the black knight drew back, trembling with fear.

Now, you must know that the Countess Champfleury on entering the wayside chapel, knelt down in reverence before our Lady's image and commenced her rosary; but no sooner had she said her first *Ave*, than she fell into a deep sleep, when the Queen of Heaven, her most merciful patroness, took her form, and came forth herself to accompany the unhappy knight to the place of meeting.

The Lord of Champfleury, struck with admiration, felt his spirits revive; and throwing himself off his horse, fell on his knees before the lady, and asked her pardon. He still firmly believed that she was his dear Mary; and the brilliant light which surrounded her figure was but to him, whose eyes were not opened to the truth, a consolatory sign of the special protection of the most holy Virgin. But the lady made a sign to him to desist; and addressing Satan in that voice so full of sweet harmony, at the sound of which all men are ravished with delight, and demons struck with fear, she said:

"Wicked spirit! didst thou dare to seek for prey in a woman who reposed her strength in me? Will thy insatiable pride never be satisfied? I come neither to chastise thy insolence nor increase thy sufferings. My object is to deliver this poor sinner from his apostasy, and to take from thee the guilty compact he made."

The spirit of darkness hung his head, and growled like a threatened dog; but he slowly drew forth the parchment, cast it down, and retired in silence.

The penitent knight lay prostrate on the earth, bathed in tears. The Blessed Virgin touched him, and he recovered what he had lost for a twelvemonth —the gift of prayer. He bitterly bewailed the enormity of his crimes, and struck his breast with deep contrition.

"Rise, my son," said our dear Lady, "and remember it is easier for God to pardon than for man to offend. But while you thus feel the depth of your misery, renounce your pride and crimes."

With this mild reproach, she conducted him to her chapel, where knelt his spouse still slumbering. On awaking, she saw, to her delight, her lord, praying by her side. Our Blessed Lady had ascended into heaven. They saw nothing but her sweet image smiling on them from the little rustic altar. The knight led his lady back to his castle, where he confessed his wickedness to her, and told her of the miraculous intervention of our dear Lady in his behalf.

From this day, the Lord of Champfleury was no longer known as a gay and magnificent knight, but his name was mentioned as a model of Christian piety and charity.*

* This legend is found in the writings of Jacobus de Voragine, an intelligent and pious man. His *golden legend* was a great favourite with our ancestors, so that it must have some merit, which it certainly has. Many writers have given the same legend of the Lord of Champfleury with slight variations. As a drama, it was very popular in the sixteenth century, when it was performed under the title of *Le Mystère du Chevalier qui vendit sa Femme au Diable*—The Play of the Knight who sold his Wife to the Devil.

Epilogue.

 REPEAT at the termination of this volume the sentiments I expressed at its commencement. I have not pretended to offer my readers as incontestable all the facts herein related.

It will be seen that some rest on doubtful authority; that the documents whence they are derived are open to the cavils of the critics. There are others, however, like that of the translation of the "Holy House of Loreto," which can admit of no doubt, after an examination of the solid proofs which have been brought forward by the most trustworthy authors. As for those less authenticated, they do not demand the same degree of confidence. They may be regarded as the pious traditions of our ancestors, which bear witness to the simplicity of their faith. They did not imagine, as men do at the present day, that it was so difficult for the Almighty to work miracles. Bossuet, even in his time, said: "Why do people wish to make it so laborious a work for the Almighty to cause miraculous effects?"

Our mediæval ancestors had, perhaps, too often recourse to the extraordinary intervention of the Deity. Many pretended philosophers have wished absolutely to deny this miraculous interference with the order of nature. Which were right? I, for one, have no hesitation in avowing (however severe some critics may blame me) that, after the example of the good St. Francis of Sales, I feel naturally inclined to believe whatever appears to me to reveal the power of the Almighty and His goodness towards men; and when some fact in the history of the saints, or in the legends of the good chroniclers, touches and edifies me, I cannot believe that the proofs upon which they rest are entirely defective and valueless. But in order to gain more credit for my words, I hasten to lay before my readers the great authority to which I have alluded. Listen, then, to the saintly Bishop of Geneva, in words so full of charm and sweetness, extracted from the preamble to the *Wonderful History of the Decease of a Gentleman who died of love upon the Mount of Olives*, related in the seventh book of the *Treatise on the Love of God*, chap. xii.

"Besides what I have said, I have found a most admirable history which will be readily believed by sacred lovers; for, says the holy apostle, Charity believeth all things; which is to say, it does not easily believe *that one lies*. And if there be no signs of falsehood in what is represented to her, she makes no difficulty in giving it credence, especially when it relates to anything which exalts and praises the love of God towards men, or the love of men to God; the more so as Charity, which is the sovereign queen of virtues, takes pleasure after the manner of princes in those things which tend to the glory of her empire and domination. Supposing then that the narrative I am about to relate be neither so public nor so well attested as the greatness of the wonder would seem to require, it loses not for that its truth; for, as St. Augustine excellently says, when a miracle is made known, however striking it may be in the very place where it happened, or even when related by those who saw it, it is scarcely believed, but it is not the less true; and in religious matters, well-disposed souls feel more inclined to believe those things about which they have the greatest difficulty."

Our intention is not, however, to disregard the rights of a sound criticism; for to it belongs the duty of discerning truth from falsehood, and of pointing out to us what is really worthy of credit. And since we show ourselves so well disposed towards it, we may hope that it will not be too rigorous towards us; and allow in our narratives, for the love of the wonderful, which distinguished the chroniclers, and especially the legendaries of the good old times.

THE END.

INDEX

TO THE

IMAGES AND SANCTUARIES

MENTIONED IN THIS WORK.

AFFLIGHEM, the Abbey of ....*Page* 288
ALBERT. Our Lady of Brebière........................ 218
BAR-SUR-SEINE. Our Lady of the Oak.................. 223
BETHARRAM, Our Lady of 217
BOULOGNE. Our Lady of Safeguard 209
BOURGES, Our Lady of................................ 183
BOURDEAUX (near). Our Lady of Buglose............... 48
BRUSSELS. Carmelite Church.......................... 59
CHALONS SUR MARNE. Our Lady of the Thorn...... 223
CHAMPFLEURY, Our Lady of 301
CHARTRES, Our Lady of 196
COMPOSTELLO. St. James.............................. 263
DAMASCUS, Our Lady of 281
DIJON. Our Lady of Hope............................. 54
EINSIEDELN. Our Lady of the Hermits................. 189
EPHESUS. St. Mary's.................................   9
GARO. Our Lady of Bethlehem 241
GUELDERS. Carmelite Church.......................... 187
HAL, Our Lady of.................................... 110
HANSWYCK, Our Lady of 30
HAVRE. Our Lady the Deliverer....................... 109
HILDESHEIM, Our Lady of 153
JURA. Our Lady of the Flowering Thorn 79

Liesse, Our Lady of ....*Page*	150
Loreto, Our Lady of	170
Marseilles. Our Lady of Safeguard.....................	205
Mexico. St. James	175
Montaigu, Our Lady of	223
Montserrat, Our Lady of	35
Nazareth, Our Lady of	167
Nice. Our Lady of the Little Lake.......................	62
Orleans. St. Paul's	48

Paris—
Our Lady's (the Cathedral)...........................	41
St. Etienne des Grés	13
St. Severin..	292
St. Julian the Poor	21
The Holy Chapel	293
Our Lady of the Hospitallers.......................	18
English Convent	18
St. Denis	192
Our Lady of Montmartre	39

Poictiers. Great St. Mary's	85
Poy, Church of	51
Portiuncula, Church of	254
Puy, Our Lady of	96
Rheims Cathedral	192
Roc Amadour, Our Lady of	91

Rome—
St. Mary Major...	248
St. Nicholas..	181
St. Augustine	284

Sarragossa. Our Lady of the Pillar.....................	262
Tersato, Our Lady of	168
Verviers, Our Lady of..	64
Vincent of Paul, St., Pilgrimages relating to	48

PRINTED BY COX (BROTHERS) AND WYMAN, GREAT QUEEN-STREET.

CATALOGUE OF BOOKS

PUBLISHED BY

CHARLES DOLMAN,

61, NEW BOND STREET,

AND

22, PATERNOSTER ROW, LONDON.

ALSO KEPT ON SALE BY

GERALD BELLEW, 79, GRAFTON STREET, DUBLIN,

AND BY

MARSH & BEATTIE, 13, SOUTH HANOVER STREET, EDINBURGH.

N.B.—All New Publications of interest in general literature kept on sale, or procured to order.

Foreign Works, not in stock, procured to order.

A choice selection of Religious Prints always on sale.

The Publications of the **CHRISTIAN BROTHERS** supplied to order.

WORKS PRINTED AND PUBLISHED FOR AUTHORS ON REASONABLE TERMS.

All the Books in this Catalogue can be procured by order from any Bookseller in the Country.

☞ Export orders carefully attended to.

NEW WORKS, AND EDITIONS RECENTLY PUBLISHED :

A Catechism of the Christian Religion; being a Compendium of the Catechism of Moutpellier. By the Rev. Stephen Keenan. Price 5s. cloth lettered.

Alcantara, Peter de, a Golden Treatise of Mental Prayer, with divers Spiritual Rules and Directions, no less profitable than necessary, for all sorts of people. Translated by Giles Willoughby. 18mo, cloth, 2s. 6d.

Archer, Rev. J., D.D., Sermons for Festivals, and a second series of Sermons for every Sunday in the Year. 2 vols. 8vo, 12s., boards.

A True Account of the Gunpowder Plot, extracted from Lingard's History of England, and Dodd's Church History of England, including the Notes and Documents appended to the latter, by the Rev. M. A. Tierney, F.R.S., F.S.A., with Notes and Introduction by VINDICATOR. 8vo, 3s. 6d.

Breviarum Romanum. 4 vols., 4to.
——————————— 2 vols., 4to.
——————————— 4 vols., 12mo, 18mo, and 32mo.

Graduale Romanum. 8vo.

Horæ Diurnæ. 32mo.

Missale Romanum. Large and small folio, and 12mo.

Office of the Blessed Virgin Mary. 18mo.

Pontificale Romanum. 3 vols., 8vo.

Rituale Romanum. 18mo.

Vesperale Romanum. 18mo.

Brownson's Quarterly Review. This Review, conducted by the gentleman whose name it bears, is devoted to Religion, Philosophy, and General Literature.

It is published quarterly at Boston, in the months of January, April, July, and October. Each number contains, at least, 136 pages, 8vo, and the four numbers make a volume of 544 pages, which will be furnished to Subscribers, at *Sixteen Shillings per annum.*

No subscription will be received for a shorter time than one year, and each subscription must be for the entire current volume.

C. DOLMAN having been appointed sole Agent for this Review in the United Kingdom, can supply it on the terms stated above. Persons desirous of subscribing to the work, are respectfully requested to forward their subscriptions to C. Dolman, either direct, or through their regular Booksellers.

Butler, Rev. Alban, Lives of the Fathers, Martyrs, and other principal Saints, compiled from Original Monuments and other authentic Records: illustrated with the remarks of judicious modern Critics and Historians. The original stereotype edition, in twelve volumes, including the account of the Life and Writings of the Rev. Alban Butler, by Charles Butler, Esq., and an Appendix, containing General Indices, Chronological Tables, &c. Handsomely printed on medium 8vo, cloth lettered, price £3.

The same, illustrated with above Forty Plates; fine early impressions, only £3 12s.

Canons and Decrees of the Sacred and œcumenical Council of Trent, celebrated under the Sovereign Pontiffs, Paul III., Julius III., and Pius IV. Translated by the Rev. J. Waterworth. To which is prefixed Essays on the External and Internal History of the Council. Dedicated, by permission, to His Eminence Cardinal Wiseman, Archbishop of Westminster. In 1 large vol., 8vo, 10s. 6d., cloth, lettered.

Catechism of the Council of Trent, translated into English, and published with the original Latin text, by J. Donovan, D.D. 2 vols., 8vo, price £1 1s., sewed. Printed at the Propaganda Press, Rome, 1839.

The same, the English Translation separate. 8vo, 10s. 6d.

Catechism of the History of England. By a Lady, price 9d.

"*Talbot House School, Richmond, 26th Nov.,* 1847.

"MY DEAR SIR,—I have been using your little Catechism of the History of England for some time past, at my Establishment. I have found it more useful than any of the kind I have ever met with, and shall be happy to recommend the work whenever I shall have an opportunity. You may make use of my name to that effect, in any way you think proper.—Yours faithfully,
"W. D. KENNY."

—— History of Germany. By A. M. S. 18mo, 6d.

"It is Catholic, and extremely well-condensed, lucid, and full enough for the purpose of an introductory outline."—*Tablet.*

—— History of France. 6d.
—— Italy. *At press.*
—— Spain and Portugal. 6d.
—— of Classical Mythology. By R. O. 6d.

N.B.—These Catechisms, being all written by Catholics, can be safely recommended for the use of Schools.

Catholic Pulpit, containing Sermons for all the Sundays and Holidays in the Year. Second edition, revised, in 1 vol., 8vo, 10s. 6d., cloth lettered.

an Appendix, containing Translations of the Greek, Latin, and other quotations. Small 8vo, price 6s.

The Appendix, adapted to suit the first editions, price 1s. 6d.

Compitum. Book II. at press. Second edition with additions.

Coombe's Essence of Religious Controversy. 8vo, 6s. 6d.

Cousins, The, or Pride and Vanity: a Tale, by Agnes M. Stewart. 18mo, fancy cloth, 1s.

Devotion of Calvary; or Meditations on the Passion of our Lord and Saviour, Jesus Christ. From the French of Father J. Crasset, of the Society of Jesus. 1s.

Devotion of the Three Hours' Agony, in honour of our Lord Jesus Christ on the Cross. Composed originally in the Spanish language, at Lima, in Peru. By the Rev. F. Alphonsus Messia, S.J. Royal 32mo, 4d.

Devout Reflections for, before, and after receiving the Holy Eucharist. To which are added, Short Preparations for Confession and Communion. Royal 32mo, 1s. 6d., bound.

Documents of Christian Perfection. Composed by the venerable and famous Father Paul, of St. Magdalen (Henry Heath) of the Seraphic Order of the Friars Minor at Douay, crowned with martyrdom at London, April 11th, 1643. Translated out of the sixth and last Latin edition into English, and published at Douay in 1674, and illustrated with a Portrait of Father Paul. 18mo, cloth, 2s. 6d.

Dodd's Church History of England, from the year 1500 to 1688, chiefly with regard to Catholics. By Charles Dodd, with Notes, and a Continuation to the beginning of the present century. By the Rev. M. A. Tiernay, F.R.S., F.S.A.

Vols. I. to V. are published, 12s. each, in cloth.

Vol. VI. preparing for press.

N.B.—Subscribers' names may be transmitted to the Publisher through any Bookseller in the country.

Dollinger, Rev. J. J. Ig., D.D., History of the Church. Translated from the German, by the Rev. E. Cox, D.D., President of St. Edmund's College, 4 vols., 8vo, £1 14s.

Dolman's Home Library of Religious and Moral Works, for popular reading; suited for gift-books and prizes, as well as for Family Reading, School Libraries, &c.

Now ready, price 8d. each volume, sewed; or 1s. cloth,

THE SISTER OF CHARITY. By Mrs. Hannah H. Dorsay. In 2 vols., 18mo., with frontispiece.

TEARS ON THE DIADEM; or, the Crown and the Cloister.

ZENOSIUS: or, the Pilgrim Convert. By the Rev. C. C. Pise.

FATHER FELIX. By the author of "Mora Carmody."

THE ELDER'S HOUSE; or, the Three Converts.

JULIA ORMOND; or, the New Settlement.

Dublin Review. Vols. I. to XVI. This Periodical, from the commencement, in 1836, down to June, 1844, inclusively, published at £9 12s., in Parts, is now offered, in sets of Sixteen vols., half cloth, for only £3 12s.

Just published, price 3s. plain, or 4s. coloured.

Houses, with the Boundaries of the Archdiocess and the Diocesses; with a plan of London, showing the Position of the Catholic Churches, &c.; together with a complete List of the Towns in which Catholic Churches are established. On a large sheet, printed in red and black.

N.B.—This Map can be had mounted on canvass and rollers, or folded up in a case.

Facts and Correspondence relating to the Admission into the Catholic Church of Viscount and Viscountess Fielding. By the Right Rev. Bishop Gillis. 8vo, price 2s. 6d.

Faith of Catholics, on Certain points of Controversy, confirmed by Scripture, and attested by the Fathers of the first five centuries of the Church. Compiled by the Rev. Joseph Berington and the Rev. John Kirk. Third Edition, revised and greatly enlarged by the Rev. J. Waterworth. 3 vols. 8vo, 10s. 6d. each vol., cloth, lettered.

Fasti Christiani; or, Rhymes on the Kalendar, by William Cowper Augustine Maclaurin, M.A., late Dean of Moray and Ross, now a Member of the Catholic Church. 8vo, 6s. 6d., cloth, gilt.

Father Oswald, a genuine Catholic story. 1 vol., 12mo, 6s., cloth lettered.

Flowers of Heaven; or, the Examples of the Saints proposed to the Imitation of Christians. Translated from the French of the Abbé Orsini. 18mo, cloth lettered, 2s. 6d.

Francis de Sales, St., Introduction to a Devout Life. 18mo, sheep, 2s.

——————— Treatise on the Love of God. 8vo, bds., 10s.

Geraldine: a Tale of Conscience. By E. C. A. A new edition, 1 vol., small 8vo, 5s., cloth lettered.

Geramb, Marie Joseph, Abbot of La Trappe, Journey from La Trappe to Rome. Second edition, small 8vo, 3s.

Gerbet, Abbe, Considerations on the Eucharist, viewed as the generative Dogma of Catholic Piety. Translated from the French, by a Catholic Clergyman. 12mo, cloth, 4s. 6d.

Griffet, Pere, Meditations for every Day in the Year, on the principal duties of Christianity. Translated from the French, by the Right Rev. Dr. Walsh. 2 vols. in one, 32mo, cloth, 2s.

Hierurgia; or, Transubstantiation, Invocation of Saints, Relics, and Purgatory, besides those other articles of Doctrine set forth in the Holy Sacrifice of the Mass expounded; and the Use of Holy Water, Incense, and Images, the Ceremonies, Vestments, and Ritual employed in its celebration among the Latins, Greeks, and Orientals, illustrated from Paintings, Sculptures, and Inscriptions found in the Roman Catacombs, or belonging to the earliest Ages of Faith. By D. Rock, D.D. Second Edition, with Additions, and illustrated with Fifteen Engravings, and above Thirty Woodcuts. In one large Volume, 8vo (nearly six hundred pages), price 16s., cloth, lettered.

Huddleston, John, a Short and Plain Way to the Church, composed many years since by Richard Huddleston, of the Order of St. Benedict; to which is annexed King Charles the Second's papers, found in his closet, with an account of what occurred on his deathbed in regard to religion; and a summary of occurrences relating to

Illustrations of the Spiritual and Corporal Works of Mercy, in Sixteen Designs, engraved in outline, with descriptive anecdotes in four languages, and a Sketch of the Order of Mercy, by a Sister of the religious Order of our Lady of Mercy. 1 vol., oblong 4to, cloth lettered, 10s. 6d.

Imitation of Christ, in Four Books. By Thomas à Kempis. Translated by the Rev. Dr. Challoner. A new edition, handsomely printed in large type, 18mo, 2s. 6d. bound.

The same, cape morocco, 3s.

Jones', Rev. J., Manual of Instructions on Plain-Chant, or Gregorian Music, with Chants, as used in Rome, for High Mass, Vespers, Complin, Benediction, Holy Week, and the Litanies. Compiled chiefly from Alfieri and Berti; with the approbation of the Right Reverend Vicars Apostolic. Beautifully printed in red and black type, in small quarto, 2s. 6d.

"We have carefully examined every part, and have found all most accurate and conformable to authentic models. We sincerely hope, therefore, that it will be universally adopted as the standard in singing at the altar, and in the Church."— *Dublin Review*.

"A perfect vade-mecum for the Priest and the Choir, where the Gregorian chant is preferred, as it always ought to be, to the unauthorised variety which prevails in most of our chapels and churches. The book is very neatly, nay, beautifully printed. We augur for it a deservedly extensive sale."— *Tablet*.

Keenan's, Rev. Stephen, Controversial Catechism; or Protestantism refuted and Catholicism Established, by an Appeal to the Holy Scriptures, the testimony of the Holy Fathers, and the dictates of Reason. Second edition, revised and enlarged. Eighth Thousand, 12mo, sewed, 1s. 6d.; cloth, 2s.

Kenrick, Right Rev. Francis, Bishop of Philadelphia. The Four Gospels, translated from the Latin Vulgate, and diligently compared with the Greek, being a Revision of the Rhemish Translation, with critical and explanatory Notes. Large octavo, cloth, 10s. 6d.

Also by the same author,

The Acts of the Apostles, The Epistles of St. Paul, The Catholic Epistles, and the Apocalypse. Translated from the Latin Vulgate, and compared with the Greek. Large octavo, price 12s. 6d., cloth, lettered.

LIBRARY OF LEGENDS.

Legends of the Commandments of God.

Legends of the Seven Deadly Sins.

Translated from the French of J. Collin de Plancy, approved by the late Archbishop of Paris, Monsignor Affre.

N.B.—These Volumes will be re-issued in Parts, price 6d. each, commencing on the 1st January.

Letters on the Spanish Inquisition. By Count Joseph de Maistre. Translated from the French. 18mo, cloth, 1s. 6d.

Life of St. Jane Frances de Chantal, foundress of the Order of the Visitation, collected from original Documents and Records. By the Rev. W. H. Coombes, D.D. 2 vols., 8vo, price 9s.

Life of St. Francis de Sales, from Marsollier. 2 vols., 8vo, 10s.

Life of the Blessed Peter Fourier, Priest, Reformer of a Religious Order, and founder in the beginning of the 17th century of one of the first Congregations of Women devoted to the gratuitous instruction of young Girls. Translated from the French of Edward de Bazelaire. With a finely engraved Portrait. 18mo, cloth, 2s.

Lingard, Rev. Dr., The History and Antiquities of the Anglo-Saxon Church, containing an Account of its Origin, Government, Doctrines, Worship, Revenues, and Clerical and Monastic Institutions. In 2 vols., 8vo., price £1 4s., cloth lettered.

"If we were asked from what source one could obtain the greatest insight into the national mind and ways of thought of the Christian Anglo-Saxons, we should have no hesitation in referring the inquirer to these pages. As a narration of facts, and expounder of the inferences more immediately to be drawn from them, there is no writer of the present day who excels the diligent, accurate, and eloquent historian of England."—*Morning Chronicle*.

"Of the Monastic Institutions among the Anglo-Saxons, Dr. Lingard has written in a spirit of candour and fairness; he points out the abuses to which such communities are liable, and does not conceal the fact that such abuses frequently prevail."—*Athenæum*.

——————— History of England, from the First Invasion of the Romans to the reign of William and Mary, in the year 1688. New edition, revised and much enlarged. This Library edition is handsomely printed in ten large octavo volumes, price £6, or 12s. per volume, cloth lettered, and enriched with a likeness of the author, engraved in the best style, from a portrait taken last year by Mr. Skaife.

"From all comments on the work, as a history, we abstain: but we may say it has achieved such a success, and obtained in the eye of the public such a position, that the possession of this new and revised edition is essential to the completion of every library. The typography is beautiful, and the work, independently of all intrinsic merit, will ornament any shelves where it may find a place."—*Morning Chronicle*.

"The labour expended by Dr. Lingard upon his subject has been enormous. He has again and again gone over it with a profound and scrutinising investigation, and although he is now, we believe, in his eightieth year, he has prosecuted his task with undiminished zeal, until he could give, in the edition before us the finishing stroke of emendation to the great occupation of his life. This edition may, therefore, be considered far superior to those which have preceded it, and in this respect will remain as a mountain of unexampled perseverance to the latest period of time."—*Bell's Weekly Messenger*.

——————— Catechetical Instructions on the Doctrines and Worship of the Catholic Church. A new edition, revised, in 18mo, price 1s.

[This work contains a short exposition of Catholic doctrine and Catholic practice, with the chief authorities on which that doctrine and practice are founded.]

Also, another edition of the same, in larger type, 12mo, price 1s. 6d.

"A beautiful little volume, written with all that sobriety of style, power of language, and force of logic for which the venerable author is remarkable."—*Tablet*.

Mac Hale, the Most Rev. John, Archbishop of Tuam, Evidences and Doctrines of the Catholic Church. Second edition, revised, with additional Notes. 8vo, cloth, 8s. 6d.

Manning's England's Conversion and Reformation compared. 18mo, bound, 1s. 6d.

——————— Moral Entertainments. 12mo, bound, 3s. 6d.

Manzoni's Vindication of Catholic Morality against Sismondi,

Memoriale Rituum, pro aliquibus protestantioribus, sacris functionibus, persolvendis in minoribus ecclesiis Parochialibus. Benedicti XIII. jussu primo editum. 8vo, 8d.

Merati, Selections from, on the Ceremonies of the Church. 12mo, 1s. 6d.

Monastic State, duties of, by De Rance. 2 vols., 12mo, sheep, 6s.

Mœhler, J. A., Symbolism; or Exposition of the Doctrinal Differences between Catholics and Protestants. Translated by J. B. Robertson, Esq. 2 vols., 8vo, 14s.

More, Sir Thomas. A Dialogue of Comfort against Tribulation, made by the virtuous, wise, and learned man, Sir Thomas More, sometime Lord Chancellor of England, which he wrote in the Tower of London, A.D. 1534. Crown 8vo, 5s., boards.

Mores Catholici; or, Ages of Faith. Eleven Books, in three very large vols., royal 8vo, price £1 6s. each, handsomely bound, in cloth lettered and gilt.

⁎ "It contains food for all minds. The wisest will find in it a strain of a high, clear, pure, and (in these days) a new philosophy. The historian and the antiquarian will find light thrown upon the manners of many times and many people. The poet will be charmed with the strains of lofty eloquence, and the many touching and beautiful stories it contains. Many, we think, will desire 'to build up their minds' upon the wisdom of the Christian schools here collected and illustrated; and none, we are sure, can read it without being soothed by its harmonious eloquence, and entertained by a diversity of pleasing and new ideas."—*Dublin Review.*

New Month of Mary; or, Reflections for each Day of the Month, on the different Titles applied to the Holy Mother of God in the Litany of Loretto: principally designed for the Month of May. By the Right Rev. Dr. Kenrick. 18mo. 1s. 6d.

New Version of the Four Gospels; with Notes, Critical and Explanatory. By John Lingard, D.D. First published in 1836. 8vo, 7s. 6d.

Observations on the Laws and Ordinances which exist in Foreign States, relative to the Religious Concerns of their Roman Catholic Subjects. By Rev. John Lingard, D.D. 8vo, 1s.

Oliver, Rev. Dr., Collections towards illustrating the Biography of the Scotch, English, and Irish Members of the Society of Jesus. 8vo, 12s., cloth lettered.

Pauline Seward, a Tale of Real Life. By John D. Bryant, Esq. 2 vols., 12mo, price 8s. cloth.

Peach, Rev. Edward, Sermons for every Sunday and Festival throughout the year. New edition, handsomely printed in large type. 8vo, cloth, 9s.

Poor Man's Catechism; or, the Christian Doctrine Explained; with suitable admonitions. By the Rev. John Anselm Mannock, O.S.B. A new edition, revised and corrected, with a Memoir of the Author. Price 1s.

"We may with great truth call this a careful and elegant edition of this most useful work."—*Tablet.*

Power, Rev. T., Instructive and Curious Epistles from Clergymen of the Society of Jesus. Selected from the "Lettres Edifiantes." 12mo, cloth, 2s.

Pugin, A. Welby. A Treatise on Chancel Screens and Rood Lofts; their Antiquity, Use, and Symbolic Signification. Illustrated with many figures of Rood Screens, drawn on stone by the Author. Small 4to, uniform with " The True Principles of Gothic Architecture." Handsomely bound, 15*s.*

——————— The present State of Ecclesiastical Architecture in England. With 36 illustrations. Republished from the "Dublin Review." 8vo, cloth, 9*s.*

——————— Contrasts; or, a Parallel between the Noble Edifices of the Middle Ages and corresponding Buildings of the Present Day, setting forth the present decay of pure taste. Accompanied by appropriate Text. Second Edition, enlarged. 4to, cloth lettered, £1 10*s.*

Ravignan, on the Life and Institute of the Jesuits. By the Rev. Father de Ravignan, of the Company of Jesus. Carefully translated from the fourth edition of the French. By Charles Seager. 12mo, 1*s.* 6*d.*

Reading Lessons, for the use of Schools; a new series, from Words of Two Syllables upwards. By a Catholic Clergyman. Fifty-six Lessons, 5*s.* the set.

Reeve's History of the Bible, new edition, illustrated with 230 Wood Engravings. 12mo, roan, sprinkled edges, 3*s.* 6*d.*

Rigby, Rev. Dr., Catechetical Discourses on Natural and Revealed Religion. 4 vols., 12mo, 10*s.*

Rock, Rev. Dr., The Church of our Fathers; or, St. Osmund's Rite for the Church of Salisbury, from a manuscript in the Library of that Cathedral. Printed for the first time, and elucidated with Dissertations on the Belief and Ritual of the Church in England before and after the coming of the Normans. Vols. 1 and 2, illustrated with many Engravings on Wood and Copper. 8vo, cloth, price £1 16*s.* Vol. 3, *at press.*

Rules of a Christian Life, selected from the most Spiritual Writers; with Letters on Matrimony: on the choice of a State of Life; and on Monastic Institutions, &c., &c. By the Rev. C. Premord. 2 vols., 12mo, boards, 7*s.*

Rutter's Help to Parents in the Religious Education of their Children. 12mo, 2*s.* 6*d.*

Set of Altar Cards, handsomely printed in red and black type, with an engraving of the Crucifixion, from Overbeck. Size of Centre Card, 12 inches by 10¼. 2*s.* 6*d.*

Sick Calls: from the Diary of a Missionary Priest, mostly reprinted from "Dolman's Magazine." By the Rev. E. Price, M.A. In small 8vo, 5*s.* 6*d.*, cloth lettered, frontispiece by H. Doyle, Esq.

Sinner's Complaint to God; being Devout Entertainments of the Soul with God, fitted for all States and Conditions of Christians. By the Rev. J. Gother. 12mo, 4*s.* 6*d.*

Smith, Rev. H., A Short History of the Protestant Reformation, principally as to its rise and progress in England, in a series of Conferences held by the most eminent Protestant Historians of the present and former times. 12mo, boards, 2*s.* 6*d.*

Soul united to Jesus in his Adorable Sacrament. 18mo, 1s. 6d.

Spiritual Exercises of St. Ignatius of Loyola. Translated from the Latin by Charles Seager, M.A., with a Preface by Cardinal Wiseman, Archbishop of Westminster. Small 8vo, price 4s., cloth lettered, illustrated with a fine print of St. Ignatius of Loyola.

St. Mary and her Times: a Poem in Fourteen Cantos. By the Authoress of "Geraldine." Dedicated to Cardinal Wiseman. Crown 8vo, price 3s., cloth lettered.

Stories of the Seven Virtues. By Agnes M. Stewart. Price 2s., cloth lettered. Containing:
1. HUMILITY; or, Blanche Neville and the Fancy Fair.
2. LIBERALITY; or, the Benevolent Merchant.
3. CHASTITY; or, the Sister of Charity.
4. MEEKNESS; or, Emily Herbert and the Victim of Passion.
5. TEMPERANCE; or, Edward Ashton.
6. BROTHERLY-LOVE; or, the Sisters.
7. DILIGENCE; or, Ethel Villiers and her Slothful Friend.

Each of these Stories may be had separately, in a wrapper, price 3d.

Stothert, Rev. James, The Christian Antiquities of Edinburgh. In a Series of Lectures, on the Parochial, Collegiate, and Religious Antiquities of Edinburgh. Small 8vo, 6s., cloth.

Tales explanatory of the Sacraments. In 2 vols., 12mo, 10s., cloth. By the Authoress of "Geraldine: a Tale of Conscience." Containing:
1. THE VIGIL OF ST. LAURENCE.
2. BLANCHE'S CONFIRMATION.
3. THE SISTER PENITENTS.
4. THE ALTAR AT WOODBANK.
5. CLYFFE ABBEY; or, the Last Anointing.
6. THE PRIEST OF NORTHUMBRIA; an Anglo-Saxon Tale.
7. THE SPOUSAL CROSS.

The Tales are told with great spirit and elegance. The Narrative never falters; and a spirit of the purest and most profound piety breathes in every word."— *Dolman's Magazine*, January.

The Bible, its Use and Abuse; or, an Inquiry into the Results of the respective Doctrines of the Catholic and Protestant Churches, relative to the Interpretation of the Word of God. By the Rev. Paul Maclachlan. Small 8vo, cloth, lettered, 4s.

The Catholic Hierarchy Vindicated by the Law of England. By William Finlason, Esq., of the Middle Temple, Pleader. Price 1s. 6d.

The Duties and Happiness of Domestic Service; or, a Sister of Mercy giving Instructions to the Inmates of the House of Mercy placed under her care. 18mo, price 2s., cloth, lettered.

The Glory of Mary in Conformity with Word of God. By James Augustine Stothert, Missionary Apostolic in the Eastern District of Scotland. Small 8vo, handsomely bound, cloth, gilt, 3s. 6d.

The Holy Scriptures: their Origin, Progress, Transmission,

The Life of St. Teresa, written by herself, and translated from the Spanish, by the Rev. John Dalton. 1 vol., crown 8vo. 5s. 6d., cloth, lettered.

The Old Tree; or Filial Piety. A Tale. 18mo, cloth, 1s.

The Pope, considered in his Relations with the Church, Temporal Sovereignties, Separated Churches, and the Cause of Civilization; by Count Joseph de Maistre. Translated by the Rev. Æneas Mc D. Dawson, with a Portrait of Pope Pius IX. Small octavo, 5s., cloth.

The Spirit and Scope of Education, in promoting the well-being of Society, from the German of Dr. Stapf. By Robert Gordon. Crown 8vo, cloth, lettered, 5s.

Thornberry Abbey; a Tale of the Established Church, cloth lettered, 3s. 6d.

" We cordially recommend it to the notice of the reader."—*Tablet.*
" It is one of the best little works, treating an important matter in a popular manner, we have recently met.—*Brownson's Quarterly Review.*

Walsingham, Francis, Deacon of the Protestant Church, a Search made into matters of religion before his change to the Catholic. Wherein is related how first he fell into his doubts, and how, for final resolution thereof, he repaired unto his Majesty, who remitted him to the L. of Canterbury, and he to other learned men; and what the issue was of all those Conferences. Forming a thick volume, crown 8vo, 8s.

Wheeler, Rev. J., Sermons on the Gospels for every Sunday in the Year. 2 vols., 8vo, 12s.

———— Sermons on the Festivals. A selection of Sermons. 1 vol., 8vo, 9s.

White, Rev. T., Sermons for every Sunday, and on other occasions. Selected by the Rev. Dr. Lingard. *A new edition at press.*

WORKS BY HIS EMINENCE CARDINAL WISEMAN,
ARCHBISHOP OF WESTMINSTER.

Lectures on the Principal Doctrines and Practices of the Catholic Church, delivered at St. Mary's, Moorfields, during the Lent of 1836. Second edition, entirely revised and corrected by the Author. Two volumes in one, 12mo, price 4s. 6d., cloth.

The Real Presence of the Body and Blood of our Lord Jesus Christ in the Blessed Eucharist, proved from Scripture. In Eight Lectures, delivered in the English College, Rome. Second edition, 12mo, cloth lettered, 4s. 6d.

A Reply to Dr. Turton, the "British Critic," and others, on the Catholic Doctrine of the Eucharist. 8vo, 4s. 6d.

Four Lectures on the Offices and Ceremonies of Holy Week, as performed in the Papal Chapels, delivered in Rome, in the Lent of 1837. Illustrated with Nine Engravings, and a Plan of the Papal Chapels. 8vo, cloth, 5s.

Twelve Lectures on the connexion between Science and Revealed Religion, with Map and Plates. Third edition, in 2 vols., small 8vo, cloth lettered, 10s.

Veronica Giuliana, whose canonization took place on Trinity Sunday, 26th of May, 1839. Edited by Cardinal Wiseman. Second edition, 18mo, cloth lettered, 2s. 6d.

WORKS OF THE PASSIONIST FATHERS.

New Litany and Prayers for the Conversion of England, price 2d.

Pious Reflections on the Passion of Jesus Christ to help the Faithful to meditate upon it with ease. By Father Seraphin. Vols. 1 & 2, 8vo, cloth, 1s. 6d. per vol.

Life of the Venerable Peter Canisius of the Society of Jesus, surnamed the Apostle of Germany, who lived during the time of the Reformers. Price 2s. 6d.

Young Catholic's Guide in the preparation for Confession; for the use of Children of both sexes, from Seven to Fourteen years of age. By W. D. Kenny. Royal 32mo, sewed, price 3d.

Young Communicants. By the Author of "Geraldine." Second Edition, 18mo, cloth, 1s.

RECENTLY PUBLISHED.

Twelve Prints, drawn and illuminated in Gold and Colours, in the early Missal style, suitable for Prayer Books, with Miniatures and Prayers, printed in Black Letter, consisting of the following:

St. Augustine, Apostle of England,
St. Catherine,
St. Philip Neri,
St. Margaret of Scotland, — Size 4 inches by 2¼. Price 6d. each.

St. Elizabeth of Hungary,
St. George,
St. Joseph,
The Memorare, by St. Bernard, in English, — Size, 4½ inches by 2¾. Price 6d. each.

The Our Father,
The Hail Mary,
We fly to thy Patronage,
In the Name of Jesus, — Size, 3½ inches by 2¼. Price 4d. each.

Any of the above may be had mounted under Glass, with ornamental Frames.

Also, a beautiful Drawing of the

Madonna and the Infant Jesus, seated under a Canopy, with attendant Angels, encircled by a floriated border, in which the figures of St. Ann and St. John the Baptist are introduced, with the following inscription beneath the Drawing:

Regina Sine Labe Originali Concepta, Ora pro nobis.

The whole illuminated in gold and colours, in the early Missal style. Size of the Drawing, 10 inches by 7, price 3s., or mounted under Glass, with ornamented Frame, 6s. 6d.

The Life and Passion of our Lord Jesus Christ, illustrated in twelve Plates, engraved on steel from the designs of Frederick Overbeck. Proofs on India paper, price 10s. the set; single plates, 1s. each. Plain prints, price 5s. the set; single plates, 6d. each.

The following well-engraved small Prints, 3d. each:
Our Saviour Knocking at the Door.

A great variety of Coloured Prints; Illuminated Prayers; Crucifixes; Altar Cards; Rosary Rings; Beads, &c., are always kept on Sale, at moderate prices.

Just Published, in demy 8vo, with numerous Plates, price 12s. cloth lettered.

A Journal of a Tour in Egypt, Palestine, Syria, and Greece, with Notes, and an Appendix on Ecclesiastical matters. By James Laird Patterson, M.A.

Just Published, price 2s. 6d.

A Letter to the Right Hon. W. E. Gladstone, M.P., in answer to his Two Letters to the Earl of Aberdeen, on the State Prosecutions of the Neapolitan Government, with a Preface written for the English edition. By Jules Gondon, Rédacteur de l'Univers.

AT PRESS.

Now in course of Publication, price 6s. each volume, handsomely bound, cloth lettered and gilt, a cheap edition of

The Letters and Official Documents of Mary Stuart, Queen of Scotland, collected from the original MSS. preserved in the State Paper Office of London, and the principal archives and Libraries of Europe, together with a Chronological Summary: By Prince Alexander Labanoff.

₊ To be completed in Seven Volumes. The consecutive volumes will be issued on the 1st of each Month until completed.

OPINIONS OF THE PRESS.

"We heartily recommend these volumes to general attention, as one of the most valuable contributions ever offered to British literature by a foreign hand."— *Quarterly Review.*

"We never saw a more carefully edited book. More patient exactness, a more praiseworthy elaborate fidelity we could not possibly have desired. We heartily recommend this valuable collection to the best attention of the students of history."—*Examiner.*

"We must in justice say that we have never seen a mass of historical documents more faithfully edited, lucidly arranged, and impartially illustrated than the collection before us."—*Athenæum.*

A Selection of Essays and Articles from the *Dublin Review*, by Cardinal Wiseman.

Audin's History of Henry VIII. and of the Schism of England. Translated from the French by Edward George Kirwan Browne. 8vo. *Nearly ready.*

The Translation of this important work has been undertaken with the special sanction and countenance of the talented author, M. AUDIN, who has not only authorized the publication but also kindly furnished the Translator with further corrections and notes.

☞ Besides the Books in this List, of which by far the greater part are published by C. Dolman, all the Books issued by other Catholic Publishers are kept on sale, as well as an extensive collection of Foreign Works, both ancient and modern, containing many of the Fathers of the Church, Early Printed Books, Theological and General Literature, and also many rare English Catholic Controversial and Devotional Works of the Sixteenth and Seventeenth Centuries, of which Catalogues can be had on application.

LONDON: C. DOLMAN, 61, NEW BOND STREET.